PLAYING AGAINST THE HOUSE

The Dramatic World of an Undercover Union Organizer

JAMES D. WALSH

SCRIBNER

New York   London   Toronto   Sydney   New Delhi

SCRIBNER
An Imprint of Simon & Schuster, Inc.
1230 Avenue of the Americas
New York, NY 10020

First Scribner hardcover edition February 2016

SCRIBNER and design are registered trademarks of The Gale Group, Inc.,
used under license by Simon & Schuster, Inc., the publisher of this work.

For information about special discounts for bulk purchases,
please contact Simon & Schuster Special Sales at 1-866-506-1949
or business@simonandschuster.com.

The Simon & Schuster Speakers Bureau can bring authors to your
live event. For more information or to book an event,
contact the Simon & Schuster Speakers Bureau at 1-866-248-3049
or visit our website at www.simonspeakers.com.

Interior design by Kyle Kabel

Manufactured in the United States of America

1   3   5   7   9   10   8   6   4   2

Library of Congress Control Number: 2015044659

ISBN 978-1-9821-1555-5
ISBN 978-1-4767-7837-2 (ebook)

For my parents, John A. and Ellen

It is not from the benevolence of the butcher, the brewer, or the baker that we expect our dinner, but from their regard to their own interest. We address ourselves, not to their humanity but to their self-love, and never talk to them of our own necessities but of their advantages.

—Adam Smith, *The Wealth of Nations*

CONTENTS

The Targets

Magic City Casino
Calder Casino and Race Course
Mardi Gras Casino

Salt Organizers

Sarah: from Massachusetts
Dan Connolly: Sarah's boss
Tom: salt in Boston

Salts

Mary: from Wisconsin
Erika: from Miami
Colette: from New York
Luke: from Tennessee

Union History

Herbert "Pinky" Schiffman:
    Miami hotel union local
    president from 1961 to 1977
Ed Hanley: Hotel union
    international president
    1973 to 1998
John Wilhelm: Hotel union
    president 1998 to 2009,
    Unite Here international
    president 1998 to 2012
Bruce Raynor: Unite Here
    international president
    2004 to 2009
Andy Stern: president of SEIU
    1996 to 2010

Unite Here Local 355

Wendi Walsh: president of
    Local 355
Alex: staff organizer
Rozaline: staff organizer
Pilar: staff organizer
Bridget: staff organizer
Andy: treasurer
Reverend Aguilar: Episcopal
    priest, organizer
Jeanette: community activist
Sam: researcher

Calder Management

Tom O'Donnell: president of
    Calder during orientation
Austin Miller: president
    of Calder after Tom
    O'Donnell
Stanley Donovan: director of
    food and beverage
Mike DiStefano: assistant
    director of food and
    beverage
Peggy: head of human
    resources
Jon: manager of Twin Spires
    Tavern
Debbie: buffet manager
Randy: buffet manager

Calder Employees

Kalia: buffet leader
Keon: dishwasher
Dylan: waiter from Vegas
Dot: concession cashier, brownnoser
Tricia: Twin Spires waitress
Donna: Twin Spires waitress
Melanie: bartender from Oregon
Becca: cocktail waitress
Ceci: dishwasher
Priya: buffet cashier, Vidya's sister
Vidya: buffet cashier, Priya's sister
Erin: buffet server
Rita: buffet server
Tasha: buffet server
String: buffet server

Mardi Gras Management

Dan Adkins: vice president
Steven Feinberg: director of human resources
Dick Trotter: head of security
Sally: food and beverage director
Rico: hired Mary
Jay: assistant food and beverage director

Frank: bar manager
Marat: manager of the French Quarter restaurant
Tim: food and beverage manager, father of Vanessa's nephew
Nydia: food and beverage manager

Mardi Gras Employees

Deirdre: bartender
Saraphina: cage cashier, committee member
Lena: cocktail waitress
Elisa: cocktail waitress
Vanessa: cocktail waitress
Grace: cocktail waitress
Lynne: cocktail waitress
Benita: housekeeper, committee member
Fabiola: housekeeper, committee member
Harriet: slot attendant, committee member
Alexis: slot attendant, committee member
Violine: concessions cashier
Alice: money sweeper, committee member
Rosalie: cage cashier, committee member
David: bartender

Brett: bartender

Tina: concession stand cashier

Dante: server in the French Quarter

Maya: guest services representative, committee member

Michael: cook in the French Quarter, committee member

Sean: porter

Lawyers and Judges

Susy Kucera: counsel for the National Labor Relations Board

William Zloch: federal judge who presided over the 10(j)

Robert Norton: counsel for Mardi Gras

Peter Sampo: counsel for Mardi Gras

George Carson: NLRB judge

AUTHOR'S NOTE

To write this story I used two years' worth of notes written on servers' pads and strips of glossy receipt paper. Whenever I wanted to write something down, I would flee to the bathroom or pull out my phone, pretend to text, and send an e-mail to myself. This is far from the most desirable method of reporting—some quotes were written down from memory an hour or two after they had been spoken—but I did my best to quote as accurately as possible. No one knew that his or her conversations with me would be printed in a book one day. As such, I have changed the names and identifying characteristics of certain people.

Part 1

GETTING IN

◎

Just west of Little Havana I saw the neon sign's giant letters burning red like a bull's-eye: Magic City Casino. I'd just consumed four times the recommended serving size of Miami's most popular legal upper, Cuban coffee, and my heart was bouncing like a racquetball in my rib cage. Sarah turned into the vast empty parking lot and pulled up alongside a row of taxis whose drivers were trying their luck between fares.

"It's going to be really hard to get a job at Neverland," she said. Unite Here Local 355, South Florida's hospitality union, was targeting three casinos for unionization. Magic City (code name: Neverland) was one of them. "I'm pretty sure they only hire people who speak Spanish. But it's worth a shot. So, I want you to go in and look around."

"Just walk around?" I asked.

"Yeah, and then, there's a bar on the left side when you walk in, I want you to go sit there and get the bartender's name. Start a relationship. Who knows? Maybe she will get you hired."

In fact, it was Sarah's job to get me hired. Sarah worked for Unite Here. She traveled the country recruiting and training

1

"salts," union activists who got jobs in non-union workplaces, intent on organizing them from the inside. I was in Miami to salt.

The thought of waltzing into Magic City and striking up a conversation with a bartender was daunting. I protested. What if the bartender is a woman? And what if she's hot? What if she doesn't want to talk to me? Sarah didn't budge. It was a push, union-speak for something more than a request and slightly less than a directive. Sarah, like other organizers, presumed any excuse to get out of a push to be a manifestation of fear. Of course, in this case, she was right. Back then, few tasks could have been more challenging than starting a conversation with a female bartender.

All three of the targets were relatively new. Miami-Dade voters had only recently approved slot machines at pari-mutuels (dog tracks, horse tracks, and jai alai frontons). Only three weeks earlier, Flagler Dog Track—first opened in 1931—had celebrated a grand reopening as Magic City Casino. Despite being largely empty of customers, the casino floor was loud and bright. Lights pulsed. Buttons blinked. The room was shaking with euphoric tintinnabulation. *Ding, ding, bling, bluuuueooorrrp. Ding, ding, bling.* I walked through the cornfield of machines with names like Kitty Glitter, Desert Spirit, Wolf Run, and Cleopatra. The people sitting in front of them, all older than forty, were transfixed. Slot machines were once thought to be a superfluous part of the gambling industry. They lined the walls of casinos, simple games for women to pass time with while their husbands played black-jack, poker, and roulette. But casino operators learned that the earning potential of slot machines greatly outmatched that of any other game. By the end of the twentieth century slot machines were the most prominent part of every casino in the country, producing twice as much revenue as blackjack, poker, roulette, and all other live games combined.

I found the bar. Behind it, to my horror, was a gorgeous

bartender. Tall and slender, her black hair braided like a whip, she was wearing a red corset and fishnet stockings. As I took a seat at the otherwise empty bar, I was struck by the dolorous realization that I had never spoken to a woman wearing a corset and fishnets.

"What can I get you?" she asked with a thick Latin accent.

"A coffee?"

"American or Cuban?"

"Cuban, please." Was it safe to consume two Cuban coffees in under an hour? I sipped what she placed in front of me, though it looked nothing like the *colada* Sarah had ordered for me on Calle Ocho twenty minutes earlier.

"How long have you been working here?" I asked with the surety of a newborn giraffe's first steps.

"Not long," she said coldly.

"I just moved here and I'm wondering who I should talk to if I want to get a job?"

Realizing that I wasn't hitting on her, she loosened up. "My manager isn't here right now. But I don't think they're hiring. They just fired, like, eight people in the buffet, and two bar backs." Sarah had warned me that newly opened casinos often overstaffed for grand openings.

"When is your manager usually around?"

"He comes by the bar around eleven. If you come back another time I'll introduce you."

I paid and asked for her name.

"Maria," she said with a smile. I retreated to Sarah's rental car, caffeine and adrenaline coursing through my body.

Inside the car, Sarah wrote down Maria's name. Sarah was constantly collecting intel on hotels and casinos. She had a list—food and beverage managers, security guards, directors of human resources—that might come in handy one day. Sarah had been responsible for getting plenty of salts hired. She believed my hiring to be a matter of societal certainty—I was a white male with straight teeth and a nonregional accent. I had been in Miami for less than a day and I was already eager to get inside. Once there, I could start making trouble.

A few months before I met Sarah, I knew nothing about unions, casinos, or Miami. I had just graduated from journalism school and landed an interview to be a research assistant to a popular historian. The interview went well. Toward the end of our conversation the historian casually asked me to pitch him a story. I'd known a few friends in college who salted. I told him about salting because it was the first—and only—good story that came to mind.

"Usually when I ask people your age to pitch me a story, they give me something that's total shit. But that's good. That might say something about your generation and what's going on in the country. You should do it." When I had asked my friends if I could write the story, they'd said no, salting was top secret. Off limits. "No, you should *do* it," the historian said. "You should salt. Then write about it."

Growing up, I knew nothing of unions. My only point of reference was the premature end of a pitiful Red Sox season in 1994. The baseball players' strike was a far cry from the battles fought between laborers and ruthless industrialists in Colorado's coal mines, Chicago's train yards, and Lowell's factories. As I became aware of unions' bloody history, I began to understand the importance of organized labor to the country's identity.

In 1935 Franklin Delano Roosevelt signed the National Labor Relations Act into law as part of a second wave of New Deal reforms that protected middle-class and poor Americans who had taken the brunt of the Great Depression. Over an eighteen-month period, from 1936 to 1937, more than three million workers unionized. By the middle of the twentieth century, almost one in three Americans belonged to a union.

In 2010, nationwide, labor unions represented 12 percent of the workforce and only 7 percent of private-sector workers. Studies proved the link between the plummeting rate of union membership and the disconcerting rise of income inequality. Unionized workers made about $200 more every week with greater access to benefits than their non-union counterparts. With the economy in shambles, why weren't low-wage workers joining in droves as they had after the Great Depression? Salting was the best way to find out. I was about to discover that some campaigns, no matter how well conceived, face anti-union strategies so insurmountable it's hard to fathom how any union organizing is accomplished.

In the summer of 2009, I told a salt I knew that I wanted in. He gave me Tom's number. Given the clandestine nature of the work it was best not to meet near the union hall, Tom said over the phone. A few days later, he sat coolly on the crossbar of his bike waiting for me near a coffee shop on Hanover Street in Boston's North End. He wore a newsboy cap atop a thicket of blond hair. Cheap sunglasses hung from the neck of his green collared shirt, the sleeves of which were rolled up, exposing the word "unity" tattooed on the inside of his left forearm.

Tom and I stepped into an authentic Italian coffee shop. As soon as we sat down, he started telling me about himself. Until recently, Tom had been working as a cook at a swanky corporate hotel in Boston. He had taken a leave of absence to work for Local 26, Unite Here's Boston chapter, as a full-time union organizer. He told me with pride that he had been one of the first salts in the city, and in the few years since the program began operations in Boston, the city's hotels had gone from

30 to 60 percent unionized. (Other salts would later say those numbers were optimistic.) Then Tom got more personal. His father was a stiff Republican and a National Guardsman who always worked two jobs. His mother was a waitress. They never had much money.

"Spaghetti with butter every night, man," he said, spinning his cup of cappuccino. "I wouldn't wish it on my worst enemies."

Just as I was thinking about how I had not asked any questions to prompt these personal details—what Tom was divulging normally took beers or years for most people to share—I realized this was not just coffee. Tom was baiting a story swap. I was now in a vetting process.

"So tell me about a time in your life when you had to fight for something," he said.

I would soon learn this verbal strategy. Sure, union organizers want to know if you have grit. But their conversations follow a kind of Socratic method; they want you to ask yourself if you have grit. There was a yawning silence while I wracked my memory for a story. I had also eaten spaghetti with butter every night, but only because everything else grossed me out. Did I have grit? Hardly. I told him about some college activism, how I'd fought apathy and all that, and made some nebulous reference to obstinate parents, which everyone can relate to. Tom didn't know my true intention was to write about my experience as a salt, which made me uncomfortable. I liked Tom. He wasn't what I had expected, a college punk who looked in the mirror and saw Che looking back. I needed to display a commitment. Organizers don't like half commitments because they don't have time to train salts who bail early.

"This is what I want to do," I said, looking him straight in his bright blue eyes. "I want to salt."

"We actually say 'intern.' No problem, it's just, 'salt' is such a loaded name." I'd learn that "salt" could mean a lot of different things to different people. For example, some unions used salts to provoke employers into breaking the law, a tactic, as far as I knew, antithetical to Unite Here's salting philosophy. "Anyway, you know the work's fucking hard, right?"

I both relished and feared the chance to work as a waiter or a bellman. I had never worked a service job, or any real job for that matter, in my life. "Yeah, I'm ready."

"Okay. There's a need in Miami, Phoenix, and Seattle."

"Miami?" I asked, unsure if I had heard him correctly.

"They're putting together a team down there. You'll be great, the hospitality industry loves us white guys. I can see you in a white linen suit. Miami Jim, they'll call you."

After Tom, I met with Becky, another member of Boston's salt team. Becky asked me the same questions Tom had as we walked around Cambridge. Like Tom, Becky approved of me, which meant I had been double-cleared. Sarah called a few days later. Sarah was one of two Unite Here staff members who worked full-time to build salt teams around the country. She came to Boston to meet me.

Sarah was my age, twenty-four, gaunt and tough like a stickball bat. She had thick black wavy hair and a hoop through her nose. She wore jeans with squiggly lines stitched up and down the legs. We ate burritos and walked around a reservoir. Our conversation had the same rhythm as my conversations with Tom and Becky—*I'll share my story if you share yours.*

Sarah was from rural Massachusetts, the kind of small college town populated by farmers, plumbers, and professors. Cows and hybrids. Growing up in a working-class townie family, Sarah was resentful of the white, comfortable, liberal lifestyle that permeated the town, even becoming disillusioned with members of her own family. She hung out with wandering street kids, hitchhiked the East Coast, and eventually dropped out of a small liberal arts college in Maryland and began salting. She never looked back. She salted for three years at a DoubleTree outside Washington, D.C. Salting gave her more than school ever had, she said. Finding the mettle to lead her coworkers and confront her bosses made Sarah, once shy and yielding, feel as if she had control of her life. After she organized the union at the DoubleTree, she joined Unite Here's staff to help build the salt program nationally.

When she finished her story, Sarah asked me questions similar to Tom's. Sarah offered me the same quiet attention that Tom had. They both used open-ended follow-ups—*Why? How did that make you feel?*—and nodded along to make sure I knew they were listening. I wasn't sure if they had ever met but it was as if they had attended the same church of conversation.

When I had convinced her that I would be a good underground organizer, she gave me what I wanted. "How do you feel about Miami?"

"Good?"

"I fucking love it. Everything you've heard about it is true. But there's more." Her eyes were wide, as if she were revealing a secret.

"Where would I work?"

"We don't know yet, but we're targeting casinos more than hotels now."

In late October, I stuffed everything I owned into my Ford Focus and headed down I-95, the air a little bit warmer each time I stopped for gas.

After Magic City, Sarah took me to Calder Casino and Race Course. We drove north along one of Miami-Dade's long avenues, past strip malls, schools, parks, and airports. In South Florida, places aren't hidden by hills or tucked into valleys. Mystery is man-made, veiled by walls and protected by gatekeepers with clipboards. An hour later we were on the northern edge of Miami-Dade, entering another vast parking lot.

The newly built casino, with its teal and yellow siding, rose out of the pavement like the Emerald City.

The grandstand, on the track's southern straightaway, was a massive structure enclosed in glass. Off to the side of the grandstand was the shell of the casino, a one-story building with the same dimensions as a Walmart. The casino hadn't opened yet so Sarah instructed me to walk around the grandstand.

"The guy who's going to be doing the hiring's name is Stanley Donovan; I think he's in charge of the food and beverage department or something. Let's not talk to him yet but you should go look around. Ask a worker about Stanley Donovan." This time I knew enough not to protest.

Unlike Magic City's casino floor, Calder's grandstand was quiet, outdated, and musty. There were walls of boxy TVs, empty cubicles, and rows of empty chairs in front of them. Calder's horses wouldn't start running for a few months. In the off-season, the grandstand had a skeleton crew to maintain the building, just enough to please the hard-core gamblers who came to wager on races simulcast around the world. They clenched their programs tightly, waiting for races to go off in the United Kingdom, South Africa, and Sweden. It was a motley bunch: white guys, Rastafarians, Indo-Caribbeans. Some would scream at the Thoroughbreds halfway around the world, urging them on. Others sat calmly with their heads resting in their hands.

I found a concession stand and was pleased to see a woman in her sixties sitting behind the counter reading a Bible. Her name was Ginette.

"You looking for the boss man?" she said when I asked her whom I should talk to about a job. She had a Haitian Creole accent. She was telling me that I would see the boss man if I hung around the hot dog stand long enough when she tensed up. "Don't look now, he's coming. Oh, and please don't tell him I told you."

A white guy with black hair walked around the corner.

Wearing a droopy suit, wire-rimmed glasses, and a cleanly shaven grimace, he looked like a basketball coach. I thanked Ginette and walked straight past the boss man, Stanley Donovan.

A few months after the target tour, we started using the code name "Disney" for Calder. It was the least creative of the code names (something to do with the general bliss of the staff when the casino first opened) and it was downright confusing with Disney World only a few hours north, but somehow it stuck. The third target, Mardi Gras Casino, had the most creative code name. Like Magic City, Mardi Gras was originally just a dog track. It was located in Hallandale Beach, a predominantly white suburb halfway between Miami and Fort Lauderdale, an area occupied by strip malls and streets cluttered with quaint homes and two-story apartment complexes. Early attempts at organizing Mardi Gras had ended disastrously, and, according to a local Haitian dishwasher whom Sarah had helped to get a job, work at Mardi Gras was grim. Thus, inspired by the casino's namesake and in remembrance of one of the grimmest scenes in recent American history, Sarah dubbed it "Superdome."

"You're not even gonna apply to Superdome," Sarah said. "They're on the lookout." She explained that a few months earlier she was helping another salt get hired at Mardi Gras. (The salt left the program soon after I had arrived.) After weeks of persistent nagging, he got an interview. When he showed up for what he thought would be an interview for a position in the food and beverage department, a sizable human being from the security department brought him to an empty room for questioning.

"They asked him who else he was working for," Sarah said, grinning with pride.

"How could they have possibly known?" I asked her.

"Because he's white, educated, and persistent." I guessed that was why I wasn't allowed to apply to Mardi Gras.

Salting is legal. In 1995, the Supreme Court unanimously ruled that workers could fulfill their obligations as employees of a company while simultaneously working for a union. As such, the concept of salting isn't a secret; companies know about it. A quick search online will yield a supposed internal Walmart labor handbook from the nineties, "A Manager's Toolbox to Remaining Union Free," which features an entire section on salting and how to recognize salts during the hiring process. ("Salts can be harmful to Wal-Mart, not only because of their organizing activities, but also because they typically feel they are 'above' company policies.") Nearly all of the information about salting on the Internet comes from the real salt experts, law firms that specialize in keeping workplaces union-free. Such firms warn companies about salts who intend to provoke clients into costly legal battles or, as many websites warn, destroy company property in an effort to shut down non-union construction sites. Nothing like the work I would be doing.

With Mardi Gras "on the lookout," Sarah told me to walk around but not to talk to anybody. The casino floor was a tumbling kaleidoscope of Fat Tuesday purple, green, and gold. Other than the New Orleans theme, everything else was the same as Magic City. The same slot machines lined the walls with the same lights and the same *dings* and *blings*. The patrons were under the same spell, slapping the same buttons in syncopation. I saw a few bartenders; a cocktail waitress glided across the floor in a corset similar to Maria's. I walked from one end to the other and back out to Sarah's rental car.

Once we had visited the targets, Sarah decided it was time to begin applying for jobs. I got a haircut and shaved for the first time in months. "Oh God, you look like a manager," she said. Sarah proceeded to shuttle me to every hotel, casino, restaurant, and bar in Miami-Dade while listening to a mix of Mariah Carey's greatest hits, the only CD she had with her. To new salts, Sarah was half college counselor and half parole officer. When she said, "I think you should," she meant "You need to." She took us shopping at discount clothing stores to find outfits—ties for the boys and short skirts for the ladies. She role-played conversations with me:

"Hi, I'm James," I would say with an all-American smile. "Are you the manager?"

"Yes, I'm Sarah. How can I help you?"

"Hi, Sarah, I'd love to work here. I'm wondering if I could give you my résumé?"

"We prefer that you submit applications on our website."

"Please?"

"I'm sorry, I really can't take it."

Blank stare.

Sarah would break character. "Get me talking. Ask where I'm from. Talk about where you're from. Talk about how beautiful the casino is. Talk about how much you love the Miami Dolphins. Anything! It's awkward because you're making it awkward."

Sarah walked me through applications, a few of which were harder than I expected. One upscale French hotel required all applicants to take a 230-question personality test. I assumed the hotel operators valued laissez-faire strictly as a capitalist concept, not a philosophy they would want their waiters subscribing to. So, as I did so many times, I answered the questions in the spirit of Boxer, the cart horse in Orwell's *Animal Farm*.

I like to challenge authority.
Strongly Disagree

I adapt quickly to changing work situations.
Strongly Agree

```
Personal feelings are very important in
a business environment.
```
Strongly Disagree

```
Napoléon is always right.
```
Strongly Agree

Other questions were more challenging.

```
I believe you first have to collect all
the information you can in order to make
the best decision.
```
Strongly Agree? Agree? Neutral? Disagree? Strongly Disagree?

Strongly agree, right? But did the hotel want me to slow down my decision making? If so, should I only agree? I called Sarah for help.

"Strongly agree," she said confidently. I moved on to the next tough one.

```
I have never been late for—
```

"Strongly agree!" she said before I could finish.

"That seems ridiculous. Do they want me to lie? Do they want someone who's delusional?"

"Believe me, it's the answer they want," Sarah said.

```
I am the friendliest person I have ever
met.
```

"Strongly agree," she said again. Delusional and narcissistic waiters.

There were questions about my decision making, my risk taking, my attitudes about safety and danger. Some questions

sounded as if they could have been asked by psychiatrists, financial advisers, or a Clint Eastwood character about to send
his daughter on her first date.

```
Self-sufficiency   is   the   key   to   being
successful.
```

The key? Sure, it's a factor, but do they want me to say
anyone who's self-sufficient will be successful? What about
teamwork? And how are we defining success? There were
questions about problem solving, motivations, shopping rou-
tines, and pride. If this hour-long psychological colonoscopy
did anything, it heightened my ability to empathize with test
monkeys and four-year-olds taking entrance exams to posh
Manhattan preschools.

I hit them all, dropping off applications, meeting managers,
filling out online applications everywhere I could. Marriott,
Hyatt, Sofitel, Four Seasons, DoubleTree. One afternoon I
walked into a self-styled "boutique" hotel on South Beach
and was immediately granted an interview with the general
manager. The hotel was opening a small restaurant off the
lobby and needed another waiter.

After looking me up and down and glancing at my résumé,
he asked me one question: "You're new to Miami, how do I
know you're not going to quit and work at a five-star hotel
in a week?"

"That's not for me," I told him. "I like the small intimate
setting here."

I was hired. I took the job for the paycheck and to get some
service-industry training while I applied for jobs at the targets. On my first day the manager of the restaurant, a middle-

aged Trinidadian man, introduced me to Pedro, the only other waiter at the restaurant.

"I'm Carlos," the man who had been introduced as Pedro said as the manager walked away. "I stopped correcting him a while ago."

Carlos was in his early thirties and handsome with thick dark stubble. He said that he'd come to the United States from Cuba only two years ago. He'd graduated from the top hospitality school in Cuba and it showed. Watching Carlos serve was like watching a figure skater. He was quick, precise, and clean. Lucky for me, he was also happy to teach. He went over the basics: never sit, never serve a drink without a tray, cut lemons like this, open wine like that. When he saw that I was genuinely interested in the work, he shared more esoteric knowledge: When setting the table, use the end of your thumb, from the joint to the tip, to measure the proper length between the bottom of the silverware and the table's edge. Serve solid food from the left, liquid from the right. He taught me how to fold napkins to look like seashells, a miter, and his favorite, the vulva. Carlos was good company and I was lucky to get a crash course from someone with his patience.

Soon, Sarah cleared me to begin applying at Magic City and Calder. I started visiting both casinos on a regular basis. At Magic City, I sought out Maria and met her manager. I put $5 in a slot machine and won $40. I chatted up Doris, a security guard, and asked her if I needed any special qualifications to work security. She guffawed and handed me a strip of paper with an e-mail address to send my résumé to.

At Calder, I looked for Stanley Donovan. In a moment of uncharacteristic temerity, I waltzed into an area marked *Employees Only* and found his office. He wasn't in it. I returned a few days later and found him by the concession stand where I'd met Ginette.

"I'm James, I just wanted to meet you. I'd really love to work here," I said with the confidence of someone who had rehearsed the line a hundred times.

"Well, we're not hiring yet. The casino isn't open. We'll be posting the jobs online as soon as we're ready."

His name tag said he was from Springfield, Massachusetts.

"I'm from around there. I grew up near Hartford and went to college in Boston." He looked at me, puzzled as to why I had decided to share such facts. "So, yeah, close to Springfield," I added.

"Well, like I said, we're not hiring yet but just check on-line."

Sure enough, Calder posted a ton of jobs. I filled out applications to be a barback, restaurant host, bartender, food server, food runner, concessions attendant, steward, and security officer. After I submitted the applications, Sarah instructed me to go back and remind Stanley Donovan.

Once again, I found him near Ginette's concession stand.

"If you applied, I'll see it," he said, a bit annoyed by my persistence.

Sarah would stay in Miami for only as long as it took to assemble a salt team. For the first few weeks I was in Florida, Sarah was living in a shabby Ramada in downtown Hollywood, a strip of bizarre food and entertainment pairings a mile north of Mardi Gras. There was a hookah joint with belly dancing, a few sports bars, a fifties diner, and a musty wine bar, which, I later found out, advertised itself as a place where "adventurous couples and singles meet." It was at the Ramada that I first met Dan Connolly, Sarah's boss and the only other Unite Here employee working full-time on the salt program.

Salting, in some form or another, has been around as long as organized labor. In the 1860s, the Rochester Trades Assembly began sending "agents" to organize non-union construction jobs. Coal miners salted throughout the latter half of the nineteenth century. Garment workers salted factories, longshoremen salted docks, and autoworkers salted Detroit. They were leftists, Mexican immigrants, Jewish seamstresses, communists, anarchists, and socialists. With no distinction between worker and organizer, these so-called agents were on the front lines of America's most harrowing labor struggles.

Nobody knew salting better than Dan. He was one of the first to revitalize the practice for Unite Here, and, after winning a union at a California Four Seasons, he went on to build the program for the union nationally. He was largely responsible for the growth of the salt program over the past ten years. (Though they were hesitant to share any concrete numbers, Sarah and Dan estimated that there were about two hundred salts working in hotels and casinos at any given time.) Dan frequented colleges and activist communities, groups of people still riding the wave of the Battle in Seattle, hungry for ways to maintain a radical existence between protests. When I talked to Dan on the phone before moving to Florida, I conjured up a picture of a brawny union man from a different era, a standing portrait of gritty America. Dan Connolly, the Irish proletarian. He may have been Irish, but the real Dan Connolly was proof that mobsters and steelworkers no longer epitomize the union profile. Dan was gentle, more bookish than brutish. He'd once wanted to work in science and children's entertainment, be the next Bill Nye the Science Guy, but after losing the fight to unionize a children's museum where he'd worked, he decided to spend his life fighting for workers' rights. He was thoughtful and you needed to listen closely to enjoy his subtle sense of humor. He wore plaid dress shirts and khaki shorts. Thin blond hair topped a face with pink cheeks. His quiet nature was deceiving. Dan was enthralled with union organizing.

Even his hobbies were evidence of a one-track mind. He loved sports and he particularly relished opportunities to talk about unions and sports together.

"Sean Payton is a scab," he'd said about the coach of the New Orleans Saints. Payton had played for the Chicago "Spares" when the Chicago Bears were striking with the rest of the NFL players in 1987. Dan was also happy to point out that Drew Brees, Payton's quarterback with the Saints, was a vocal leader in the NFL players' union. Dan used his knowledge of sports to broaden his skills as an organizer. The first time I met him, he asked me if I had any brothers or sisters. When I told him that I was close to my older sister, he gestured approvingly. "I've been reading about John Wooden. You know Wooden? The famous UCLA basketball coach? He'd ask his recruits if they got along with their siblings because it's a sign of how they would perform as team members."

Dan would casually make such connections in conversation. Sometimes it would be sports, other times pop culture: "If people watch *Mad Men,* they'll know how to get hired at corporate hotels. The old, sexist world actually hasn't changed in these places." Or religion: "I want to know more about Jehovah's Witnesses and Mormons and how they organize, because they just seem to be so damn good at it."

On a brilliant Miami winter afternoon Dan, who had been busy starting a salt program in another city and had come to Florida to check on Sarah's progress, asked me potential interview questions from a list that a salt in another city had seen on the desk of a human resources employee.

"Tell me about a time you went above and beyond for a customer," Dan asked, his expression devoid of irony. I gave him the story I had prepared with Sarah.

"I was working at a high-end restaurant as a waiter. An elderly couple came in for their fortieth wedding anniversary. They were sweet, dressed in a suit and a poufy dress. Well, before they had even ordered drinks, Manny, a clumsy busboy, spilled water all over the gentleman. I, of course, apologized profusely and told Manny to do the same. I got permission from my manager to offer the couple complimentary glasses of champagne. While pouring the champagne, I slyly asked what their wedding song was. The gentleman told me it was 'Dream a Little Dream of Me' by Louis Armstrong and Ella Fitzgerald. I downloaded the song and played it over the restaurant's speakers as I brought out a complimentary chocolate cake, again approved by my manager. They were overjoyed. Carl and Henrietta still go to that restaurant every anniversary. I like to think I played a small part in that." When I finished, Dan cracked a smile and chuckled.

"Too much?" I asked.

"As crazy and corny as you sound, you can't do too much. They eat this shit up."

Dan was right. One salt wrote at the top of his résumé: "Guests love me and so will you!" He got hired. Another salt told me that when he was interviewed to be a cook in a hotel he had used the line: "I believe the most important ingredient I cook with is love." He got hired. A Chicago salt told me she used a fake story similar to mine but hers involved a diner across the street from a hospital and "going above and beyond" for a man's dying wife. It was clear that Sarah and Dan wanted me to do anything possible to get hired, but there was something holding me back that they didn't know about. I knew, as a journalist, my deception had boundaries. Obviously, I was already in a gray area of journalistic ethics, but legally I knew that I couldn't lie my way into a paying job. Sarah would spend an hour editing my résumé and I would reedit it before submitting it to the targets. I could not use the story of Carl and Henrietta's anniversary, but more than a year later, I gifted it to a salt who used it during an interview at Magic City. She was hired.

Dan showed me an evaluation form from the human resources department of another corporate hotel.

```
This candidate:
Lacks  a  smile,  occasionally  smiles,
frequently smiles.
```

I smiled until my cheeks were numb. It took me a while to get comfortable with the corny character I was playing. I feared my enthusiasm might out me as a subversive. Dan assured me otherwise.

"Salts are like crack for these hospitality companies," he told me. "They look at us and say, 'This person is too good to be true.' And they're right. We are too good to be true. But they can't resist. They just have to shoot up." Dan fired off a few questions that Sarah had already prepared me for.

"What would you do if you had a problem with a coworker?"

"Outside of work, I'd try to make him or her feel more comfortable. I don't think the workplace is an appropriate venue for personal issues."

"Do you have reliable transportation to work?"

"Yes."

"Do you have a scheduling preference?"

"No."

"We think you'd be more valuable to our management team, how does that sound?"

"I hope to be on the management team one day but I want to start in the trenches and work my way up. I want to earn it."

"When are you available to start?"

"Right now."

Dan listened intently to each of my answers. He added ideas that might give my story extra flair. "Say you're a quick learner. Quick learners save companies time and money. Most importantly, remember getting hired is all about selling your story." Obviously, the story I'd tell a hotel manager would be different from the one I had used during the salt vetting process, but the principle, as Dan explained, was the same.

"We, as the middle and upper class, are told from day one to create a story. It's bullshitting. Your story, just like a politician's story, is based on the convergence of two things: your life and the job you want. Up until this point, how has your life prepared you for this job? As long as you put those two things together with everything you say, you will be okay." It was better advice than I'd gotten from my university's career center. We sat in silence and thought of ways to tie the casino industry to my life. At some point Dan gave me a list of typical interview questions with exemplary answers that another salt had put together. At the top it said: "Remember, the less you have to lie the better."

"You grew up in Connecticut, right? They have casinos there. You ever been to Mohegan Sun or Foxwoods?"

"Nope."

"Okay. But you remember seeing that they are doing well on the local news and you think the same thing will happen in Miami but bigger, right? I mean you can say you went there as a customer, right?"

"Right." I filed the story away to use in an interview.

Dan and Sarah loved their jobs. They loved teaching young idealists how to get hired in an industry that coveted hokey and repressive conventionalities they actually despised. While the job required a certain level of perception and judgment, there were plenty of people who could have done the day-to-day work that Sarah did. What Sarah brought to the job was stubborn resolve and loyalty to Unite Here. To Sarah, there was no other job, no other union, no other fight. She believed that the labor movement, with Unite Here at the helm, had the ability to influence all of the world's maladies. The union gave Haitian workers enough money to send to relatives, daughters a chance to become scientists, janitors the opportunity to retire, and perhaps most importantly, history had proven that unions were a way to grow the middle class.

In Miami, Sarah struggled to recruit new salts. People drifted in and out of the program. There were college activists who were intrigued. They would fly to Miami for a weekend, but after a few endless afternoons in Sarah's rental car, they would fly home, never to be heard from again. There were former members of Local 355 who needed jobs but didn't understand why Sarah was so pushy. There were Miami activists who got tired of Sarah's showing up at their homes unexpectedly. Sarah believed in the power of salting because it had helped her develop so much as a person. (She was the happiest when she was telling recruits about the time she summoned the courage to confront her bosses at the DoubleTree and her coworkers had her back.) Sometimes, what most would consider friendly banter felt like work because she would sneak in inane pushes. I stopped mentioning friends' names in front of her because she would always push me to recruit them. Such interactions made it easy to feel like a number in her recruitment folder. She couldn't understand why a burgeoning activist would do anything other than salt. Office jobs might as well have been Plato's cave and she didn't know—or care—why people chose to stay in the dark. I listened to Sarah tell college students about her experience as a dropout. She thought of herself as an enlightened twenty-first-century progressivist who saw college for the sham she thought it truly was. Which fit her own story. Sarah had found her dream job without college, and she was good at it. Sarah was dogged. She continued to recruit salts by following up on every lead she got. When an organizer in Milwaukee sent word through Unite Here that he had a recent college graduate interested, Sarah made a trip north to meet her.

Mary was a smiley Wisconsinite who grew up on a farm

out where the roads don't bend—the Wisconsin State Fair occupied a line on her résumé. As such, Mary knew about horses and hard work. She attended a big state school but left after a tuition hike. "It was pretty hard to look at them building a brand-new football stadium when I couldn't afford another semester," she told me later. She transferred to a cheaper college in Milwaukee. While there, Mary got involved with Unite Here. Sarah met up with Mary in Chicago and took her to a massive Unite Here protest. At the protest, two hundred people were arrested outside a Hyatt in support of ninety-eight housekeepers who had been fired from Hyatt hotels in Boston. Afterward, moved by this extreme act of solidarity, Mary committed to salting. A month later, she quit her job waitressing at a movie theater that doubled as a restaurant and moved to Miami against her father's will.

Sarah and Dan believed salt teams should be comprised of both locals and out-of-towners. With Mary and me committed, Sarah concentrated on finding salts in Miami. She put together a few conferences billed vaguely as organizing trainings for "young activists." At the trainings, Sarah would illustrate the importance of unions by comparing the average workloads and wages of housekeepers in cities with high and low union densities. San Francisco's hotels are 85 percent organized. Their housekeepers make $19 an hour. They clean twelve rooms a shift. Housekeepers working for the same hotels in Phoenix make $7.75 an hour. They clean twenty-one rooms a shift. Only 2 percent of hotels are unionized in Phoenix. Miami housekeepers clean fifteen rooms a shift. They make $10 an hour. At that point in my union education, the disparity in the numbers was to be expected.

Sarah had a way of stating facts that were too obscure to refute or so inane they weren't worth checking. ("Those cranes lifting storage containers off freight ships were the inspiration for the big walking things in *Star Wars*." *False*. "Did you know Dolly Parton's husband has never seen her perform live?" *Ev-*

idence inconclusive.) But when it came to union knowledge, Sarah generally got things right. One of her factoids left me dumbfounded.

"Housekeepers are more likely to suffer injuries on the clock than coal miners," she said, pausing and waiting for the disbelief to sink in. I wrote this down to check later. I was amazed by what I found. Housekeepers *are* more likely to suffer injuries on the job than coal miners by more than one percentage point. Hotel mattresses are as heavy as they are comfortable. The repetition of lifting, lunging, scrubbing, pushing, standing, and twisting can have ruinous effects on the body. But on average, housekeepers make less than half of what coal miners make annually. Sarah and the other organizers who spoke at these trainings used these examples to explain that the union wasn't simply about raises; it was also about long-term health, workload, and a good pair of shoes.

I met Erika at one of Sarah's trainings. She was a punk rocker working at a shampoo shop in the mall. She had grown up in Miami. Her father was a therapist and her mother taught at a small university. Erika's hair was bleached blond with a pink streak. She had cartoonish tattoos around her shoulder and the leather straps of her gladiator sandals wrapped around an unfinished skull tattooed on her shin. She was loud and enthusiastic. I could hear her across the room, making everyone around her laugh. It wasn't long before we were talking and she told me about how her recent marriage would affect her Mexican husband's immigration status. Then she invited me to a punk show at Churchill's, a dive bar famous for its live music. Erika's demeanor could switch between professional and a somewhat ironic bubble-gum Valley girl with surprising ease. Both seemed incongruous with her punk rock style, which made her all the more exotic to everyone around her.

Whether in professional mode or Valley girl mode, she was always encouraging. When I told her that I was looking for an apartment, she took my phone number. "Don't you worry, baby boy. I'll hook it up. Loves it!"

It was impossible not to like Erika. I was happy when she joined us as we traversed Miami-Dade in Sarah's rental car. Mary and Erika began visiting Stanley Donovan and the bartenders at Magic City. Sarah also allowed Mary and Erika to dress up and visit the bar at Mardi Gras. They were told to find a manager, Rico, who would "*love* you girls." The team grew closer. Sarah and Mary moved into a house off Biscayne Boulevard. It was across the street from Erika's apartment, on the fringes of Little Haiti and a stoplight away from the walls of Morningside, a ritzy neighborhood next to Biscayne Bay. The house itself was massive with oceans of sunlight and a yard with tropical shrubbery as tall as a lamppost. The union would never use members' dues to fund a salt house so Sarah, being the only one with a steady paycheck, paid the lion's share of the rent. Sarah was certain more salts would follow and they would eventually fill the other bedrooms.

Living in the salt house wasn't an option for me. I was constantly updating my notes and didn't want to risk exposing my writing. I signed a month-to-month lease on a studio apartment with an ocean view. Sure, the building was decrepit, filled with cockroaches and mold, but I wanted to live near the ocean as I was starting to feel like my time in Miami might be short-lived. After a month of applications, I was discouraged and skeptical of the program. I was told I'd be unionizing a workplace in Miami and that process still felt distant and abstract. After trainings or long days in her rental car, the salts talked about Sarah and her pushes like we would an overbearing boss at the office. I wondered if my blind faith in Sarah's plan was just an exercise in liberal disorganization or, perhaps, something worse. I had heard former salts describe Unite Here's salt culture as exploitative and cultish.

Relief came in an e-mail I received while working the breakfast shift at the boutique hotel.

Dear James,

I would personally like to congratulate you for being selected for our interview process. After reviewing your application for your desired position, we would like to move you to our next step in our selection process in joining our Food & Beverage team here at Calder Casino & Race Course.

Best Regards,
Mike DiStefano

Mary and Erika also got interviews with Mike DiStefano. On the day of my interview, I met Sarah at a McDonald's inside a Walmart near Calder. I was wearing a gray suit. She had on her squiggly jeans. We ate fries and went over a few warm-up questions.
"Why do you want this job?"
"Why did you move to South Florida?"
"Where do you see yourself in five years?"
She approved.
"You're ready."

Mike DiStefano greeted me outside the grandstand and escorted me into the building and down the hallway. He led me through the door marked *Employees Only,* unaware of the fact that I had already looked behind this curtain, and showed me to a conference room, where we sat across from each other.
"I see you have a Connecticut area code," he said. "I just moved down from Connecticut. I worked at Foxwoods." With

that, I decided not to bring up my home state's casino industry. Mike was clean-cut, in a suit and tie, late thirties, but could have passed for late twenties. He was white with a tourist tan. Later on, one of my coworkers would describe him as "Joel Osteen with a Kool-Aid smile." He was a likable guy, certainly more affable than his boss, Stanley Donovan. Just before the interview commenced, Stanley walked by and Mike called him in to introduce us.

"I know James," Stanley said. "This is the guy I told you about."

Mike looked as if he had no idea what Stanley was talking about. Stanley looked at Mike as if to say, *Cover for me.* Apparently, I would have gotten the interview regardless of my courtship of Stanley.

At first, Mike did the talking. He showed me a blueprint of the casino floor where the buffet, restaurant, and concessions stand would be located.

"We really want everybody to be able to work every job, but you'll probably be good for the high-end restaurant, the Twin Spires Tavern. I mean, it's not a hundred-a-head Foxwoods here, we're talking more like a hundred bucks for a four-top." I bobbed my head to acknowledge the industry language. When he was done describing the food and beverage layout he looked around the blueprint, searching for something else to tell me.

"Oh! I almost forgot." He pulled out a piece of paper with interview questions. "What does 'on the rocks' mean?"

Cake.

"What do you do if there's an overserved couple?"

Training kicked in.

"How many ounces in a standard pour for a glass of wine?"

"Eight?"

"It should be about five. You keep pouring eight, you'll be fired," he said, sneering.

"Give me a bottle and a glass and I'm sure I'll pour five."

I nailed a few more restaurant questions thanks to Sarah and my guardian angel, Carlos. Then Mike asked if I had any questions.

"There are a couple of casinos opening around here, how is this one going to separate itself?"

"With people like you," he said, clearly pleased with my presentation.

There were no congratulations. Mike shook my hand and passed me off to a seamstress, who fitted me for a uniform. I was surprised by the sleek look of it, a dark clay-colored tunic with a mandarin collar and black dress slacks. After being fitted, I went to the human resources office to fill out paperwork.

Calder contracted an independent health clinic to administer drug tests to new hires. The clinic was twenty minutes away and looked like any doctor's office. Objectively, it's easy to understand why companies require drug tests. No one wants to hire an employee who might be tripping on peyote when the fire alarm goes off. A year after I was hired at Calder, the salt team worked hard to get an unemployed Local 355 member a job there. He smoked weed two or three times a day so when he went to the health clinic for testing, he taped a bag of Clean Stream synthetic urine around his thigh, and once in the privacy of a bathroom stall, he popped a tab that warmed the yellow liquid and poured it into the cup. He passed and quickly became one of management's favorite housekeepers.

Mike DiStefano's interviews with Mary and Erika went just as well. Erika was hired as a bartender and Mary as a waitress in the Twin Spires Tavern.

Not long after I was hired at Calder, the security guard I had talked to at Magic City, Doris, called. I had landed an interview with the head of security. While security wasn't part of Unite Here's beginning unit, Sarah believed I could get my foot in the door and transfer to a food and beverage job. At the very least, the interview was a chance to collect some intelligence to pass on to future salts trying to get jobs at Magic City. Sarah didn't know what to expect from a security interview so she consulted a salt who had worked in hotel security. He told her that low-level security jobs depend on communication and the ability to defuse situations that might make a scene. Deep down, I still hoped they would teach me how to spot card counters and maybe some jujitsu.

On the day of the interview, I waited in the security office and listened to the dispatcher say "Bravo" and "Charlie" into a walkie-talkie. The head of security showed me to his office. He was young with tightly cropped hair and a goatee. He was stern and spoke with a subtle Latin accent. He had spent the last four years as a Secret Service agent. All of the security guards at Magic City wore red polo shirts and blazers. His blazer looked tailored. Sitting down, I realized how eerily similar this was to the scenario Sarah had described at Mardi Gras: a young, white, educated, persistent salt gets an interview with the head of security. Was I about to be interrogated about the union?

"Okay, you good to go?" he asked as he held up a list of questions. "Do you believe you have the courage to save someone's life?" I felt like he had pulled the trigger of a clown gun. I was relieved and stifled an urge to laugh.

"Yes, absolutely," I said, tightening my eyebrows in an attempt to make myself look more like Steven Seagal.

"Good to go. What are five words you would use to describe yourself?"

"Effective, sociable, loyal, trustworthy, and strong-willed."

"Good to go. What would you do if two guests were in a confrontation?"

"I would immediately defuse the situation." I was about to give him the rest of the script I had prepared but he cut me off.

"I like your language."

"Thank you."

"What would you do if you saw a coworker smoking marijuana?"

"I would immediately report him to my superior, because that is a mistake that affects all of us." I startled myself with the professionalism—and guile—of my answer.

"Good to go. What would you do if you heard a fire alarm?"

"Direct the guests to the nearest exits."

"Actually, we make sure it's a real fire first. Don't want to mess up someone's hot streak." He smiled. "Why do you want this job?"

"The casino industry is growing. It's going to be big. I'm from Connecticut, they've got Foxwoods and Mohegan Sun up there and they are huge. I think Miami can be bigger—"

"Good to go. We're expanding by seventy-five percent soon." I could tell he was warming to me. "Have you ever done drugs?"

I shifted in my chair. "No . . . well . . . like, *ever*?" I regretted the response immediately. Sarah would be so disappointed.

"Yes, *ever*."

"No, no. Never."

He grinned. "Are you sure?"

"Yes."

When he ran out of questions he sent me down the hall to a room where a paramedic administered a piss test. After I passed, I went back to the security office to fill out some papers.

"Did you pass?" he asked me.

"I'm good to go."

I had the job.

Rico at Mardi Gras had loved Mary, and not long after her Calder interview, she got a job as a waitress in Mardi Gras's

French Quarter restaurant. After two months of calculated, persistent work, Sarah had managed to get salts hired at all three targets. I was officially a believer. Sarah consulted the leadership at Local 355 and decided that Erika and I would start a campaign at Calder while Mary began a campaign at Mardi Gras. New salts would be moving to Florida soon and it would be our responsibility to get them hired at Calder and Mardi Gras to bolster our numbers. Finally, it was time to salt.

Mariah Carey's "Honey" was playing as we drove across Biscayne Bay toward the Fontainebleau hotel, one of Sarah's favorite places to take salts when they first arrived in Miami. The Fontainebleau was one of Local 355's oldest, biggest, and prettiest shops. The hotel has a grand history. Elvis, drug smugglers, Gleason, Sinatra, *The Sopranos,* real mobsters, murder plots, presidents, and (my favorite) a wall built to cast a shadow over a competing hotel's pool next door.

Inside the lobby, crystal chandeliers dangled from the ceiling like giant inverted birthday cakes. The floor radiated electric blue. Golden columns surrounded a circular bar with a glowing pink pillar at its center. The Fontainebleau was the Miami of my mind's eye, an unapologetic partnership of pomp and paradise.

"Any chance I'm going to work here?" I asked.

"Nope, sometimes we put interns in places that are union but we need new shops in Miami."

"What other hotels are unionized?"

"The Miami Beach Resort and the Westin Diplomat," Sarah said. I waited for her to continue. There were more than one thousand hotels in South Florida. Only three were unionized? I had heard Unite Here represented as much as 80 percent of hotel workers in cities like New York, Chicago, Las Vegas, and

San Francisco. Because Miami had as many, if not more, hotel rooms per capita, I figured the density would be comparable.

The comparison between Miami and Las Vegas is natural. Two hot cities swollen with tourists looking for sun during the day and bass-thumping debauchery at night. Yet the difference between the average hotel worker's compensation in Vegas and Miami is substantial. The average Vegas housekeeper makes about $16 an hour. The average housekeeper in Miami makes about $10. Las Vegas's Culinary Workers Union Local 226 (a Unite Here local) was founded in the 1930s. Throughout the twentieth century Local 226 battled the two other giant forces on the strip: the mob and corporations. (In 1977, the head of Local 226 was found naked in a "shallow grave" thirty miles outside of Las Vegas.) Through it all Local 226 continued to build its membership and won major strikes in the seventies, eighties, and nineties. Today, Local 226 boasts a membership of fifty-five thousand. Many workers on the strip are homeowners who can afford to save for college and retirement. Unions in Las Vegas enjoy a tremendous amount of political capital—presidential candidates don't go to Vegas for the shows.

Like Vegas, Miami's hospitality local was incorporated in the 1930s, the dawn of American destination tourism. Up until that point, Florida's major industries—railroads, sugar, tomatoes, and shipping—relied on cheap labor, and slave labor before that. The hotels, in accordance with the area's other local industries, often forced their staff to work seven days a week without benefits or overtime pay. As such, hotel owners were extremely hostile toward the union. The union's newsletter printed a call to action: "Members from other cities who come to Miami and obtain employment in hotels which are in the process of being organized can be very helpful to us in securing the required majority before the union can legally demand recognition." The union was looking for salts. Aware of management's animosity toward organizers in South Florida, the newsletter requested that members coming to Miami drop off their membership cards at the local's office to avoid being found out.

Miami, like the rest of the country, brimmed with labor activism throughout the 1950s. As unions grew, they were able to hire full-time staff organizers, political organizers, negotiators, consultants, researchers, lobbyists, office managers, and public relations specialists. Salts were no longer a staple of the union campaign. Recognizing the growth of the hospitality industry in Miami, the international sent money and organizers in the hopes of establishing the city as a hotel union stronghold in the South. There were strikes, negotiations, and rallies with as many as 15,000 in attendance. By some estimates, at its peak, the union grew to represent nearly half of all hotel employees in Miami during vacation season.

In 1961, Herbert "Pinky" Schiffman, a professional boxer turned bartender turned union leader, was elected president of a healthy Hotel Employees and Restaurant Employees local in Miami. He was stout, with a slick comb-over and drooping earlobes. The walls of his office were adorned with civic awards from the community and pictures of the pugilist president alongside Frank Sinatra, Jackie Gleason, and Senator Scoop Jackson. One union member described Schiffman as a "tough guy" who would "give you the shirt off his back." He spoke in short, punchy sentences like he was doing a postfight interview. With his tough attitude, for the first fifteen years of his tenure, Pinky managed to maintain, even grow, the local's membership. But Pinky didn't stay out of trouble.

In 1975, Pinky was found guilty of intimidating an Atlanta Hyatt hotel manager into providing him and other union leaders with a discounted rate. (Under federal law unions and companies cannot exchange "things of value.") In 1978, a report drafted for the White House titled "Organized Crime and the Labor Unions" cited Schiffman as "an associate of several southern organized crime figures." Given the rampant corruption of unions, the fact that Schiffman was never publicly linked to the Mafia in South Florida is surprising. South Florida had long been popular with the mob before Schiffman arrived, and while the leadership of other unions could be found mingling with La Cosa Nostra, members of the hotel local's leadership were more often victims of racketeering than willing participants. Nevertheless, Schiffman wasn't squeaky clean. In addition to his position as president of the local, he was a vice president of the international. The president at the time was Ed Hanley, who, like Schiffman, was a former bartender. Hanley is best remembered as a brilliant and committed organizer who had many alleged ties to organized crime. Under Hanley, a congressional report found the hotel union to be one of the most corrupt in the country.

In 1979, Schiffman was part of a trio of union officials—including the international's secretary treasurer—indicted for misappropriating union resources when they used the union jet for a salmon fishing trip to Quebec. (The union had paid $2.5 million for the jet at Hanley's insistence.) The union's pilot was also ordered to fly to Quebec City to pick up ladies in "evening" attire and shuttle them to the resort. While his miscues certainly harken back to a time when union leaders abused their power, the list of Schiffman's indiscretions is paltry compared to the massive corruption scandals at other unions throughout the latter half of the twentieth century. What's more, as far as the record shows, Schiffman's improprieties weren't necessarily the reason the South Florida local began to crumble.

In 1976, Schiffman led an enormous, disruptive strike on Miami Beach. It was December, the high season in South Florida, and five thousand workers picketed eleven hotels—including the Fontainebleau—to demand contracts with better wages. Some said it was the changing demographics in South

Florida that put pressure on Pinky to call for the strike. When Pinky first took office, less than 20 percent of Miami-Dade's population was foreign born. By 1976, there were more Cubans and South Americans than ever in Miami and much of the local was Latino. The strike was a terrible disaster. By the time it was called off, not only had the union failed to win what they asked for but four hundred workers, who had struck with the understanding that they would be put back to work, weren't rehired because Schiffman and Hanley (who had been brought in to negotiate with the hotels) had "mistakenly" forgotten to include a provision that guaranteed that all strikers would be rehired.

Schiffman was forced out of his presidency because of "financial irregularities," and the local was put under the trusteeship of the international. The day after the court ruled the hotels weren't required to rehire four hundred strikers, Pinky left his apartment building in a suit and tie. While president of the local, Schiffman had a chauffeur. Now he was renting a '78 Buick LeSabre. Car bombs were in vogue in Miami and Pinky knew how to check his car for explosives. On that morning Pinky either didn't check or the bomb under the hood of his car was well hidden. When he opened the driver's-side door of the car the bomb triggered. The blast broke windows on all three floors of Schiffman's apartment building and knocked the toothbrush from a woman's hand as she stood in her bathroom. The bomb launched Pinky to the ground but, miraculously, he escaped with only cuts and bruises. An anonymous caller left a message at a local newspaper: "Next time we won't miss." Investigators never determined who was responsible—Pinky had drawn the ire of many in Miami—but the papers speculated the bomb had been placed on behalf of the workers who had lost their jobs because of Pinky's poor leadership. Though Schiffman moved out of Florida, he continued to serve as the vice president of the international and would soon be vice president of the San Diego local.

Meanwhile, Local 355 plunged into thirty years of mediocrity and infighting. To make matters worse, hotels shut down operations for renovations until contracts expired, fired union leaders, or waited for workers to strike and then hired non-union replacements. Business wasn't great, either. In the eighties, hotel owners began blaming the negative media attention that came from the Mariel boatlift, drug shootouts on highways and in strip mall parking lots, and riots in Overtown and Liberty City following the acquittal of white police officers who killed a black motorist in their custody. By then, Local 355 was a shell of what it had been in the 1950s. In 2000, more than half of Miami-Dade's population was foreign born. The local didn't do much to welcome the city's new workforce. It struggled to recruit Cuban workers, who were wary of anything that resembled communism, and Haitian workers, who had no desire to draw bull's-eyes on their backs. Even after Miami Beach cleaned up and experienced a renaissance as a popular tourist destination, Local 355 continued to flounder. With only about two thousand members, and accusations of corruption flying among top leaders, in 2007, Local 355 was once again put under trusteeship of the international.

Before I got hired, Sarah took me to meet Wendi Walsh, the woman who had been put in charge of Local 355. We drove to a nondescript office building next to the highway a few miles south of Calder. While Pinky's union hall had been on South Beach, close to the hotels, Local 355's office was far from the beach, closer to North Miami, where much of the membership lived. The office's decorations were limited to a few framed photos of union workers and posters from past campaigns. There was a main room, a kind of lobby, where the office secretary had a desk. There were a few private offices, each no larger than a small bedroom. Cubicles lined a hallway. Staff and membership meetings were held in a large conference room at the end of the hallway. Dan Connolly, Sarah's boss, had told me that he didn't like visiting the international's office in Manhattan because it was too fancy. Unions shouldn't be spending money on decadent offices, he told me. Offices should be decorated with flyers and pickets. They should be gritty. Local 355's office wasn't decadent and it certainly wasn't the sort of place Pinky and his pals would hang out. There was no cigar smoke or pictures of celebrities or politicians on the walls. Johnny Friendly wasn't smacking somebody over a money-strewn pool table. The office was more suburban than gritty. Without the union posters, boxes of buttons, and conference room labeled *War Room,* one might have mistaken Local 355 for a small insurance agency or accounting firm.

That night, the office's conference room was filled with airline catering members, the workers who load food onto airplanes. Sarah ushered me into Wendi's office and quickly closed the door because she didn't want anyone who might one day work at a casino or visit a casino—or have family members work at a casino—to recognize me on the job and scream, "I saw you at the union hall!" Through the office walls I heard a few people start to clap . . . *clap* . . . *clap.* Then others joined. Soon it sounded like a room full of people clapping in unison. *Clap, clap, clap.* People began chanting, "*Sí, se puede! Sí, se puede!*" It was how they ended every meeting, Sarah said. The "union clap" was inspired by Cesar Chavez's "unity" or "farmworker" clap. When the chanting subsided, Wendi joined us in her office.

I didn't know what I was expecting, but she wasn't it. Her energy and simple, stylish wardrobe made her seem younger than forty-two. She was bony with deep eye wells and dark hair that hid a few streaks of gray. She had a stiff posture and a sharp jaw. Wendi welcomed me to Miami. We did the clan thing: "You're a Walsh? I'm a Walsh!" She of the Worcester line, I of Scranton lineage.

I had heard that John Wilhelm, who succeeded Ed Hanley as president of the international in 1998—and sold the union jet on his first day—had handpicked Walsh to fix troubled locals. She had just finished overseeing fights with hotels—and another union—for Local 25 in San Antonio and had spent the year flying between Texas and Miami. "I thought they were much closer than they actually are," she said. Soon Wendi would be making weekly drives to Orlando to administer the overhaul of Local 362, which represented workers at the real Disney World.

Wendi said that she had grown up in a middle-class family, working hard for a living in Worcester. She attended Boston University and went on to work at Harvard and Stanford, before entering a PhD program in psychology at Yale, where she studied self-stereotyping and its effect on female students' math performance. (After he graduated from Yale in 1967, Wilhelm supposedly answered an ad in a New Haven newspaper, "Wanted: labor trainee, person willing to work long hours for low pay in order to learn to be a labor leader. Must be unmarried.") Much to the displeasure of her adviser and the Yale administration, Wendi began organizing the graduate assistants into a union. Wendi knew that if she had any hope of working in academia after her PhD, she would have to make good with her superiors by giving up her work with the union. Instead, she turned down two eminent postdocs and spent the next fourteen years organizing workers and graduate students in New Haven. In a story about Yale's union fight, *The Nation* wrote about Wendi, "The lessons she learned in academia were about subordination to the job market and to her professors; organizing taught her what it meant to live a thinking life." Wendi was easygoing and sharp, magnetic even. Without much effort, she could explain complicated concepts and strategies in smart, simple, compelling sound bites. She was like a politician who didn't care about politics and wasn't afraid of dropping an f-bomb every now and then.

"Miami is going to be a scrappy fight," she said that night. "Who knows what they're going to pull, but they will pull something. In San Antonio, they brought in professional union busters. In Miami there will be characters; I'm picturing union-busting Yosemite Sam."

The three targets, along with the other recently opened casinos in the area, had entered into what are known as card-check and neutrality agreements with Local 355. Traditionally, union votes involve an election day supervised by the National Labor Relations Board, an independent arm of the government charged with enforcing the National Labor Relations Act. Under card-check agreements, unions are free to collect signatures throughout the duration of the contract and present the cards to employers whenever they see fit. Companies are expected to honor the signatures and enter contract negotiations with the union. Card checks are often coupled with neutrality agreements, which forbid companies from engaging in anti-union campaigns. Often, they require employers to provide a list of employees' names and addresses to the union, and allow union organizers access to employees on the casino's property. In return, the union forfeits its right to mount a public campaign against the company. No boycotts or picket lines.

Once Local 355 and the casinos entered the agreements, the casinos enjoyed the backing of the union as they lobbied Tallahassee and Florida voters to legalize slot machines. By entering into an agreement with the union, the casinos were telling lawmakers that the jobs they were going to create had the potential to be unionized. Unite Here committed more than $100,000 of resources to the voting initiative with the understanding that the casinos would uphold their end of the card-check agreements.

Union organizers use the time that card checks afford them to visit workers at their own pace and argue that traditional elections provide too many opportunities for companies to mount anti-union campaigns. A study done in the nineties showed that card check elections were nearly twice as likely to succeed than NLRB elections. Because of this, those interested in dealing a final blow to organized labor have pushed to outlaw card-check agreements.

The Miami casino targets, in an attempt to get out of the agreements, hired legal teams that used the law like a house of mirrors, bending reason and intent to suit their goal. The family that owned Magic City, the Havenicks, argued that the patriarch, who had been in charge of the casino since 1977, was no longer representing the casino when he signed the contract a year before he died. An arbiter found the argument lacked a "factual basis." Magic City Casino lawyers also tried to argue that the card-check agreement expired far sooner than the date originally agreed upon because the contract should have retroactively included the years the dog track operated lottery dispensers that looked similar to slot machines. Once again, an arbiter found the company's argument bogus. Calder's lawyers had tried, unsuccessfully, to argue that their card-check agreement was unenforceable because the slots initiative hadn't passed on its initial vote in Miami-Dade. Slot machines weren't legalized until a second vote. Local 355 had supported both votes. Mardi Gras flat-out refused to abide by its card check, claiming the list of employees it was required to supply under the agreement constituted a "thing of value," citing the same law that Pinky Schiffman violated when he forced a hotel manager to offer him a discounted rate. Of course, the intent of the law is to prevent collusion between union officials and company executives. In 2010, a court ruled that the agreement was valid and ordered Mardi Gras to comply. At the same time, the National Right to Work Legal Defense Foundation, an effective and well-funded anti-union organization, had somehow been connected with Martin Mulhall, a landscaper at Mardi Gras. The NRTWLDF, with Mulhall as its plaintiff, had filed charges claiming his and his coworkers' names were a "thing of value." The case would eventually make its way to the Supreme Court and had the potential to invalidate card-check and neutrality agreements across the country. Unions let out a sigh of relief when, in December 2014, the Supreme Court dismissed the case. Wendi explained how essential the neutrality agreements were to Local 355's growth.

"We have no power here," she said to me the night I met her. "Right now it's all smoke and mirrors. If those contracts expire before we have a chance to organize, we're fucked. I'm probably going to die in Florida, that's how long it's gonna take."

Part 2

THE HORSE TRACK CAMPAIGN

In January 2010, we gathered for our first official salt team meeting in Sarah and Mary's living room before orientation at Calder. At first, Sarah explained the basics of salting. A salt's job is to identify the workplace leaders, figure out whom they lead, and then get information about the leaders. If we won over the leaders, we would win their followers. Sarah called this "mapping" the workplace. Workplace maps look like the web outlines middle school students use to organize ideas. Get a twelve-year-old to do a web outline of his school's social cliques and you'd be halfway to unionizing the seventh grade. Once we identified a leader—almost all of whom were women—we would start to court her. We needed to learn her story and her issues at work. Then we would pass along the information to a union organizer without the company, co-workers, or leader ever knowing. The union organizer would visit the leader at her home, armed with the intel, hoping to recruit her to the leadership committee.

Before we could identify and get to know the leaders, we needed to build a master list of all the employees eligible for unionization. Under the neutrality agreement, the casino was required to supply the union with a list of employees' names and addresses only after the union requested it. But requesting a list would have tipped the company off. Instead, we decided to build our own reliable list.

Sarah put a piece of butcher paper on the living room wall and wrote "goals" at the top. She split the paper into four columns. In the column farthest to the left, she wrote our names: James, Mary, Erika.

"James, how many names are you going to get?" Sarah asked.

"Ten?"

"Ten? I could get ten names at the Starbucks across the street." She wrote twenty next to my name in the second column. "How many phone numbers?"

"One?"

"Come on. How about ten? And ten addresses?" She filled in the next two columns. She had the same conversation with Erika and Mary. Erika seemed to be the most excited about the challenge.

"Time to be the social butterfly that everyone knows you can be, baby boy."

Most importantly, Sarah wanted us to get socials. Socials were a salt's bread and butter. They were chances to have conversations with coworkers outside the workplace. People were never completely at ease at work. Off-duty, they were free to say whatever they wanted. Salts used socials to vet potential leaders through "clearing." In order to clear a leader, we had to answer four questions:

1. What's her story?
2. What are her work issues?
3. When has she proven that she will fight for what she believes?
4. What is her relationship to management?

Each leader needed to be cleared by two salts before a union organizer would visit her house with the information that the salt had provided. Often, entire salt meetings were spent brainstorming ways to get coworkers to hang out. My notes from one salt meeting read: "Drinking, cooking, rides home, beach, ask 'best pizza in Miami?,' drinks, church, employee parties."

"I want each of you to have a social by the end of orientation," Sarah declared.

My first day of Calder orientation, January 11, 2010, was cold—forty-five degrees in South Florida feels like twenty everywhere else. The buildings don't have heat and people don't have clothes for that kind of weather. I joined about seventy-five shivering new employees in a makeshift classroom on the third floor of Calder's grandstand. Construction on the casino would finish in the coming weeks, we would begin work, and the casino would open soon after. The room was mostly quiet. People were on their phones, avoiding eye contact with the strangers around them. Erika was the loudest person in the room, gabbing with the people sitting around her. At Sarah's behest, Erika and I had staggered our arrivals to avoid anyone even subconsciously linking us. At nine a.m. sharp, Tom O'Donnell, the president of Calder, entered with a gust of energy, as if he were Tony Robbins and we had paid to learn his secret to success. He wore a suit, was mostly bald, and sported a wide, neatly pruned mustache.

"Welcome to a winning experience," he proclaimed. "Winning experiences," we learned, was the new employee motto at Calder. O'Donnell had coined the maxim. As Calder "team members" we were not in the "service industry," he explained. Instead, we were facilitators of "winning experiences." We were given a stack of papers that explained the "culture of

Calder." We would need to make other changes to our lexicon, the president informed us. He read from the employee handbook:

```
Instead of customers, we like guests.
Instead of management, we like leadership.
Instead of turnover, we like retention.
Instead of they/them, we like We.
```

I couldn't help but wonder what had inspired O'Donnell's doublespeak. As I read about the corporate service industry, I learned that its Orwellian, or Rumsfeldian, approach to language had been inspired by a much more insidious force, Disney. Employees at Disney's parks are "cast members" and employee-only areas are referred to as "backstage." Cast members use the "Disney point" (a minimum of two fingers) to direct guests. Disney is so famous for its service that it created a consulting group, the Disney Institute, which has taught teachers to squat to connect with students at their eye level and inspired a children's hospital to employ a ukulele player to greet patients. O'Donnell didn't mention the Disney point but he told us that we should always walk the guests to the bathroom. It was clear that he, like so many other executives, was trying to tap into Disney's magic.

Miami Gardens, where Calder is located, is Miami-Dade's northernmost municipality. Calder is located in the heart of Miami Gardens, an area that had been known as Carol City up until it was folded into Miami Gardens in 2003. Some residents still lovingly refer to Miami Gardens as Carol City. Today, Miami Gardens is known as the home of Rick Ross, the Dolphins, and Trayvon Martin. About three quarters of Miami Gardens' 107,000 residents are black, making it Florida's largest city in which the majority of the population is African-American.

More than half of the new employees at orientation were black and at one point O'Donnell told us that, as a former high school teacher in New Jersey, he knew all about diversity. He pointed to the front of the room, where the management of the company stood, and said, "We've got a Jamaican in charge, an Asian, and, well, we've got a diverse group of people here." He didn't point to the thirteen other members of the "leadership" who were all white. Two of the fifteen managers at the front of the room were women. O'Donnell's willingness to address diversity was unexpected and seemed like an earnest, if unsuccessful, attempt at welcoming the group.

O'Donnell was adamant about the importance of the workers on the casino floor. We were "the face" of the company working on "the front lines" of the business. We were the best of many applicants, he reminded us more than once.

"Look, eighty-eight percent of our guests leave with less money than they come with," he said, turning out the pockets of his pants. "So we need to rely on service to bring them back." Though O'Donnell had grossly oversimplified the percentages—even guests who won big spent their winnings, thus, ultimately, almost all guests left with less money than they came with—we understood his point. How do guests decide between two casinos offering the same slot machines? While there were many factors—location, food service, acts of God, misconceptions about odds and statistics—one could argue that the friendly service of workers "on the front lines" could attract guests more than anything O'Donnell did in his office.

Later, O'Donnell introduced what he described as "the best video I've ever seen on the service industry." The lights dimmed and a film that could only be described as the *Red Dawn* of corporate orientation videos played.

"My friends don't understand why I drive thirty miles out of my way to get tools that I could easily buy online," said a handsome fortysomething as he walked up the steps to a quaint country general store. "Hey, Rick," said the matron behind the counter as she prepared Rick's "usual" with a smile. As Rick sat with his coffee and pastry, he began to daydream and found himself in the Gulag Café, a dark coffee shop with a wrought-iron counter. The patrons waited in a long line to order from a Soviet-themed menu. "Uh, I guess I'll have a Karl Marx?" a confused customer said. Behind the counter a woman with fluorescent hair, a nose ring, and a bad attitude scowled. She looked like Erika. Rick woke from his day-mare. He was back in the country store sitting next to some old men playing chess. The video was clearly meant to encourage us, employees of a casino owned by a publicly traded company, to emulate the laid-back and personal service of a locally owned, small-town general store. This was how we were to treat customers in a capitalist society, a message that was lost on almost everyone in attendance as they'd taken the film as an opportunity to nap or continue playing games on their phones.

After the video, O'Donnell orchestrated a kind of pep rally. Before opening, the casino needed to pass a state safety test that was scheduled a week after orientation. In a month's time Super Bowl XLIV would kick off in the Dolphins' stadium down the street from the casino. O'Donnell had started a crusade to maximize employee effort, pass the safety test, and open in time for the big game. The food and beverage department had nothing to do with the state test yet we were given buttons emblazoned with O'Donnell's campaign slogan: "Yes, We Can!" Before he left for the day, O'Donnell led us in a chant, "*Yes, we can! Yes, we can! Yes, we can!*"

When orientation resumed, Peggy, the head of human resources, guided us through the company's policies and procedures. She was blond, in her fifties, dressed in a conservative suit, and stood at the front of the room clutching a packet of papers. On her LinkedIn profile Peggy described herself as a "human capital manager" and a "change maker . . . Experienced in driving business processes for maximum results." She reminded me of an algebra teacher I didn't get along with in high school. She did her best to explain the "points" system. Points were demerits, and should an employee accrue enough points, he or she would be fired. The subject seemed to bring our group to life. "When do the points get wiped? A year from when you get each point or on January first?" "Do you get points if you're late because your car broke down?" "Can we challenge the points?" My coworkers wanted to be sure that management would be reasonable; they wanted to have a say in the process. It was a legitimate concern but one that was put to rest by section 2-10 of the employee handbook: "Since employment with Calder Casino & Race Course is based on mutual consent, both the team member and Calder Casino & Race Course have the right to terminate employment at will, with or without cause, at any time." The points were meaningless.

A little while later, a young bartender raised her hand.

"I was over at the Isle and we had the union. I know managers don't like the union, but will we have it here?" she asked, blithely unaware of the hazard in her question. Peggy went rigid. She took a deep breath and lowered the employee handbook she had been reading from. The neutrality agreement forbade Peggy, and anyone else in management, from making bias statements about the union.

"That's a great question," Peggy said coolly, collecting her thoughts. "We have an agreement that says we legally are not allowed to have an opinion about the union. We can't tell you we do or don't want a union, that's up to you guys." It was the first time she or O'Donnell had acknowledged any difference between workers and management.

"One union showed some interest a while ago but we haven't heard from them since then," Peggy continued. "The one thing I would just like you to think about is, what do you gain from having a union?"

Nobody said anything.

For Peggy, the timing of the question couldn't have been better. She segued into the benefits Calder offered, which were very good compared to other low-wage jobs at places like McDonald's, Pizza Hut, and Walmart. We would have access to a 401(k). Over the past three decades companies have increasingly replaced pensions with 401(k)s so that employees, not employers, bear the financial risk. The coworkers I knew who signed up for the 401(k) believed this job would be different from their past service jobs. They were the same coworkers who disenrolled from the 401(k) program once they realized that financial foresight was a luxury for people who had money left at the end of the month. Most surprising was the casino's promise of paid vacation. Through a system of accrual and various other guidelines, I could earn twenty-one days' paid time off throughout the year that could be used for vacation, sick days, or any other days I couldn't come to work. Peggy also went over "blackout" days, major holidays and a handful of big horse races, which no one was allowed to take off. Management, Peggy told us, looking over her glasses, would be dubious of anyone who called in sick on a blackout day. There would be no holiday pay on blackout days. "It's the sacrifice we all make in the casino industry," she told us.

On average, union workers are paid about 15 percent more than their non-union counterparts, a divide that widens during a recession. The difference in Miami, and anywhere else union density is low, isn't so wide. Generally, the tide rises in cities with high union density because non-union employers know that offering competitive pay and benefits is the best way to remain union-free. When I first arrived in Miami, unionized casino servers working for tips could make anywhere from $4.19 to $10 an hour with guaranteed yearly raises. Non-tipped employees at union casinos generally made $8 to $13 with guaranteed raises. At non-union casinos, most "frontline" employees made $7.25 to $12.

Depending on the plan, health insurance for a single person could range from $5 to $40 every two weeks. But for a family, insurance could cost anywhere from $78 to $194; throw in another $45 for dental and it would have been impossible for someone on minimum wage to pay. At the Isle, a unionized casino, family coverage cost less than $30 and would soon cost even less. Health insurance is by far the most important benefit to workers in the United States. The union's goal was to get free health insurance for families. While pay and insurance are important components of any union contract, seniority rules and protection against indiscriminate firing are equally, if not more, valuable benefits. Such benefits reduce workplace turnover, the kryptonite of service union campaigns.

A full quarter of Americans work jobs with an average lifespan of less than a year. If a union were to start a campaign at a fast-food restaurant in 2009, on average, organizers would watch the entire restaurant's staff move on (and then some) within twelve months. Depending on the job market, turnover in the service industry can average anywhere from 50 to 124 percent. (The years leading up to the Great Recession turnover averaged about 80 percent.) Some percentage of turnover can, of course, be explained by firings, both justified and needless. But the majority of turnover is voluntary. Workers move on to the next job because they are offered more hours, a shorter commute, or they simply need time off to care for their kids. Job security and stability are always a little bit farther.

Back at orientation, I took our first break as an opportunity to introduce myself to a coworker. Across the aisle and a few rows in front of me was a short guy with a boyish face and a patchy beard. He wore cerulean Air Jordans that matched his throwback Marlins cap. He wasn't talking to anyone so I approached him, assuring myself that social confidence was like adulthood—everyone was faking it.

"I'm James." I offered my hand.

"What it do, James. Name's Keon."

Keon was twenty-four and lived in Miami Gardens. He had been hired as a steward—a dishwasher, janitor, porter, move-this, clean-that. He was a gentle guy who talked in hip-hop po-etry: "I needa gain a measure of perspective before I confront the melee that is them dishes." As a steward, Keon would make minimum wage, $7.25 an hour. If they were scheduled for a full forty-hour week, which they rarely were, my minimum-wage coworkers would be paid $15,080 a year. If Keon had kids, he would have been officially under the poverty line. We talked for a minute about the Dolphins and the Marlins and the Gulag Café. Keon was relaxed and affable. I wasn't the only one who felt at ease around him. It wasn't long before Keon had a crew of stewards who looked up to him.

We ate lunch in the grandstand's restaurant overlooking the horse track. Calder first opened as a horse track in 1971. In 1999, Churchill Downs Inc., the company that owns the Ken-tucky Derby, bought the track for $87 million. Horse racing wouldn't start for another three months. A backhoe was dredg-ing the pond in the middle of the grass. I sat at a table with Dylan, a white guy from Las Vegas who had moved to Florida a few months earlier, and Jordon, a Jamaican-American a few years younger than me. Both had been hired to work in the Twin Spires Tavern, Dylan as a waiter and Jordon as a buser. Jordon had a heavyweight wrestler's build and his face was in a perpetual grimace. He had been a part-time cook at a Denny's before getting hired at Calder. He started busing tables at Denny's, trying to get more hours, but he still didn't make enough to support his newborn son. He quit Denny's to try other jobs, "some legal, some not so much." He hoped he would make enough at Calder to "give up that other stuff." Jordon's intimidating frame and mischievous "other stuff" were completely incongruous with the goofy coworker I witnessed singing along with Madonna's "Like a Virgin" as he wiped down tables.

O'Donnell, the president, made a curtain call at lunch and visited each table asking if he could get anybody anything. When one worker half-jokingly asked for a cup of coffee, O'Donnell howled. "I wouldn't even know where to look!" It was the kind of calculated kindness that made workers wary around the casino's top brass.

Churchill Downs Inc., has a market value of $2.5 billion. At the time, the company owned four tracks and two casinos as well as off-track betting facilities, online gaming operations, and various other gaming businesses. Documents filed with the IRS showed chief executives at Churchill Downs had compensation packages worth tens of millions. Opening a new casino, an $85 million investment, would only be entrusted to someone with a history in gaming, management, and finance. O'Donnell's charisma, confidence, and clothing sent a clear message: *I have power.*

Erika was sitting at the cool kids' table making all the cocktail waitresses and bartenders laugh. I overheard her scheduling her first social. "Girl, how much longer you working at the bar? What days do you work? I'm gonna come get a drink!" At one point, someone passed me a sheet of paper and instructed me to write down my name, number, and address. Erika's name was at the top and I knew she had created it. I looked up and she winked at me from across the room.

I confessed to Jordon and Dylan that I knew little about casinos or horse tracks. As a Las Vegas native, Dylan was our expert. His mom worked at a casino on the strip and he liked to play the slots from time to time. Dylan said he was dying to go bet on jai alai. With the sport's popularity quickly vanishing and almost every venue in the country closed, Florida was home to an astounding seven jai alai venues still open for business. I jumped at the opportunity.

"You mean the guys who throw the ball at the wall?"

"Yeah, it's over in Dania Beach."

"Oh, we're definitely going. What's your phone number?"

It would be my first social.

Once we finished with the large orientation group, we split off into departments. I joined my food and beverage brethren. We were given another set of papers. This one coached us on how to provide winning experiences in the food and beverage department. Mike DiStefano and Stanley Donovan read each point aloud. The list was exhaustive and sometimes abstract.

```
Hospitality is felt.
Hospitality is heart and soul.
Make the atmosphere fun!
```

There were some concrete tips. Particularly in the section titled "Moments of Truth."

```
Speak clearly, make eye contact and smile.
Take beverage orders within five minutes.
Up sell. If a guest asks for a vodka and
    grapefruit ask them if they want Abso-
    lute [sic] or Grey Goose.
```

The food and beverage department's policies on tardiness, absence, seniority, appearance standards, and discipline were reasonable. Infractions would result in "coaching and development," followed by a verbal warning, a first written warning, and a second written warning, and then disciplinary action (points) would be taken. Somewhat naïvely, I wondered how these policies would be enforced. They weren't. I never saw any of the policies in action.

We went to pick up our uniforms from the seamstress. While we waited, Dot, a concessions cashier, nodded toward Erika. "I'm surprised they let her work, it's just not professional." She was talking about Erika's visible tattoos. I tried my uniform on. The mandarin-collared shirt fit fine, but I think I was given someone else's pants. They were wide and baggy. I looked like Aladdin, which I thought was kind of cool. I never had them resized.

The Twin Spires Tavern waiters were sent to a storage closet where computers were set up to teach us the operating systems we would be using to place orders. Dylan was in my class, along with a middle-aged white woman, Tricia, and Kalia, a young black woman from Miami Gardens who would be working in the buffet. Tricia had the dark, taut skin of someone who used tanning beds on the weekdays and went to the beach on the weekends. Her hair was in a tight ponytail and her bangs were gelled and coarse like sawgrass. She looked, spoke, walked, and worked like a softball coach. She was married to a police officer and had four daughters.

Kalia was about my age, sweet, and giggly. She had a three-year-old son, Leo, at home. She grew up in St. Louis, and after a stint in Tulsa, she moved to Florida. Before Calder, she said, she had worked as a receptionist at the University of Miami. I wasn't good with the operating system and neither were Tricia and Kalia. We all relied on Dylan, who had used the same system at another job. Though I knew Erika had probably gotten their names and addresses, I passed around my own contact list. "Just in case you need someone to cover for you."

Jon, the manager who would be overseeing the Twin Spires Tavern, joined us for a portion of the training. Jon was in his fifties but an achy walk and smoker's cough made him seem older. He had a balloon head with bulbous earlobes. His thinning hair was slicked back in fragile lines and formed small curls at the back of his neck. He wore large wire-rimmed glasses. He looked like a villain in a Dick Tracy comic. He had a New York accent and a deep milky voice that drew out vowels. Though he wasn't very good with computers, he repeated the few directions he knew about the operating system like a substitute teacher reading the instructions left by a sick teacher. Jon had worked at restaurants in New York and Florida and before Calder he had worked at the Isle, a unionized casino north of Fort Lauderdale. He seemed friendly enough and I felt a childish desire to do well by him. It felt good when, after I successfully placed a fake order, he gave me a pat on the back.

Before orientation finished, we went on a tour of the casino. The building was 104,000 square feet and looked like a warehouse on the outside. The vast majority of the building was one room filled with 1,200 slot machines. My coworkers *ooh*ed and *aah*ed as we walked through the rows of machines.

"It's just absolutely beautiful," Dot whispered as she spun in circles.

There were hundreds of cameras encased in tinted bubbles covering the ceiling like barnacles on the hull of a ship. Knowing that my every move would be monitored was unsettling. But there were places to hide. I would soon learn to take notes in the bathrooms and service stations where surveillance couldn't spy.

◎

In late January, the casino opened and we were given "Yes, We Did!" buttons. There was a party. Tom O'Donnell cut the cake. With hundreds of newly employed workers in a sparkling new building, it was hard to escape the excitement. Orientation had inundated us with reasons to be thankful for the opportunity to work at a first-rate establishment in an industry poised for growth. We were all investors in this venture, ready to contribute in our own small ways. That attitude was doubly noticeable among the tipped employees, who, among the workers on the "front line," stood to benefit the most from the droves of customers we were told would be coming through the doors. The Twin Spires Tavern, we presumed, would be a hit in Miami Gardens. The restaurant opened without any fanfare. One minute we were opening boxes of new silverware, the next we were standing at the hostess's podium scanning the casino floor like children waiting for birthday guests. The other waiters were Dylan, Tricia, and Donna, a server who had worked with Jon at the Isle Casino. Jordon bused the tables. My first table on opening night was Tom O'Donnell and his family. I was cripplingly nervous, a maladroit subject before the king. He asked where I was from and if I had any serving experience. I told him Connecticut and was happy to be able to say that, yes, I had experience. Yet another reason to give Carlos, the waiter at the boutique hotel, a big fat kiss. Training for the Twin Spires servers had been minimal, so I improvised. O'Donnell asked if the sweet Thai sauce on the Bang Bang Shrimp was hot. I knew it was a test. I didn't know the answer. Graciously, he waited while I asked the chef. "It's got a bang, but it's not too hot," I told O'Donnell when I returned. He didn't order the Bang Bang Shrimp. He tipped 20 percent. A few nights later I served O'Donnell while he sat with a middle-aged white man with thick gray hair and a flat nose. He was Dan Adkins, the head of Mardi Gras Casino, who came to congratulate O'Donnell on the grand opening.

Dylan and I met at the jai alai fronton just south of Fort Lauderdale. Inside, there were a few hundred seats set up like a large theater. (Most of the seats were later ripped up to make room for slot machines.) The court was like a large, green stage. The players were stage left with baskets on their hands. They flung a goatskin ball, or *pelota,* off a granite wall at stage right. They continued flinging the *pelota* until one of them missed. It was a simple sport, like the wall-ball I played as a kid. There were about fifteen people in the audience and the only sounds were the thwack of the *pelota* on the wall and the drunk racist guy who periodically shouted at the players, "Go pick some fuckin' tomatoes!" We placed a few bets. I chose my players based on how cool their names sounded. Xabat Urizarbarrena. Endika Madarieta. Hormnetxea. Some of the players were from Basque country in the north of Spain, where the game had originated. Others, I'd heard, changed their names to sound like they were from there. It was good to sip cold beers and ask Dylan as many questions as I wanted.

Dylan had finished a few years at the University of Nevada, Las Vegas, but he didn't have the money or time to continue. His father, who had moved to Miami years ago, had run into money problems. Dylan agreed to move to Florida temporarily and help his father out. They were both living with Dylan's grandmother in a retirement community; Dylan slept on the couch. Since moving to Florida, he had been working under his dad at a cemetery but that work had dried up. Dylan loved movies and the Houston Astros. He had no desire to stay in South Florida. He wanted to move back to Vegas, where "there was real money."

Drinking beer and watching jai alai with Dylan—a white

male twentysomething who, like me, enjoyed baseball and action movies—wasn't exactly the kind of boundary-pushing experience I'd assumed socials would be. At the next salt meeting, I told Sarah and the rest of the team that I liked Dylan, but it was clear he was not the kind of leader we were looking for.

"He really likes you, James," Erika said about Dylan.

"Good, you will lead Dylan," Sarah said. I was okay with that. I figured Dylan would be back in Vegas by the time we were collecting signatures.

Erika had started hanging out with the bartenders and cocktail waitresses and she'd decided that I needed to clear a bartender named Melanie.

"Melanie is definitely a leader and she's super tight with this cocktail waitress Becca. You know, the really thin white girl? We need to get you on a social with them, baby boy." Erika said she would invite Melanie and Becca to a bar where I would meet them.

"How does Melanie feel about the union?" Mary asked.

"That doesn't matter," Sarah said before Erika could answer. Convincing anti-union leaders of the union's merit was a task for a later date. For now, we needed to concentrate on identifying the leaders. Guessing whether someone is pro- or anti-union is nearly impossible. Liberal or conservative, black or white, gay or straight. None of it means anything when it comes to the union question. This was especially true in a place like Florida, where so few workers knew anything about unions. I had coworkers ask if we were already unionized at Calder. Some coworkers wondered if the union was going to be organized by management. Others didn't know what a union was. On both sides of the issue, people were uninformed or misinformed. As such we had to discount workers' initial opinions.

"At some point, the company will do something to piss off everyone you work with. It's inevitable," Sarah said. "You need to be there for that person when it happens." Sarah's method depended on a come-to-the-union moment and it was our job to welcome them with open arms.

The salt team was growing. Luke, a young, happily aimless vagabond with a rawhide drawl. He had recently graduated from the University of Tennessee and was just as excited to talk about the revolution as he was to go out and meet cheerleaders. I once heard his college classmate lovingly refer to him as a "mack-tavist," because a protest was just as much about exercising his right to free speech as it was an opportunity to hit on like-minded women. Colette was also new. She'd moved to Miami after graduating from Yale. She had been offered a job at a global nonprofit, but, her senior thesis on black communists still on her mind, she was emboldened to deviate from the nonprofit pipeline. Colette lied to her successful Nigerian parents and told them she would be putting her Ivy League degree to use as a full-time staff union organizer. The ends of our salt meetings were used to figure out ways to get Luke and Colette hired at Mardi Gras to work alongside Mary. Almost immediately, Colette was hired as a cocktail waitress and Luke was walking through aisles of slot machines as Mardi Gras's new cheery slot attendant.

At one meeting, Sarah passed around a stack of papers called contact sheets. There was a Cesar Chavez quote on the top of the first sheet: "The fight is never about grapes or lettuce. It is always about people." The sheets were bisected with lines forming a grid with headings in each section.

Basics - Address, contact info, past jobs,
    union experience, shift, job position.
Friends and groups at work
Story - Home, family, past, relationships,
    struggles.

Their goals and dreams
Issues
Awesome conversations
Pushes
Relation to management
Trust?

Sarah told us to fill in the sections as much as possible for as many coworkers as we could. The sheets were a way of quantifying the value of each of our relationships and would help us to remember important details to pass on to staff organizers when they began house visits. I was always taking notes about conversations, but the idea of sharing these notes with staff organizers, many of whom we didn't know well, irked all of us.

"It's completely up to you whether or not you want to give organizers the notes," Sarah said. "I just want to make sure you remember details."

Wendi joined us for the latter half of the meeting. At the end she saw one of the sheets Sarah had passed out. She pulled Sarah aside.

"So, you need to get those sheets back from everyone. These are part of the case and we can't be handing them out. It's just that, if anyone were to find out about . . ."

Sarah nodded her head compliantly. Wendi didn't have to say anything more.

I didn't understand it at the time, but Wendi was worried that if the sheets were to fall into the wrong hands, they could be used as ammunition in Unite Here's very public, bitter, and embarrassing breakup. While battles between unions and companies are charged with passionate animosity, nothing rivals the carnage of warring union siblings.

The Hotel Employees and Restaurant Employees International Union (HERE) was financially decimated after September 11, 2001. The union had already been in dire straits financially. When the service and hotel industries started to recover—with hotels, casinos, and stadiums opening all over the country—HERE had plenty of new organizing opportunities but no money to organize. The Union of Needletrades, Industrial, and Textile Employees (UNITE) once had a larger membership than any labor union in the country, but it had been losing workers to cheap labor abroad for decades. But UNITE did have money. The union controlled the Amalgamated Bank—formed by garment workers in 1923—which had more than $4 billion in assets and whose profits contributed millions of dollars to the union's operating budget each year. The two unions' leaders, John Wilhelm (HERE) and Bruce Raynor (UNITE), met for the first time on a picket line at Wilhelm's alma mater, Yale. They hit it off. They were both savvy, Ivy League educated (Raynor attended Cornell), and well liked in the labor community. In the early seventies Raynor had worked on the campaign to organize textile workers in the South, an effort made famous by the 1979 film *Norma Rae*. By combining UNITE's assets with HERE's membership potential, the newly renamed Unite Here could take on organizing campaigns across the country and bring service industry unions up to the numbers and standards of textile workers before globalization. The unions merged in 2004.

Under the merger, Raynor and Wilhelm shared the executive responsibilities of the new union. Their partnership didn't last long. The two leaders had very different ideas about growing Unite Here's membership. Raynor attempted to undo the merger and reclaim UNITE's independence, along with its bank. None too pleased, Wilhelm and the rest of Unite Here fought back. Then the largest service union in the country got involved.

The Service Employees International Union represents 2.1 million workers, second in size behind the teachers' unions. Some experts argue that under its last leader, Andy Stern, SEIU sacrificed the value of membership in the name of growth. For many, Stern's focus on growth was impetuous and detrimental to the rest of the labor movement. I heard Unite Here organizers badmouth SEIU just as much, if not more, than hotel companies. Unite Here's collective resentment for SEIU reached a boiling point when Stern, still in charge of SEIU, supported Raynor's attempt to secede from Unite Here. Eventually, Raynor managed to defect, taking one hundred thousand apparel workers with him. They formed a new union, Workers United, which would officially be a part of SEIU. To Unite Here, it was an all-out act of war. The unions raided each other's shops, claiming each other's territory as their own. There were public accusations of corruption and greed. Offices were broken into. Wilhelm accused Stern and Raynor of hiring a private investigator to look into his family. To outside observers, it was chaos. To anti-union observers, it was bliss. The two largest service unions in the country were spending millions on legal fees, public relations, and damage control. They were like hungry rats devouring each other.

Though much of the battle between SEIU and Unite Here had already been fought before I arrived in Miami, there were still tremors. In November 2009, the *New York Times* published an article about Unite Here's use of "pink sheeting," the practice of documenting workers' and organizers' stories—which sometimes included personal details—as a catalog for future pushes. According to the article, "organizers said the question sheets were no longer pink, had been renamed 'motivation sheets,' and contained such questions as, 'What risks or difficulties has your target undergone in her/his personal life?' " The sheets Sarah had passed out were, in fact, pink sheets. The article quoted multiple former organizers at Unite Here who were made extremely uncomfortable by bosses who had used personal information gathered from pink sheets to "manipulate" them. "Several organizers likened pink sheeting to a practice that Cesar Chavez used when he embraced a mind-control practice developed by Synanon, a drug rehabili-

tation center founded in Santa Monica, Calif." Chavez's asso-
ciation with Synanon was a stain on the activist's illustrious
life. The "drug rehabilitation center" was more akin to a cult.
According to the article, twice over the past two years Unite
Here had issued orders banning the practice of pink sheeting.
Wilhelm claimed the entire controversy was manufactured by
SEIU.

I continued taking notes, and while no organizer ever asked
for my notes, the salts often debated whether or not our work
was in an ethical gray area. For the most part, we all agreed
that our goal justified any of the white lies we told. Aside from
getting jobs at places that didn't necessarily square with our
educational backgrounds, we rarely did anything that could
be characterized as definitively deceitful. I was genuinely interested in every coworker I went on socials with. Not everyone felt the same way. One salt, who didn't last long, flat-out
told me, "You guys don't fucking treat people like people."
She went on socials only when they were convenient or happened "naturally." If I had let relationships develop naturally
I wouldn't have hung out with the woman whose husband
proudly displayed his collection of Confederate curios, the
dishwasher who said "faggot" just as often as "fork," or the
guy who used me for rides to his girlfriend's house. People
who accused the salt program of manipulation, or claimed
we were being disingenuous, left me wondering what kind of
progress society would make if everyone waited for everything
to develop naturally.

Within Unite Here, salting was one facet of the intense organizing philosophy that was practiced at a handful of locals
around the country. Some locals squarely rejected the culture
of pushes, pink sheets, and the expectation that everyone be
On the Program. A former salt, speaking to labor journalist
Steve Early, praised Unite Here and its leadership while also
bemoaning its "very hierarchical, military style of organizing.
They expect you to follow the program and the program is

decided by the staff, not the workers." "The Program" was a vague label only used by people who considered themselves On the Program when describing people who weren't receptive to pushes or who had gone rogue. More than an inability or unwillingness to further Unite Here's goals, Off the Program connoted actions that might be detrimental to the entire labor movement. Off the Program could be supporting the wrong candidate, taking vacation time during a campaign, getting a job at a different union, or running for president of a local without the international's blessing. If you were Off the Program, somewhere someone was pretending to be you, role-playing a conversation about how to get you back On the Program. Being On the Program felt good because, more often than not, it worked. Being On the Program meant you were in formation, flying toward the target.

Wendi showed up at a few more salt meetings. She would come toward the tail end and listen like a principal doing teacher evaluations, adding a few thoughts here and there. From what I could tell, Wendi didn't take days off. Not even weekends. I was happy to have her at our meetings, because as good as Sarah was at getting people hired and starting salt teams, she didn't know much about the larger goals of Local 355. Wendi gave us some insight. She told us that, over the past two years, Local 355's membership had increased by 50 percent. Her goal was to increase the membership by another 50 percent over the next two years. The challenge with new organizing was that Local 355 needed to maintain the few shops it already had control of while simultaneously running new campaigns. All on a limited budget. Still, Local 355 desperately needed to organize new hotels and casinos because executives at the unionized shops wouldn't feel pressure to renegotiate contracts while their competitors were union-free. It was an exhausting, desperate cycle.

I asked Wendi, why Calder? We already had relatively good benefits. There were so many other service industry workplaces that didn't have health care or paid time off. Without the union, she said, benefits and pay would come and go. While South Florida was still fairly new to Wendi, she understood the way big companies operated. She knew "innovative" business decisions, like installing self-serve soda fountains or subcontracting housekeepers, were just ways to chip away at labor costs and invariably screwed workers.

"If you think about it, these companies know their employees are at their mercy. Whether it's part of their plan or subconsciously, the companies take advantage of that. If a company is scamming you a couple of hours a week on your paycheck, you go to human resources and report it. They say, 'Oh yeah, we'll look into it and include it on your next paycheck.' The next pay cycle comes around and those lost hours still aren't included. So you go to them again and they say, 'Oh yeah, well, we looked into that and we think you may have gotten it wrong.' But you know you didn't get it wrong. And they know that you don't have the time off or the money to hire a lawyer and get that money from them. So it's gone. Lost. That's the kind of control they will give up with a union. The final say." I'd heard some version of this before; companies weren't afraid of the dollar cost of unions—though it certainly hurt—they were afraid of surrendering control.

At the end of one salt meeting, Sarah told us that our new lead, Alex, would be arriving in Miami soon. He was moving from Sacramento, where he had been organizing casinos. I met Alex for the first time at Jimmy's Eastside Diner on Biscayne Boulevard among neglected art deco motels with neon lights and hourly rates. Jimmy's is the kind of place where the waitresses call you "sweetie" and "honey," except in Miami they're more likely to call you "*papi*" and "*mi amor*." Sarah introduced Jimmy's to all of the salts. It was part of her tour, her way of making us feel a little more at home—diners have a way of doing that. For the first few months, Jimmy's was the default location for the team's postmeeting lunches. In addition to the home-style ambiance, the team liked Jimmy's because it was conveniently located a few blocks north of the salt house.

Alex had barely arrived from California when Sarah set up meetings with each salt to introduce us to our new lead. He was a little more than six feet tall with long sinewy limbs. His hair was on the long side of bald, barely more than shaved. He had a firm jaw speckled with dark, wiry facial hair styled in a haphazard Vandyke. He wore small gold hoops in the lobes of each ear and baggy khakis with an oversized short-sleeve polo shirt. This was Alex's look. He had perfected it. He needed to appear professional while keeping it baggy, never betraying his '90s street spirit. Alex and Sarah slid into the booth across from me.

"Good to meet you, dude," Alex said. He rested his laptop bag below the table and pulled out a yellow notepad. "So you work at Disney?"

"Yeah, I work in the high-end restaurant."

"Nice. And how many people work there?"

"Three cooks, a buser, four waiters, and a hostess." I rattled it off as quickly as possible, hoping to impress him.

He wasn't impressed. "What are their names?"

"Dick, Brad, Jim, Jordon, Tricia, Donna, Dylan, Lucia, and me."

"Last names?" He was writing everything down.

I had to think. "Strong, Sommers, Green, Dixon, Polansky, Meenan, Moyers, Valasquez."

He still wasn't impressed. Rudimentary knowledge of the workplace was fundamental and expected. An organizer not knowing coworkers' names would be like a coach not knowing his players. Alex wrote down everybody's name and position. He added notes next to each of the names when I offered specific character information. Tricia: Four daughters.

Husband cop in Hialeah. Dylan: From Las Vegas. Lives with grandmother and father. Lucia: From Uruguay. Used to work at Superdome. When people take meticulous notes it can mean one of two things: the note taker values what you're saying and wants to refer back to the notes at a later date or the note taker is enacting some rote schoolboy performance for himself or others and the notes will never see the light of day again. I hoped Alex's compulsion was a sign of the former. When he finished writing down my coworkers' names and details, he put his pen down.

"So what's up with you, dude? What brought you here?" He leaned back in the booth and folded his arms across his chest, adjusting the sleeves on his shirt, ready to listen.

It was time to tell my story, again. I stuck to the basics. Blissful childhood in Connecticut. Was exposed to social justice movements in college. Grad school. Got in touch with friends who had salted and was put in touch with Sarah. Four months later I'm drinking coffee at Jimmy's.

Alex kept the rhythm of my story with *mmm-hmm* and *uh-huh*. He was following along, engaging me, getting some kind of energy out. After I finished, he gave me an abridged version of his story.

"Well, I'm excited to be here and to get to know you, man. I'm really amped about this shit. Just so you know, I swear like a motherfucker. Wendi already told me to cut it back in front of the staff." He'd been organizing a casino near Sacramento that was mostly staffed by Punjabi workers. He'd worked with salts before but never salted. He wished he had. Alex believed that salting was the purest form of organizing. "Sometimes," he later told me, "I just want to quit my job as an organizer and salt." He had enough faith in the Miami program to donate $600 to help pay rent on the salt house. Before Sacramento Alex had worked on hotel and casino campaigns across the country, mostly in California. He'd been a union organizer since he was twenty-four, and before that he had worked as a political organizer in Oregon on a congressional campaign. That's where he had met his wife, Jill. Neither Alex nor Jill had any friends or family in Miami. The only reason the two of them had moved across the country was "the revolution." Alex didn't use that word lightly. When he talked about "the revolution" he was always referring to a specific blueprint: a better world through better jobs.

That first day at Jimmy's, Alex's story was nearly as dull as mine. The closest he came to inspirational was the same hypothetical that Sarah harped on when she made her Florida recruitment pitches: What if Miami were organized? How would that change Florida and the country's political landscape? Sarah would indulge in the hypothetical retrospective: "If Miami was organized, George Bush wouldn't have been elected," she would confidently state. "There wouldn't have been any need for a recount. And there wouldn't be two wars going on right now." That assertion was so off the axis of time and reality that it wasn't worth debating. Florida was simply a next step for Alex, and though he didn't share his full story at Jimmy's, I was eager to learn more about what drove his revolutionary ambitions.

Alex went back to his notepad. Under the heading "James," he wrote "Goals" and underlined it. He was even tougher than Sarah when it came to goals and accountability.

"So, can we map your restaurant?" he asked me.

"We've got some strong personalities."

"Well, strong personalities don't necessarily make them leaders. I mean look, man, this restaurant is really fuckin' small, so it shouldn't take long for you to map. How are you gonna get to know people?"

I told him that Tricia and Donna were the two biggest presences.

"Donna from the Isle?" Alex asked as he flipped back through his notepad looking for her last name.

"Yup," Sarah said. She looked at me. "We just found

out Donna was a leader at the Isle. The first time someone house-visited her she threatened to shoot him with her gun."

Sounded like Donna, though I would have expected her two massive pit bulls to do the intimidation for her.

"Okay, how do you spend more time with Donna?"

"I don't know. She smokes a lot."

"Where does she smoke?" Alex asked. "Out back probably, right?"

"Can you start smoking?" Sarah asked through a wry smile. Alex laughed.

"Seriously, dude, don't start smoking. But you should be spending more time with Tricia and Donna. And what about"—he flipped through his notepad—"Melanie?"

I told him that Erika would be making arrangements for us all to go to a bar together.

"Erika can't be there when you clear her. She has to feel good talking to you, not you *and* Erika." I told him I would clear Melanie on my own. He made a note of it.

"Okay, listen." Alex put his hands forward and splayed his fingers evenly on the table. "Before we can really map the whole casino, we need a better list." Since orientation our list had topped off at about seventy-five names, not even half of the workers we suspected were eligible for unionization.

"Let's get creative. We need to start getting a shit-ton of names. So, what can we do to get a lot of names at once without it being too weird? Because we aren't going to get anywhere just collecting them one by one." Sarah was good at employing salt tradecraft to build the list one by one. "Ask about the neighborhood they live in," she told me. "A few days later you can ask for a street, say you think you know someone on that street, then ask for the number." If that didn't work, she had other tricks: *"Look! Isn't my driver's license picture funny? Can I see yours?"* But Alex wanted a big score.

"I could start a softball league?"

"Yes! That's good, dude!" Alex's voice shot up a few registers. "That's how you need to be thinking. I love this shit. What else? And why aren't you taking notes?" He wanted me to be taking this as seriously as any other profession. "You need to start bringing something to write your goals down. Anyway, could you try to get everybody's birthday and address and say that you like to send out birthday cards?"

"I'm all for being creative, but I think people already know I'm not the birthday card guy."

"Okay." Alex twisted his wedding band and then adjusted another ring on the ring finger of his right hand. "What holidays are coming up? You could send out cards."

"Valentine's Day passed and I think Erika already sent out a few cards. St. Patrick's Day is coming up."

"Do it. Walsh, right? You're Irish. That's Irish, right?" He was laughing maniacally. "You can do that, man! People will know you as the Irish dude who really, really loves St. Patrick's Day." He was hooked on the idea and there was no talking him out of it. If people already knew I wasn't the birthday card guy, I had to think of a passable reason to be the St. Patrick's Day card guy.

"I guess I could tell them it's some kind of annual family competition to see who sends out the most St. Patrick's Day cards?"

"Perfect. I love it." Sarah couldn't stop giggling. Under "Goals," Alex had written: "Melanie," "softball league," and "St. Patrick's Day cards."

We finished our coffee, talked about Kobe Bryant's ankle and Alex's wife, who didn't have a job in Miami but had a few ideas. Before we left, Alex made one final point.

"We're going to start meeting on a weekly basis one-on-one, but we can't meet here. Too many people. You guys can hang out here, but you can't be seen hanging out with a union organizer." He was right about Jimmy's. While I never saw anybody I worked with, I ran into customers a few times. Alex was always concerned about security. At first, it seemed gratuitous. He didn't want us to meet in public or talk about salting with our non-union acquaintances. Eventually, I realized that his concern wasn't about keeping salting under wraps, which seemed to be the case with Sarah; it was about keeping the union campaign underground. In Alex's mind, the preparation that organizers did before a campaign went public was the most valuable weapon against anti-union tactics. Jeopardizing that underground foundational work could be the difference between an efficient blitzkrieg and the kind of sophisticated anti-union campaign that would end in a black hole of legal battles.

"These companies will start slitting throats," Alex said. "Slitting throats" was Alex's way of describing the act of firing someone to kill a union campaign. Alex's heavy-handed language and liberal use of profanity were endearing. He didn't want to write poetry about the revolution, he wanted to organize the shit out of it.

"But it's illegal for them to fire someone for union activity, right?"

"They can fire you for whatever the hell they want. You have no protection there. 'Oh, James is doing union shit, so we'll just make up some other fuckin' bullshit to fire him for.' Then we have to go to court, and it's this big deal. It's just not worth it, man. Let's win this way."

The casino's employee entrance was unremarkable and looked like the back of any hotel or restaurant. A loading dock, a bench, displaced banquet chairs. Smokers. The smoke curled alongside employees' conversations about the Dolphins, LeBron, fishing, children, grandchildren, and work. The backdoor break was a level playing field. Cashiers and managers. Cooks and cocktail waitresses. Haitians and Peruvians. Newports and Marlboros. They'd toast their lungs while giving their knees a breather. Past the smokers, I would scan my ID and enter the casino.

With its tile floors and green lockers lining the walls, the main corridor in the back of the house looked like a high school hallway. The hand scanners were to the left of the entrance, next to security dispatch. I would enter the last six digits of my social security number and place my hand around a few small rods that magically read my fingers and confirmed "Walsh, James" was clocking in for work. It was busy around the hand scanners during shift changes. A couple of housekeepers would be waiting until the last second of their shifts, because every penny counted.

By spring Erika and I had nearly completed the employee list. I had gotten twenty people to sign up for a softball team that I knew would never materialize and I sent out my St. Patrick's Day cards. At first people thought I was crazy. I told them St. Patrick's Day cards were customary in my Irish family, which was a lie. I had a friend design something I could print and mail out. "Castles were built one stone at a time," the greeting said at the top. But the list still had one gaping hole: the housekeeping department.

Calder subcontracted its housekeeping, which meant housekeepers didn't have the benefits we had as Churchill Downs employees. Subcontracting has been around for more than a century. Around the turn of the twentieth century, it was called the "sweating system." Companies would enlist competing contractors who would squeeze every bit of work they could out of their employees. When garment workers began unionizing, they recognized the plight of the "sweaters" and they made it a point to organize not only the company factories but also the sweatshops. The housekeepers at Calder were almost all older Haitian workers. I was friendly with one, Stéphane. He was in his seventies and wore black wing-tip shoes at work, the kind of dress shoes that would have made my twenty-four-year-old body ache after a few hours. Stéphane said he always wore them during his shifts, which could run as long as twelve hours. He made $8 an hour. Many housekeepers didn't speak English and they always worked alone, so it was hard for us to know how many there were and even harder to map them. One night I stood guard while Erika snuck into the housekeeping manager's office and snapped a picture of the schedule. Our list was complete.

The dinner-shift waitresses would punch in with me. "I owe, I owe, it's off to work I go," Donna used to sing, like Debt-y the dwarf, as she marched down the hallway. With hand scanners and cameras in all directions, there was no covering for someone who was late. At Calder, managers had easy access to employee attendance and detailed breakdowns of sales. If there was any question about an employee's performance, management could go to the surveillance department and queue up the footage. We were ever aware of the eye in the sky, the surveillance department. We all knew the department monitored us, the employees, just as much as it monitored guests. I wondered if management ever used the cameras to casually evaluate job performance. Technology that excited me as a sports fan—computers that monitored a shortstop's range or a point guard's defensive coverage—would soon be available to gauge the efficiency of service industry employees. UPS monitors when its drivers open and close their doors, buckle their seat belts, and start their engines. When will security cameras in restaurants count how often a waiter visits each table and how many coffees he or she can carry? When will facial recognition software measure customer satisfaction?

While I knew surveillance could see me, they couldn't have known my mission. From the moment I got to work until I left, I tried to interact with as many employees as possible. In this, I was efficient. Like climbing aboard the *Pequod,* there were salutations the world over.

"*Hola, mi cabroncito.*"

"*Hola,* Lucia."

"Hi, booboo."

"*Bonjour,* Jeannette."

"*Wha gwan.*"

"What up, John."

"Hey, boy."

"Hi, Vidya."

"What's good, Keon?"

"Can't call it with a bullhorn."

"Hi, *bebe.*"

"Hi, Astryde."

"Hey, Melanie."

"What's up, baby."

It was out of character for me to arrive anywhere with trumpets of hellos. I prefer to blend in. If I hadn't been so determined to build relationships with my coworkers, I would have faded into the echo of the workweek. After a few weeks of playing this character, I became him. My social disposition was born anew, conditioned to be convivial. I would stop my conversations with Dylan to ask unfamiliar coworkers for their full names as they walked by. "At first I thought it was really weird," Dylan once told me. "Now I just think it's hilarious and kinda cool."

My introductions only got me so far. I needed socials. Erika had come through with Melanie, a bartender, and one night I met them, along with Becca, at a bar not far from the casino. Erika distracted Becca while I slid onto a bar stool next to Melanie. She was in her early forties and had bleached blond hair that waved and curled. Her West Coast aura was tethered by her low raspy voice.

"Shot of Patrón and . . . what do you want, baby?" she asked me.

"Whiskey?"

"And a shot of Jack." She shook her handbag looking for a light. "Oh, he's in the biz too, honey," she said to the bartender. Melanie knew this scene—what liquor was in the well, which bartenders gave discounts, the guy running the illegal poker game in the corner. Melanie was just as likely to work here as she was to drink here.

She lit her cigarette. We threw back the shots. She cursed the bad bets she had placed on the NCAA basketball tournament and ordered another shot of tequila. I ordered a grilled cheese. I asked her questions, the answers to which I already knew from Erika's briefing. Melanie had grown up in the Pacific Northwest and talked about it like it was Bethlehem. *In the name of the Vedder, the Cornell, and the holy Cobain.* After another round of shots, we turned to see Erika on a small stage singing karaoke. She performed the Cranberries' "Zombie" as if it were the finale of a Broadway show.

"She's like Julie Andrews or some shit," Melanie said.

Before Florida, Melanie lived in Vegas and cocktailed on the strip. They called her Square Tray because she was the only waitress whose tray had four corners. She started dating a poker dealer and they moved into an Extended Stay America together. When his gambling addiction reached its zenith, she convinced him to move to Florida with her. Her sister, a stripper in Key West, would be able to help them out. But they couldn't escape the casino lifestyle. They worked on one of those cruise-to-nowhere casino boats together, along with a few other Calder employees. Melanie told me it was a SunCruz ship, the casino cruise line that enjoyed a spell of notoriety after the lobbyist and fraudster Jack Abramoff purchased the company. A few years later, the company went bankrupt. When the casino boat was shut down, Melanie's boyfriend got a job as a poker dealer at the Hard Rock. She got a job cocktailing at Mardi Gras.

"I fucking hated that place," Melanie said about Superdome. She never told me if she was fired or quit. Becca, who had also worked at Mardi Gras, was more forthcoming.

"I was fired because I wouldn't fuck Rico," Becca said, smiling. I recognized Rico as the man who had gotten Mary a job at Superdome.

Seeing that Melanie and Becca had warmed to me, Erika left. I stayed and played pool. Becca was about my age, freckled, pretty, and played pool like Paul Newman in *The Hustler*. She stumbled around the table, sinking every shot, pausing only to visit her cigarette and her whiskey. Becca was hardworking and great with customers. But other cocktail waitresses might have also added "white" and "slim" to the list of qualities management liked about her.

Any misgivings about whether or not I had gained Melanie's trust, at least for a few blurry hours, were erased when we got onstage and sang "The Weight" together in front of a handful of regulars who, unaroused by the spectacle, barely looked up from their drinks. *And, Aand, Aaand you put the load right on me.*

"The money sucks at Calder now. It better pick up when the horses start running," Melanie lamented after our duet. For months now, management had been promising a boost in business when the horses started racing at the end of April. Horse-racing season lasted until winter. Melanie was in debt and worried she wouldn't be able to make her car payments. I asked about other jobs she had worked and my heart danced when she told me that she had worked in a union hotel. I wasn't supposed to bring the union up, but now that Melanie had, I asked what it was like.

"Fucking awesome," she said before ordering another shot.

I fled to the bathroom to hide from another shot and texted

Erika about the encounter. After a few more games of pool and another forty minutes of March Madness, Becca and Melanie drove away. I tried to sleep the booze off in the backseat of my car but eventually called Colette for a ride.

When Sarah moved to another city to build a new team, Alex took over. At the next meeting, he quizzed me on Melanie's issues. I told him her story, how slow business was at the casino, how she had proven she could fight by forcing her gambling-addict boyfriend to move out of Vegas, even though he found a way to keep gambling in Florida. I told Alex that she was pro-union and wary of management. He was skeptical of Melanie's leadership potential—as was I—but we all agreed she was trustworthy, and, because we knew Melanie was pro-union, we didn't need to worry about her squealing to management. Alex drew two check marks next to Melanie's name, which meant she had been double cleared. It would be a while before an organizer actually visited her.

The goal was to double-clear ten leaders before staff organizers started house visits. Looking at the list of employee names, Alex decided it was my responsibility to make headway in the buffet. I was one of four white servers who worked in the Twin Spires Tavern and there was only one white server who worked with about fifteen black, Latina, and Caribbean servers in the buffet. I don't think Mike DiStefano and Stanley Donovan sat down and said, "Let's put the white servers in the upscale restaurant and all other ethnicities in the buffet." They didn't need to have that conversation. Out of eight food and beverage managers who supervised a mostly black and brown staff of bartenders, cooks, and waiters, only two were people of color. The division was a stark example of the racial prejudice found throughout the restaurant industry. Alex challenged me to use the divide as a way to connect with the women in the buffet.

"You know you get preferential treatment for being a white boy," he told me. "You should be the one to agitate them about that. They'll respect you for it."

I spent the first thirty minutes at work preparing the Twin Spires Tavern for the night ahead. I polished silverware, warmed up dinner rolls in an oven, set the tables, stacked crates of glasses, plated butter shaped like racehorses, cleaned the coffee machine, and filled the ice bin. I enjoyed prep work. The routine gave me purpose. The Tavern was slow. On most nights, Calder's gamblers preferred the wings and burgers at the fast-food concession stand or the all-you-can-eat buffet. Because of this, the restaurant had a skeleton crew. Jon, the manager, usually sent two or three of the four waiters home early so that one of us had a chance to make some money, which meant the odd Saturday rush would result in pandemonium.

Any experienced waiter will tell you about "the zone," the focus the job takes when you're in the weeds and one order away from walking off the job or punching a rude customer in the face. I would walk back and forth between the kitchen and the dining room repeating tasks in my head: "Napkins at table five, refill at three, well vodka cran at two, fire apps at six." In these blurry moments time warped and the shortest nights were a string of never-ending disasters. "Where's my food?" asked the least-empathetic patron of all time. "It'll be right out," I said, struck by the heart-stopping realization that I had forgotten to place his order. A cook, who had yelled at me earlier for letting artichoke dip get cold in the window, bailed me out by dropping everything to make the food I forgot to order. I made small talk with the guests. "You're of a higher pedigree than most people here," one guest told me, trying to pay me a compliment while insulting my coworkers. "Glad to have good service," someone else said after she ordered. "Much better than that bitch bartender with the tattoos," she added. Another customer stopped me on one of the Tavern's busiest nights. "I have to tell you, I was a professional server in my country. What you are doing right now is offensive to my profession. I spend a lot of money here and I want to let you know that I could have you fired. One word and . . ." She slit her own throat with her thumb. "I won't tell your manager this time but next time I won't be so forgiving." I attributed the slow business and the customers' impatience to their desire to spend as much time as possible in front of the slot machines.

Calder was designed with traditional bits of gambling sub-terfuge—the casino floor was a maze of machines without a window or clock in sight. Vegas folklore about ploys to keep guests gambling—pure oxygen and gambling aphrodisiacs wafting from the vents—pales in comparison to what the industry has actually done to keep gamblers in front of their machines as long as possible. Sitting in plush ergonomic chairs, guests probably didn't consider the millions that had been spent designing the machines with which they engaged. In her book *Addiction by Design,* rather than studying gambling addicts themselves, MIT professor Natasha Dow Schüll studied the effects of slot machine design on gaming addictions. Modern slot machines are outfitted to grease the subliminal and draw out "time on device," TOD, the most coveted metric in the industry. Companies with names like Immersion Corporation use phrases like "haptic feedback technology" and "vibro-tactile profiles" to design systems called ContinuePlay and Capacitive Touchscreen System. Gambling executives openly refer to the machines in their casinos as "cash cows," "golden geese," or "mousetraps."

At first, it was easy to dismiss impolite regulars as feckless. I knew nothing about slot machines and even less about their appeal. Day after day I would watch the same customers in a trance hitting buttons, losing money, and wasting away their health. I wrote them off as irresponsible or genetically disposed to addiction. What baffled me the most was the fact that slot machines required zero skill or gamesmanship. They weren't video games that reward coordination, or poker, which theoretically allows players the opportunity to maximize their winning potential by reading and toying with opponents. People who play slots surrender to chaos. By law, slot machines are required to pay out a minimum percentage, varying from state to state, over their lifetimes. While casinos control the long-term percentage average payout of their slot machines—hence the advertisement "The loosest slots in town"—even when the average payout is 90 percent, gamblers are losing 10 percent of their money. Furthermore, casinos don't have control over which slot machines hit, when they hit, how much they hit for, or how often they hit. Yet that formulaic uncertainty was enough to transfix my regulars.

"Ever been to Vegas?" Walt, a regular, once asked me. He was disappointed to hear that I hadn't. He had been struggling to explain why he spent so much time at the casino. He paused and looked down at his drink and tried again.

"You ski? When I was a kid I'd go skiing in Killington, Vermont. There was so much fucking snow. Covered every tree, every leaf. It was beautiful. Marvelous. Being at the top of that mountain, you couldn't think of anything but where you were. It was perfect. That's Vegas for me. All my troubles go away."

My conversation with Walt was the first time I realized winning didn't matter. Regulars were chasing a feeling, not a jackpot. The feeling was like nostalgia but stronger. My epiphany was validated when I researched the interplay between slot machine design and gambling addiction. When a gambler plays slots he enters a fog. He focuses on navigating out of the fog but slot machines are bottomless and unending. The fog lasts as long as he is willing and able to sit, slap, and pay. Each game, each slap, each bet lasts only three to four seconds. That means he can place as many as 1,200 bets per hour. (Far more than the number of horse races he can bet on or hands of poker he can play in a day.) *On to the next one,* the brain says. Jackpots provide shots of euphoria in the form of dopamine, the chemical responsible for pleasure and motor skills. *On to the next one.* The brain wants to find more dopamine in the fog. A bell goes off; *It must be a sign.* The lights flash; *That must be good. On to the next one.* The screen blinks, and despite the fact that it was a losing spin, the bell rings and the lights flash simultaneously. *We're close now. On to the next one!* I saw customers try to reason with machines. Some people prayed. One lady tapped the buttons in bursts of seven, always seven. Another woman waved her hands over the screen, summoning some voodoo slot god. There were people who tried to use logic where there wasn't any. They watched a machine "get fat" while someone else played and jumped on the machine as soon as it was free, hoping it would "pop." They were unaware or, more likely, unwilling to accept the certainty of the odds' stubborn randomness. There is no methodology or reason. The bells, whistles, and lights aren't horns and lighthouses warning of danger in the fog; they are Sirens calling gamblers deeper.

At first the fog is cathartic. It provides relief after a long workweek. Like a cozy memory, it's a way of forgetting a troubled relationship or health problem. Before long the fog is a way to escape a dinner date or an appointment. Sometimes, as was the case for a woman at Mardi Gras Casino, the fog is thick enough to leave your grandkids in the car while you slap the buttons. Get deep enough in the fog and you don't care about the money; pausing for jackpots becomes a hindrance. *On to the next one.* Forget about the odds, the money, or the future, because the fog, like a memory, is a constant in an uncertain present.

Studies have shown that just about anyone who plays slot machines regularly is doomed to get lost in the fog. That's the point. On average, problem gamblers who prefer slot machines become addicted within one year of play. Problem gamblers who favor other types of gambling take three and a half years. And addicts pay. Government-commissioned studies in the United States, Canada, and Australia have shown that problem gamblers are responsible for 30 to 60 percent of slot machine revenues.

Florida required all casino employees to take a "responsible gaming" seminar. A few months into the job, I joined a group of coworkers on the third floor of the grandstand. The woman who ran the seminar told us that only 1 to 2 percent of people who came to Calder could be considered gambling addicts.

"Where'd you get your numbers, lady?" Rita, a buffet server who was sitting next to me, said under her breath.

We were told that we would never get in trouble for reporting a suspected gambling addict to management. We were also told about the "self-exclusion" program, by which compulsive gamblers, in an attempt to de-incentivize play, could put their names on a list that legally allowed the casino to withhold future jackpots more than $1,200. The player loses the winnings. Self-exclusion was enforced casino by casino, not state- or county-wide, so a gambling addict who wanted to participate in the program would need to put his or her name on each casino's list. Five years of publicly available Florida slot machine revenue data showed that pari-mutuel casinos paid out $8.8 billion in winnings. Over the same time period there was one monthly filing of $5,408 in self-exclusion money. Save for the few stories about cocktail waitresses calling security because someone smelled like a toilet, I never saw a casino employee take action to address a guest's gambling addiction.

While the worst addicts probably didn't stop to eat at the restaurant or the buffet, we all knew who the problem gamblers were. We saw them every day. They were the regular-regulars. There was Mrs. Peltz, who fancied herself a crab leg connoisseur even though she would break the crab legs, suck on them, and then toss them, still full of meat, into a bucket. She was there at least four days a week for more than a year.

Perry and Paula, a married couple who came almost daily, tipped well for months. However, soon $7 tips became $5, then $1. Perry started tipping with silver dollars and spare change. One casino host—one of the women (and they were almost all women) responsible for babysitting VIPs—told me that sometimes Paula would call and beg her to send Perry home.

There were plenty of customers who seemed to be more responsible. They only showed up on weekends. It was easier to serve those guests because I didn't feel like I was nourishing a habit. There was the Chinese-Jamaican man who always ordered "da linguini but I don't want no parsley on it." He told me that he owned a few grocery stores in Jamaica, which made him a walking stereotype I was previously unaware of. He always had a friendly word for me and was forgiving when the cook occasionally put parsley on his linguini. There was the wealthy tan woman in her seventies who, late in life, took an interest in erotic art and opened a museum on South Beach with one of the largest collections of chiseled penises and orgies on canvas in the world. There was the actress who played the mom on *Family Matters*. She always tipped well. There were truckers, horse trainers, police officers, teachers, and accountants. Most treated me with respect. I didn't mind people who were quiet, or indifferent, or bizarre. The wretched ones got to me, depending on the night. Of course, only one thing mattered when the final bill came—the tip.

It was inevitable that, when talking about tips, ethnicity would come up. One night in the privacy of the kitchen, I complained about a bad tip. Donna, who was white, asked if the guests had looked like her husband.

"What?" I asked, genuinely confused.

"Did they look like my husband?" she asked while opening her server's pad to show me a picture of her black husband.

"You believe that?" I asked her.

"I know I had to set my man straight," she said.

Miami's diversity is its beauty and the source of much of

its friction. Because many of my coworkers had friends and family of different ethnicities, they often felt jokes based on specious stereotypes to be all in good fun. I heard black waitresses call their Indian coworkers "dot heads" and "Osama." I heard one white server justify a joke with a racist punch line by saying, "It's funny! I call my black friends niggers and they call me a redneck!" There were Asian jokes, Haitian jokes, and jokes about people from Tierra del Fuego to Canada. Aside from letting my white coworkers know that I was not okay with their using the n-word around me, I tried to ignore the color commentary. And still, the prevalence of the *black people don't tip* stereotype was suffocating. I was only beginning to understand its complexity. When I started picking up shifts in the buffet, my black coworkers talked to me like the politically correct Yankee that I was.

"Niggas don't tip," Natasha, a black server in the buffet, said to me. A few years later, I watched the exact same exchange acted out on *Louie*. A white guy looks to a black woman to validate his understanding of racial stereotyping only to find out he knows even less than what he thought he knew. I went so far as to conduct my own studies, documenting ethnicities and tip sizes in the hope of proving my coworkers wrong. They dismissed my study on account of its small sample size. When I looked for a legitimate study, I was horrified to discover that the most professional studies showed that, generally, African-Americans tip less. Subsequent studies have sought to find reasons for the disparity by factoring in all kinds of controls like socioeconomic levels, the quality of service, servers' biases, and the awareness of tipping percentages among black diners. The studies also proved that the prevalence of the stereotype was immensely disproportionate to its truth.

In all of my conversations with coworkers about stereotyping, no one ever placed any responsibility on management, owners, or investors. Every so often the issue of tipping comes up in the news. Sometimes it's a fancy Manhattan restaurant that has abolished tipping or college football fans stiffing waitresses in their rival's town or pictures of receipts with tips too good to be true. I have been to dinner with Europeans who malign the singularly American custom for being illogical. I have defended it, knowing the feeling of empowerment that comes from a good tip. A tip is merit pay in its purest form, a reward for a job well done. But when that satisfaction fades, the reality is that too many sociological, psychological, and chemical variables make a person a good or bad tipper. What's left is a surreptitious way for companies to transfer labor cost onto consumers in the name of "enhancing customer service." Michael Lynn of Cornell University is a leading expert on tipping in America and his solution is simple: either pay servers more or apply auto-gratuity to the bill. Some servers will continue to provide exceptional service and others will continue to ignore you. But it will eradicate a mechanism through which prejudice passes from table, to person, to language, and to culture.

When I told Alex that I was grappling with this issue, he responded quickly, like a mechanic who knows it's a fried spark plug before he pops the hood.

"No shit, dude. That's why we fight for auto-grat."

At Calder, it seemed as though everybody was a bad tipper. I blamed it on gambling—$5 on the table was $5 that wasn't going in a slot machine. The only time I knew how much I would make were the shifts at the concession stand, where I made minimum wage, $7.25 an hour. That was the magic number. I used it to determine the value of every dollar I spent. Thirty-six dollars for gas = five hours of work. Ninety dollars for groceries = twelve and a half hours of work. If I decided to take the Florida Turnpike instead of Twenty-Seventh Avenue to get to work, my first twenty-five minutes were spent paying off the toll. As a tipped waiter, I was making more than my minimum-wage coworkers. Over the first few months, I went home with an average of $61 a night. If business had kept up, combined with my $4.19 hourly wage (thanks to new legislation in Florida, tipped employees would soon receive a $0.04 raise) I would have made about $24,000 a year before taxes. We were making so little that our managers rarely gave us a hard time about reporting our tips. My biweekly pay stub indicated that Calder assumed my tips covered the difference between my hourly server wage and the minimum wage. More often than not, my tips would cover minimum wage. (Eventually, Calder would pay all servers the non-tipped minimum wage.) However, night to night this wasn't always true.

"If we don't make enough in tips between two pay periods, will Calder supplement the difference?" I asked Jon, the Tavern manager.

"That's a good question that I don't know the answer to," he told me. "And I'm not going to ask management because it's a negative question. I don't have a problem with you asking, but if I ask management it would be like me assuming we will have more slow nights and that is negative."

I remember thinking Jon was either evasive or spineless. Back then I didn't realize that although Jon made more money than the servers and he didn't have to rely on tips, he didn't have it easy. Any given week, he had to work more than forty hours without overtime pay. Every few weeks he needed to work night shifts to supervise the concession stand and the bars. Jon knew that he could be replaced at any time by one of the many food and beverage employees capable of doing his job. He blamed the casino and service industries for his bad back and two failed marriages and he didn't want his job at Calder to ruin his third. The fact that Jon was afraid to ask management my "negative" question was a shining example of the chasm between management and tipped employees.

Once an elderly guest caught me off guard and asked me if I wanted to be the manager of the restaurant.

"No," I told the guest. "I wouldn't want to have to fire people."

"Those are the best kinds of managers," he responded. "Because the ones who want to do all that are a bunch of assholes."

Alex continued to push me to make friends in the buffet. On slow nights I would visit the buffet to get to know the servers. This required me to walk through the dish room, which connected the Tavern to the buffet. The industrial dishwashing machine sounded like a jet engine. To keep the noise out, Keon, the hip-hop poet steward I had met at orientation, would wear headphones and sing along while he scrubbed. *Heard that she fucking LeBron, but shit . . . I don't know.* Whenever Jon, Mike DiStefano, or Stanley Donovan walked through the dish room Keon would switch to Negro spirituals—*Wade in the water, wade in the water, children.* He said it was the quickest way to get white managers out. Erika had told me that Keon had been in trouble with the law a few times but hoped a steady job would keep him on the straight and narrow.

Ceci, a stout Peruvian woman in her late fifties, worked next to Keon. Her pastel eye shadow, applied liberally, said more about her exuberant personality than her all-white uniform. After receiving my St. Patrick's Day card, Ceci proceeded to give me cards on Easter, my birthday, Thanksgiving, and Christmas. Next to Ceci, Ginette scrubbed the large, heavy cookware. Ginette was Haitian and about the same age as Ceci. She had five adult children, three married and two college age. Despite the fact that she had lived in the United States for thirty years, Ginette didn't speak much English. Neither did Ceci. They both understood English, though.

During Calder orientation, Haiti was hit by a massive earthquake that killed two hundred thirty thousand people. Months later, I asked Ginette about her family in Haiti.

"I know three family die," she said. "Two children in school. One cousin, home."

"Bad. Bad. Bad," Ceci said.

Ceci and Ginette didn't talk to each other much—Ceci told me this was because they didn't get along, not the language barrier—but despite personal differences, there was a sense of solidarity in the dish room. Both women wore ripped latex gloves that did little to prevent their fingers from pruning within the first hour of work. They looked out for each other whenever one of them snuck a plate of food or sat down while on the job. They helped each other lift heavy pots and laughed together when Stanley Donovan walked through the dish room wearing sneakers with curved platforms meant to exercise and tighten his glutes.

Alex had told me to ask any older Haitian or Latina women to take me to church. He called it a "slam dunk" social. So I asked Ceci. She understood what I was asking but she couldn't respond fully in English.

"You. Write. Call." I wrote my name and phone number on a piece of receipt paper and she stuffed it into her bra. Later that night, as I was getting off my shift, I got a call from an unfamiliar number.

"Is this James?" a young woman asked in perfect English. "My name is Daniela and my mother tells me that you'd like to come to church with us?" We arranged to meet that Sunday for Mother's Day mass. Slam dunk, indeed.

After checking in with Keon, Ceci, or Ginette, I would walk through swinging silver double doors into the Tropical Gardens Buffet. The buffet's decor was just as busy as the casino floor's, clearly meant to contribute to a sense of euphoria. The carpet was a panoply of spiraling radiant colors. Jazzy lights illuminated fake plants and the walls were painted pink, yellow, and green. It was hard to hear the music piped in over the slot machines in the casino, but in the buffet John Mayer and Bananarama were always crystal clear. The buffet itself wasn't large. There was an Italian station with pasta, a carving table, a home-style spread of potatoes, a pizza oven, an Asian station with a wok, a salad bar, and some desserts.

When the buffet first opened, at least one cook tended to each station. Not long after the grand opening, management made major cutbacks to the kitchen staff. Cooks dropped more quickly than anyone else during the first year. They were fired or, more often, they quit because their hours had been cut so drastically. Eventually, only three cooks worked the entire buffet. During peak hours, they would scuttle from station to station. The food got cold. Managers tried to help, but still, dishwashers were summoned to do jobs they weren't hired, trained, or paid to do.

"It's all part of their plan," Keon told me the first time I saw him working a buffet station. "You think they gonna pay some nigga ten dollars as a cook, when they can just have one of us do it for seven twenty-five?"

One afternoon, I heard the executive chef berate a facilities worker—not a member of the kitchen staff or the food and beverage department—who said he wasn't allowed to fix a piece of broken machinery because of "union rules." (The facilities worker was a member of the International Brotherhood of Electrical Workers.) The chef had asked him to do somebody else's job. In that moment, I understood the chef's frustration. Such turgid union rules are often cited as a prime example of how a union can hamstring a business. But hearing Keon's logic, the rules made sense. The "not my job" edict protected workers from doing two jobs at once without proper compensation and encouraged employers to hire more employees.

Unlike the Tavern, the buffet was open most of the day with a break between lunch and dinner. The servers worked hard clearing plates, resetting tables, fetching tea, coffee, water, and sodas. The tips were bad. Usually a dollar, sometimes five, other times spare change and lint. Other times nothing.

Intimidated by the buffet servers, I tried to ease into the scene by hanging out with the cashiers at the front, who were almost all older than the servers. The cashiers didn't like hustling for tips, running around the floor, or staying late to wait for lackadaisical guests to finish at the end of the night. They were gentler. I got to know Debbie, the buffet manager, so she wasn't suspicious of me. Debbie was one of the nicest managers at Calder. (Alex would tell us to complain about the good managers because this would endear them to executives.) Debbie cared for the women in the buffet and, as the lone female food and beverage manager for some time, was particularly aware of Stanley Donovan's demeaning management style. Debbie loved casinos. On her nights off, she would spend hours on end gambling at Hard Rock, Seminole, Mardi Gras, or Gulfstream. Debbie liked me, which allowed me to mingle with the cashiers whenever I wanted. I started by talking with two sisters in their forties, Priya and Vidya. They were Indo-Guyanese, the largest ethnic population in the South American country. They immigrated to the United States in their early twenties. Neither of them was much more than five feet tall.

"When you cook, what kind of food do you cook?" I asked Priya.

"Lots of stuff. You like chicken curry?" she asked with a soft Caribbean accent.

"I want to learn to make chicken curry! Can you teach me?"

She smiled, surprised by my intensity. "I can cook for you, I'll bring you some food."

"No, no. I want to *learn*. I'll come to you. I'll buy the ingredients."

There was some more hesitation. "Okay. We can teach you. I'll have Vidya come."

"Are you around this week? How about Tuesday?" People were tickled when I asked to hang out, and they would almost always agree right away, but when I took it a step further and tried to make concrete plans, suspicion and wariness would kick in. My coworkers would inevitably pause to consider my motives. *Is he asking to learn to cook chicken curry because he wants to kill me in my own home?* Or, more likely: *Does he want to sleep with me?* The latter was much more of a problem for female salts. Erika, Mary, and Colette regularly deflected the advances of male coworkers who assumed that their relentless desire to hang out meant it was on. Dan, Sarah, and Alex explicitly forbade salts from having relationships with coworkers. It was part of the salt contract. This was never much of an issue for me. If I thought a girl liked me I would use that attraction to get a social, but of course women don't have the same expectations as men on dates. One gay coworker was downright flabbergasted to learn that I wasn't gay, which was understandable because I had gone to a gay club with him. I don't think he had ever known a straight male coworker so keen to hang out. "So you're not gay?" he said after his first drink. He checked in a bit later. "Are you sure? Not even just a little?"

Priya committed to the cooking class and a few days later I drove to her apartment for my lesson. It was in a two-story building shaded by tall palm trees behind the Hollywood courthouse. The two-bedroom apartment had lime-green walls and was impeccably clean. Priya shared it with her twenty-one-year-old son. She was wearing jeans with a pink stripe up the sides and a tank top with a floral pattern. Shortly after I arrived, Vidya showed up wearing the exact same outfit. They had gone shopping together recently and, independent of each other, had chosen that afternoon to showcase their new outfits. They were embarrassed. I laughed with them. Vidya had come straight from her other job at a middle school cafeteria, where she made sandwiches and worked the register, and her health insurance was free.

"Today was okay, no food fights. I tell you, boy, I hate those food fights."

Vidya didn't mind either of her jobs—cashing out kids by day and senior citizens by night—she just didn't like working both of them.

Priya barely let me do anything in the kitchen. She showed me the ingredients as they went in: *jeera, garam masala,* curry powder, chili pepper, and a hunk of garlic. She used a knife like a battle-ax to cut up the bony parts of the chicken and washed it in vinegar. She let me peel the potatoes.

While we waited for the chicken to cook, Priya told me about her life. She came to the United States when she was seventeen as part of an arranged marriage. Her husband was twenty-five. At first, they wrote letters. He asked for her picture, and her mom took her to have a professional portrait taken. She sent him the picture, and in the next letter, he asked her to marry him. Priya went with her mother to Trinidad to meet the man and his family. She didn't know it at the time but her future husband's family was also meeting six other potential wives. Still, he chose her. They married and moved to Florida. Even now, after the divorce, she thought of him as more of a father figure than an ex-husband.

Vidya moved to Florida in 1988 and immediately went to work at a McDonald's. Since then she had worked only in the service industry. She had seen her fair share of difficult managers but few were as cantankerous as Randy, a food and beverage manager at Calder. Both sisters despised Randy, who was in his early thirties and had dark baggy crescents under his eyes. For a while, Randy didn't let Priya take bathroom breaks during her shifts, until Vidya stepped in.

"Not because she's my sister but because sometimes you got to set the manager straight," Vidya said emphatically. In Priya's home it was clear that Vidya was the leader. Unfortunately, she didn't lead anyone else in the buffet. While I liked Vidya, she needed to lead more than just Priya to earn herself a spot on the committee. When I told Alex that Vidya only led Priya, he added the sisters to the same bubble as Dylan—I would be in charge of leading them. The social helped me gain their trust, and at the very least, I'd learned how to make chicken curry. The search for a leader in the buffet continued.

Erika and I were both drawn to Erin, a server who said she was a mix of Puerto Rican, Mexican, German, and Irish descent. Short and irreverent, Erin made everyone laugh in the buffet, which, I thought, earned her respect. She was a single mother with two sons, ages two and eight, and they all lived with her parents. One night I saw her standing out back smoking a cigarette wearing a kid-sized backpack. In one of the company's tacit acknowledgments of its own miserly pay, Calder had a back-to-school drive and gave away backpacks full of school supplies to employees with young kids. I asked Erin how she got by as a single mom.

"Gotta do what you gotta do," she said while stamping out the butt of her cigarette.

After work one night Erika and I talked Erin into going for drinks at an Irish pub. She convinced her mother to watch her kids. I was shocked to find out Erin—who could have passed for seventeen—was my age. The way she had soothingly calmed her kids down before bed on her cell phone made her seem older. After only one drink, she was candid about life as a single mother.

"Don't get me wrong, I love my kids, but if I could just shove 'em right back up there, I would."

Erin found out she was pregnant after the father began his first stint in prison. Erin's parents drove her and her newborn home from the hospital the day she gave birth. Once there, her parents went into their bedroom and locked the door in what was either an act of disgust or an attempt to teach her a hard lesson about parenting.

"The baby cried all night. I cried all night. I called the hospital and a lady, a nurse or a receptionist, calmed me down and told me the baby was fine."

When Erin's boyfriend got out of prison, she got pregnant again. Erin and her kids moved in with him, but he started getting high, drunk, and angry. When she told me this, I immediately recalled the time Erin had shown up at work with a black eye. I later found out that it wasn't her boyfriend who had hit her, but his brother. I was happy to hear that she had moved back in with her parents.

"You wanna know what I do to get by?" Erin whispered. "I sell pills."

Erin told me she had an arrangement with her sister's husband. She would visit a doctor at a pill mill, or one of the many "pain clinics" that could be spotted in strip malls; get a prescription for oxy; and then give the pills to her brother-in-law to sell. At the time, Florida was at the height of its painkiller problem. In 2010, because of lax regulations, doctors in Florida purchased 90 percent of the oxycodone in the country. Since then, the state has increased regulation and enforcement. For Erin, it amounted to an extra $250 a month, which helped pay off her credit card debt and car note.

Erin had a crew at work but they hovered around her because she was funny and erratic, not an anchor of stability or reason. She wasn't angry or fed up with Calder, minimum wage, Stanley Donovan, or the fact that we were required to work on holidays without holiday pay. Erika had another social with Erin at which she claimed to be pro-union. With that in mind, Erika and I cleared her for a house visit, but we knew we still had not found our leader in the buffet.

While I was assigned to lead four people—Dylan, Lucia,

Priya, and Vidya—Erika had a small army of people she could lead. Erika made friends effortlessly. The charisma that made her so popular at Churchill's, the punk bar, made her an all-star salt. We weren't going to win if only Erika and I were leading the way. By our estimate, there were about two hundred twenty workers eligible for unionization. With each leader responsible for ten workers, we would need twenty-two leaders to cover the whole casino. Our aim was ten to fifteen leaders. With Alex pushing me, I had no choice but to hunt for socials like a college freshman looking for a party. Alex would check in after my shifts.

"Did you get a social?"

"No."

"Why not?"

"Because Taylor said she was busy this weekend."

"Dude, you know that's not an excuse."

These conversations were brutal. I started bombarding my coworkers with requests to hang out just to get Alex off my back. Throw enough lures in the water and something is going to bite. Socials started filling my schedule. I went to dive bars, Hooters, and a Jamaican jerk joint. I went to the batting cages, bowling, and a baby shower. I had coffee with Ivan, a bartender from Slovenia who, at some point or another, had worked at every hotel between Miami and Fort Lauderdale. Wanting to avoid the line at the popular strip club King of Diamonds, where strippers were scheduled to box each other, I went to a dingy strip club next door with a group of cocktail waitresses. We were accompanied by a Calder VIP who handed out stacks of $1 bills. Jean-Louise, a cook, taught me to make *griot,* a Haitian dish made from pork shoulder. While I was cutting up pepper, thyme, and garlic to add to the *griot,* I learned that Jean-Louise had left her drug-addicted husband when she was pregnant with her second child. As one of the only female cooks, she wasn't so much offended by the misogyny in Calder's kitchen but was tired of it. Jean-Louise dreamed of becoming a full-time caterer but even at $13.75 an hour, one of the highest food and beverage wages at Calder, she wasn't saving enough to realize that dream. I went to one gay club with a slot attendant named Sam and another with Rodney, who was a cage cashier. I managed to sashay around the dance floor while prudishly avoiding close contact. I learned that Sam, the slot attendant, had "Lucky You" tattooed above his nether region. I also learned that he made $11.50 an hour when he worked at the Isle, the unionized casino. At Calder, he made $8. Lucia took me to a religious ceremony based on Nichiren Buddhism at a new-age retreat center in a posh suburb. I chanted alongside her, "*Myō hō ren ge kyō. Hōben-pon. Dai ni.*" Driving to and from the retreat center Lucia talked about her ex-husband, who had gambled away their savings playing pool. She also told me that, in addition to the $9 an hour she was making at Calder, she got by with the $600 a week she made cleaning the mansion of a cookware tycoon in Aventura. But when the pay was cut to $360, she couldn't manage her home-loan modification payment, her credit card debt, and the money she needed to send to her sick father in Uruguay. Lucia was considering taking another job as a maid in West Palm Beach. In order to tutor a cocktail waitress, Patricia, in algebra, I spent hours refreshing my math skills. I went gambling at Mardi Gras, Hard Rock, and Gulfstream. I spent an afternoon doing sit-ups and push-ups with Chris, a slot attendant and amateur boxer. I was sore for weeks. Ceci, the Peruvian dishwasher, took me to Mother's Day mass with her family. It was in Spanish. When the priest asked all the mothers to stand, I also stood up. Everyone in our pew laughed at me. Afterward, we ate skirt steak and *papa a la Huancaína* at Ceci's friend's house.

I got to know Ceci's diabetic daughter, Daniela. She was only thirteen but talked to me with the honesty and thoughtfulness of someone much older.

"I want to be a doctor," she told me while driving from

church to lunch. "My father died a year ago, and since I have diabetes, I want to learn how to take care of people."

Even when coworkers didn't open up and gush about their personal lives, socials forced a familiarity that fostered comfort and confidence. I realized just how much Ceci trusted me when she called me as she was leaving work. She was hysterical, gasping to use the little English she knew.

"You. Come. Get me."

She was waiting for me when I pulled up alongside Calder's loading dock. She was crying. She gave me an address in South Miami and explained that we needed to go get Daniela. Forty-five minutes later, we pulled up to a house. Ceci went inside. A minute later, a man exited the house carrying Daniela and arranged her in the backseat of my car. Ceci followed, yelling at the man who had carried Daniela out. Daniela's eyes were rolling into the back of her head, and she was heaving and shaking. When I asked Daniela what was wrong, she didn't respond to me. Ceci got into the car.

"Go. Hospital!"

I drove one block, pulled over, and called an ambulance. Daniela had gone into diabetic shock. When the paramedics arrived they rushed her into the back of the ambulance and Ceci went with her to the hospital. Daniela was in the hospital for days. I still don't understand exactly what happened that afternoon, why the people inside the house hadn't called an ambulance themselves. I visited Daniela and Ceci in the hospital. Daniela translated for her mother.

"My mother wants to thank you for saving my life."

Even if Daniela had been on the brink, I didn't save her life. When Ceci called me I didn't know the gravity of the situation. I almost told her that I was busy, when, in fact, I was lying on my couch reading a book, enjoying my day off. The only reason I hadn't was because I knew Ceci. Her family had welcomed me and our socials had created a bond strong enough for Ceci to trust me in a dire situation. Some might argue that our relationship was built on a falsehood, but I knew early on that Ceci's vote didn't mean much. She wasn't a leader in the dishwashing room. We had an honest friendship.

Business got even slower in the Tavern. The restaurant cut back and was open only four nights a week. Then three. The rest of the Tavern's employees fled. Dylan moved back to Vegas. Tricia quit and started working at a diner a few miles down the road. Donna got a job waitressing at the Hard Rock. They were all looking for something better. *On to the next one.*

Finally, management shut down the Twin Spires Tavern. I would be transferred to the buffet. Jon rounded up the buffet servers and told everyone about the changes.

"Twin Spires has been repurposed for special events only. We're going to be making some changes," he said. "We're a business. It's all about the bottom line here. We all need to make sacrifices."

I switched out my long-sleeved clay-colored mandarin-collared shirt for a short-sleeved celery-green shirt. Debbie, the buffet manager in charge of scheduling, put me on the buffet schedule. As the new guy in the buffet, I was the odd man out, and my presence would mean fewer tables for the rest of the servers. At most restaurants across the country, this kind of redistricting would have been considered an act of institutionalized terrorism. Figuring out the right number of servers is a challenge. If there are too few, the servers become overwhelmed, and service goes down, along with tips. Conversely, too many servers can lead to resentment, which can affect both the quality of service and, again, tips.

The most unwelcoming of the servers was Rita, a white woman nearing sixty, whose loose skin and hobbled step made the bitter glances she gave me throughout my first shift all the more frightening. Others were quieter about their misgivings.

Tasha and String (so named because she was wire thin) were quiet around me. When I entered the side service station, the small nook where servers spent the majority of their time and were generally free to be themselves, they acted as if I were a manager. They would quickly hide their cell phones or stop gossiping.

Kalia was the kindest of all the servers. "Run the butter chips under the hot water to soften 'em up," she told me. She had other bits of advice. "See the lady with the tight pants, look like she's wearing a diaper? She's all yours. She's gonna ask for hot tea, lots of lemon. He wants a Diet Coke. She'll ask for a steak knife, it's the only thing she uses to eat. It's nasty. I'd take them but I'd throw up my lunch. They're gonna leave you three dollars and a messy-ass table." Kalia was right about everything. At the end of the night I mentioned to Kalia that Rita was giving me the cold shoulder.

"Don't worry about her," she told me. "She's just runnin' out of her happy pills." Rita dealt with her arthritis and other ailments with trips to the same kind of pain clinic Erin went to.

I tried to win over the buffet bloc by showing them that I was a good coworker. I took the tables nobody wanted, helped servers who were in the weeds, and stole food from the buffet for coworkers who were too scared to do it themselves. Eating from the all-you-can-eat buffet was strictly forbidden. I would stand guard while they ate cookies, pizza, and pasta in the side station—we rarely touched the prime rib. As the only white guy in the buffet, I experienced more latitude. Other servers were scared to slip up. I sometimes wondered how long I could hide in the bathroom taking notes (or playing solitaire) before a manager would yell at me. The other buffet servers knew I could get away with more. I wanted to renounce this advantage, or at least confess to it. The tangible ways of showing other servers that I was a good coworker only got me so far. I was still an outsider. Within my first few days of serving in the buffet, a surly regular had started requesting that I take care of him. "All the others are animals," he told me. One night, after someone else had brought him drinks, he walked into the service station, and in front of all of my coworkers, he pointed at me and said, "I want *him* to serve me!" There was a stiff silence when he left.

"You think I don't know he wants me because I'm white?" I said. The words hung in the air. The ladies looked at each other and started chuckling.

"At least you know it," String said.

The buffet band started to loosen up around me. They talked about the men in their lives, their kids, and each other. I talked about the dating scene and the differences between the Northeast and Florida, and, surprising myself, I was open about my time in college. I looked forward to work because I had made friends.

Weekends in the buffet went from busy to hysterical when Stanley Donovan introduced the all-you-can-eat crab legs and prime rib nights on Fridays and Saturdays. The line for the buffet snaked onto the casino floor and stayed that way all night. Like doughboys in the trenches, we readied the service station for the deluge. We polished buckets of silverware, checked sugar caddies, topped off the salt and pepper shakers, brewed coffee and iced tea, stockpiled napkins, water glasses, straws, more napkins, crab crackers, steak knives, tea bags, and more napkins. In these calm moments, conversation was natural and fluid. Someone asked Erin how her date was.

"It was good 'til I found out he's married." Everyone but Erin laughed.

"You should try church," suggested Delphine, the buffet's resident proselytizer.

"I ain't gonna meet nobody at no damn church. And I sure as hell ain't gonna meet nobody at work wearing this fucking uniform."

We talked about money.

"I really need to make a hundred tonight."

"I need to make a thousand but I'm not keeping my fingers crossed."

We talked about car trouble, kid trouble, and the casino's promotions.

"You see they giving away a year's worth of groceries?"

"When we opened they gave away a Lexus, now they giving away groceries."

Once the cashiers started seating customers, we didn't have time to talk. Despite the preparation, we never had enough supplies and by midshift each server would have ten tables barking for something we didn't have: "How come *they* got crab crackers and *I* didn't?" "How the hell does a buffet run out of napkins?" "Young man, I can't seem to remember where I'm sitting, can you help me find my table?" I don't know how many miles I would walk a night, but I was always sore the next morning. When I was hired, I had purchased a pair of black tennis shoes because I was too vain to wear the bulky industry sneakers favored by the rest of the waitresses. After a year at Calder, the soles were so distressed that they formed a U when I wasn't wearing them.

During the rush the service station was busy but quiet. There wasn't time for conversation, only mutters of contempt for a piggish customer, a lethargic coworker, or the faulty coffee machine. There was contempt for a guy on the news who beat his grandkids, an itchy knee brace, an estranged boyfriend who kept missing child support payments, a bad back, or a manager who wouldn't approve vacation time. "This is a fuckin' hard way to make a living," Rita liked to say in these moments.

As the last of the hungry customers trickled into the buffet on Saturday, the shift would reach its denouement. The servers would count their tips even though everyone already knew what they had in their pockets.

"You break a hundred dollars?"

"Not yet."

"Back-to-school comin' up, a hundred fifty dollars for them uniforms."

The optimism at the casino's opening, the idea that all Calder employees would profit from the casino's success, was long gone. This wasn't the job that would end the job search. Buffet servers would serve five tables and make $8 during a slow day shift, then work themselves haggard for $100 that night.

Stanley Donovan's obsession with cost cutting didn't help. The casino had opened fat and now it was time to get down to fighting weight. Smaller glasses, cheaper butter, fewer hours. There were firings across the board. First it was the cooks, then the top sous chef, and then it was the executive chef. No one was replaced; their work was just redistributed. If job security in the food and beverage department was any indication, Calder's business must have been in dire straits. Yet, according to a quarterly report for shareholders, Calder Casino "continued on pace to meet [its] expected $80–100 million in annual gross gaming revenue."

Buffet work wasn't bad work, just bad money. There was some sense of satisfaction at the end of the night. But the satisfaction of a job well done, the relief of surviving another deluge, disappeared when tips were tallied. On some nights, frustration led to panic. At one point or another, I watched Erin, Kalia, String, and Tasha—people not prone to expressing self-pity—shed tears about their finances. Each crinkled dollar bill left on the table was a reminder of car payments, gas, groceries, and the pressure of providing for their children. One night Liz, a buffet server, couldn't help but let it all out. Standing in the service station next to the coffeepot, she started bawling. She had heard about another round of layoffs. Kalia rubbed Liz's back.

"I don't wanna be graphic but I've had diarrhea all week," Liz said, her sobs turning to giggles. "I mean, I don't know what I would do if I got fired. I gotta work. I can't sleep in my car."

After one of these busy nights Kalia got everyone's attention, especially mine. Donovan had instituted a new policy that required buffet servers to get a manager to check the cleanliness of our sections before signing a sheet of paper allowing us to go home. (I blatantly disregarded this policy most nights and nobody ever mentioned it.) When Randy, the manager Priya and Vidya detested, nitpicked the cleanliness of Kalia's section, she pushed back.

"Randy, why are you trying to give me a hard time right now?"

Randy was shocked Kalia would challenge him so publicly. "Kalia, I don't like the tone of your voice. If you want to have this conversation one-on-one we should do it in the managers' office."

Kalia knew that was a losing proposition. She wanted witnesses. "Nope, we're gonna have this conversation right here with everybody listening." Randy walked away. Nothing came of it. (Soon, Randy would be fired after surveillance noticed he'd been tipping himself out of the cash registers.)

After one slow weeknight shift, Kalia asked me for a ride home. It was raining and I told her I would pull my car around.

"I ain't made of sugar," she said, following me into the rain.

Once inside my car, I asked about her past. She shared without hesitance or hyperbole, which was refreshing. Kalia didn't remember much about her father or her early childhood in St. Louis. She just knew he was a drug dealer, and when she was four, he owed somebody money. "I'm pretty sure the guy reloaded and kept shooting after he was dead," she said about her father's murder. With her dad dead, Kalia lived on and off with her mom and her aunt. Her mom was an addict who went in and out of shelters throughout Kalia's childhood. Kalia didn't notice until she was seven. That's when she started recognizing the shakes her mom got when she smoked crack. When she was a teenager Kalia hurt her back in a car accident. Her mom stole her painkillers. Kalia and her brother moved around. Albuquerque, Phoenix, Los Angeles, San Antonio. When she was fifteen, her mom got locked up in Phoenix for pawning stolen jewelry to finance a fix. Kalia and her brother moved to Miami Gardens to live with an aunt. Two thousand miles away from her mother, Miami Gardens felt like home to Kalia. She liked the jobs she had and she liked the fact that the city was mostly black. She was more comfortable here than any of the places she lived in while following her mom's habit.

For eight years, Kalia worked as a receptionist at a gym at the University of Miami medical complex. She told me that her son, Leo, was asthmatic and needed frequent medical attention when he was young. Often, appointments would run over and she would be late for work. That's why she had been fired. She didn't sound vengeful, she knew her bosses had no choice. But she didn't have a choice either. She spent a year on unemployment, always looking for jobs, but it was hard to find a job that paid better than her unemployment checks.

"I left sure money for this not-so-sure money," she said about tips in the buffet.

Now, with Kalia in her midtwenties and raising a son, her mom came to visit them in Miami Gardens. Her mom had cleaned up. Otherwise, Kalia wouldn't have let her near Leo. Kalia agreed to let her stay as long as she remained sober. While it helped that her mother could watch Leo while Kalia was at work, she wasn't contributing financially and Kalia talked about her mom's sobriety with quivering uncertainty. I asked Kalia how she could afford to take care of Leo and her mother with $25 in her savings account and a job in the buffet.

"With some luck and a whole lotta prayer." Kalia wasn't a religious woman and it was the only time I heard her mention prayer.

Leo, like many if not all of my buffet coworkers' children, received health care through Medicaid or KidCare, a low-cost, state-subsidized form of health insurance for minors. Their mothers were insured through one of their jobs or didn't have any health insurance at all. It was hard to blame them. Pulling in $20,000 a year or less, how could they justify spending $2,700 a year to cover their kids when there was a cheaper alternative? Add another $900 if they wanted vision and dental. I asked one waitress how she paid for a recent trip to the hospital.

"Easy, I don't pay the bill," she said.

"What about your credit?"

She rolled her eyes in a way that told me everything. She didn't care. She wasn't planning on financing a new car or a home any time soon. At the time, a full 23 percent of Florida's population was uninsured—only Texas and Mississippi had higher percentages than the Sunshine State.

I enjoyed my socials with Erin and Melanie, and my cooking lesson with Priya and Vidya, but they hadn't struck me as people who wanted and knew how to fight. Kalia was the first to tell Liz that she needed to stand up to the husband who had been accusing her of cheating. (Liz was incapable of stealing sugar cookies from the buffet, much less infidelity.) Kalia comforted Gabriela, a Brazilian waitress, when her daughter decided not to move to the United States. She stood up to Randy. Kalia was even-keeled but excitable, smart but humble, angry, and empathetic. I was elated when Alex agreed that Kalia would be the first leader to get a house visit.

A few months in, litigation between Local 355 and Mardi Gras had stalled, so Alex and Wendi decided to focus on Calder. Alex asked the Mardi Gras salt team to transfer to Calder. It was hardest for Mary, who had a connection with her coworkers in the French Quarter—Mardi Gras's Twin Spires—but she agreed. With three salts already practiced in the art of job applications, it didn't take long before Luke, the Tennessean, was roaming the floor as Calder's bright-eyed slot attendant and Mary and Colette were the newest cocktail waitresses.

With five salts working at full steam, we cleared leaders faster than ever. Mary cleared Keon and became good friends. Erika established herself as the strongest leader among the bartenders. Colette cleared slot attendants, a slot technician, and a cage cashier. Luke was making inroads with the slot technicians.

I was meeting with Alex one-on-one once a week. During these meetings I started to notice his tics. He bobbed his head, twiddled his thumbs, and muttered assent when it wasn't needed. He liked symmetry. He wore a ring on his right hand to balance his wedding band on his left. He had hoops in both lobes that he would massage while thinking. During meetings he would pull up both of his socks to make sure they were the same height. Even when he was relaxed, I would catch him glancing at his rolled-up sleeves to make sure they were level on his forearms. The tics were hardly noticeable to anyone who wasn't paying close attention. Otherwise, Alex was mild mannered, focused, and respectful of the people and space around him. These small habits were quick-release valves, methods of burning pent-up energy when he wasn't knocking on doors, having tough conversations, ever so slowly building a movement.

Growing up, Alex believed he would be dead by twenty-one. The first time he told me this I was struck by how confident he sounded. He hadn't dreamed about his death like Idi Amin; it wasn't some soothsayer's omen. His death, he was convinced, was a matter of statistical certainty. Alex, at a young age, was a cool realist growing up in a dangerous reality. Indio, California, two hours east of LA, is more than 75 percent Latino, the majority of whom have Mexican roots. In some ways, Indio cultivates its Chicano heritage with public murals and festivals that celebrate Mexican culture. These days

Indio is known as the home to Coachella, one of the biggest, most profitable music festivals in the country. When Alex was growing up, before the festival, Indio was famous for its gangs.

Gangs recruited from the hallways and cafeterias of Alex's high school. He was thirteen the first time one of his friends was killed. Alex didn't get choked up or overly sentimental when he told me. That's just how it was in Indio. Ethnically, Alex was white and Mexican, and he remembered getting profiled by security guards and police officers. After his best friend was killed, Alex's community held a car wash to raise money for the burial. "It wasn't enough for a tombstone," he said. "I don't think they got that for, like, three years."

Over those next three years, Alex started to see his friends and family fall in with the neighborhood gangs: Campo, North Side, South Side, and a plethora of smaller gangs and affiliates scattered throughout the city. It wasn't until later in life that he appreciated the way gangs operated. The powerful ones were tightly organized with leadership and loyalty at the heart of their functionality. But as a teenager, Alex never took the time to appreciate the gangs' efficiency; he was too busy avoiding them. Before he was eighteen, he had been shot at, had guns pulled on him, and seen a man stabbed in the neck. At parties he and his friends were ever aware of the vibe, always ready to leave when the mood turned turbulent. They traveled in packs and drank their beers out of heavy forty-ounce bottles just in case they needed makeshift weapons. It was hard to picture Alex holding such a bottle, a weapon. He was passionate and gentle.

Alex's parents kept him from trouble and urged him to focus on academics. He played varsity basketball and captained the high school swim team. He earned an athletic scholarship to play water polo at a small private college an hour north of Los Angeles. It wasn't until the omnipotent anxiety was gone that Alex noticed what had been gnawing at him throughout his adolescence. He hoped to pass that realization on to his friends. The university's proximity to Indio allowed him to maintain relationships with friends and family who were caught up in the gang activity. Friends would use his dorm as a safe haven if they wanted to get off the streets for a while. Even when he left California for work, Alex still kept in touch with them. He would get letters from his cousin who was in Pelican Bay State Prison, the infamous supermax facility in the northwest corner of California. Alex had the letters sent to the union office instead of his house, "just to avoid any trouble." His wife, Jill, was the one who pointed out the seemingly obvious connection between his history with gangs and his work as an organizer. He wasn't entirely convinced a link existed, but he understood why Jill might believe there was one. The sense of community, the organizational structure, an outlet for the energy. Alex got it all from the union.

Alex relished the challenge of a house visit. There was nothing better for him than knocking on someone's door and debating, teaching, and convincing people to fight for themselves. I learned a lot about house visits during my time with Local 355. House visits required union organizers to get in the door, get workers talking, establish a relationship with them, and, ideally, convince them to commit to more than just signing a card. Local 355 needed workers to become leaders, which meant getting them to attend meetings, trainings, protests, and house visits. On each visit the organizers worked their way through this ambitious agenda, looking for ways to push and pull the conversation. They weren't looking for needles in haystacks; they were trying to turn straws of hay into needles. The work wasn't easy.

"Of course, they've made up their minds before you sit on the couch," Wendi said to me during a training on house visits. Wendi had been to a million house-visit trainings and believed organizers should be coached, but she had been thinking about a study she read in graduate school. Published in the *Journal of Personality and Social Psychology,* the study examined snap judgments. A famous social psychologist asked Harvard students to watch short video clips of teaching fellows. Some of the videos were only two seconds and none of them had audio. The students were then asked to evaluate the teachers based on fifteen different characteristics. The study found an uncanny correlation between these "thin slices," or snap judgments, and evaluations done by the teachers' actual students at the end of the semester. I asked Wendi how her PhD work in psychology influenced her work as an organizer. She guffawed and said something about those days being ancient history. She rarely talked about Yale, and when she did, she talked about her time organizing the graduate assistants, not her course work. Wendi didn't actually think house visits were won or lost in the first two seconds but she wanted to train her staff to be as effective as possible in those meetings. Most often, that didn't mean getting signatures, it meant starting an honest conversation, agitating, and eliciting a serious commitment.

"The most important thing you can do is make a big ask," Wendi told us. "'I want you to join the revolution, not just come to an event.' People trust honesty, not a union rep."

Ready to recruit the Calder campaign's first serious leader, Alex knocked on Kalia's front door. Kalia lived in a small one-bedroom apartment five miles south of Calder. She answered her door in a do-rag and sweatpants. A few people were asleep on the couches in her dark living room. She joined Alex on the porch, where they talked for the next two hours. Alex didn't need to coax Kalia. She was angry and direct. She couldn't stand the way Randy pushed people around and she knew Randy was just an extension of Stanley Donovan's management style. She was angry about scheduling, pay, and insurance. Alex loved what he heard.

"The visit could not have gone better, dude," he told me afterward. He didn't ask Kalia to sign anything. He didn't even ask her to join the committee. The only thing he wanted was another meeting. Most Unite Here organizers made it their policy to avoid asking workers to sign anything on their first visit. The big ask required more of an investment.

Alex's meeting with Erin did not go so well. They sat on the porch outside Erin's parents' house for an hour and a half on a sweltering afternoon. Alex tried to get Erin to tell him what she had already told me and what I had told him. How she was not making money and not getting enough shifts. But Erin told Alex there were no problems at work. She liked Calder. Alex left Erin's house sure that she was not going to be a leader in the campaign.

The first time Alex visited Melanie, she didn't answer the door because she thought he had been there to repossess her car. The next time he visited, Melanie greeted him with open arms. "Where the hell have you been? I've been waiting!" But Melanie's enthusiasm didn't make up for Alex's concern about her ability to hold a job and stay focused. It also made Alex nervous that Melanie had a tough time keeping a secret.

"I just can't wait for the fucking union to come knocking on my door, I don't know what's taking them so long," Melanie said to me soon after Alex visited her, unaware of the fact that I knew about the visit. "I have a friend out in Vegas and, shit man, they have it good there." I knew Melanie wasn't talking about a friend. She was talking about Marc, a Unite Here member in Vegas who had taken a leave of absence from his job to help Local 355. "When we get the union, man, I'm gonna be like Norma Rae." She held an imaginary sign over her head, imitating Sally Field as Norma Rae standing in the middle of her factory and hoisting a piece of cardboard that said "Union."

Unlike Melanie, Kalia was subtle and productive. On Alex's second visit, Kalia agreed to become the campaign's first committee member. The next day I went to work expecting to see Kalia grinning like a fourth grader with a secret, but, had I not known she had been visited, nothing would have tipped me off. After workers agreed to become committee members, Alex would start them off with simple, sometimes unnecessary tasks meant to instill confidence and test their reliability. He told Kalia to collect the last names of people in the buffet. I almost laughed out loud when Kalia flipped my name tag, which had only my first name, to check my slot license for the spelling of my last name. Eventually, Alex gave Kalia more challenging missions. He encouraged her to agitate her coworkers. Published in 1971, *Rules for Radicals* is widely regarded as the organizer's bible. In it, Saul Alinsky wrote that it is the organizer's job "to agitate, introduce ideas, get people pregnant with hope and desire for change." Watching Kalia agitate was a revelation.

"I was talking to a friend who works at a union casino and she makes twelve dollars an hour plus tips," Kalia said to a group of buffet ladies around her. "Hey, Kim, you think we're ever gonna get a raise?"

"Hell no."

"I wonder how we could change that."

For the first time in the campaign, I bought into salting, leadership, and the endless potential of good organizing. If we could find twelve more Kalias at Calder, we would surely win the campaign. She even tried agitating me. When I told her I was pissed off that I had to work Thanksgiving, Christmas, and New Year's, she added, "Without holiday pay." She told Alex about "this kid James" in the buffet. He might be right for the revolution, she said. Kalia started to pick up on my agitation and organizing. Once, I said South Florida, not just Calder, needed to change. She looked at me with a smirk and said, "You sound just like someone I know." I pretended not to hear her and walked away. It felt good to have an ally in the buffet even if we couldn't talk freely about it.

Alex pushed Kalia even farther. She organized a buffet "social" at Chili's. While there wasn't a lot of organizing at the dinner, I watched as Tasha, String, and a few other employees deferred to Kalia. Kalia's leadership hit an all-time high when she invited the same crew of servers to her home for a barbecue.

I could smell the burning charcoal and chicken as soon as I pulled up on a hot afternoon. Kalia's apartment, even smaller than what I had pictured, was bustling. Her son, Leo, entertained the kids, who ran around the dirt yard before disappearing into the living room to watch a Disney movie. My coworkers' boyfriends stood off to the side, passing a blunt and talking about the Heat's playoff run.

"Celtics too old, can't keep up," Slim, String's fiancé, said. His nickname also derived from his slender build.

"Heat don't got nobody to cover Rondo though," Torrance, Kalia's boyfriend, said.

"LeBron could cover him, right?" I asked. They weren't listening.

I was a bit uncomfortable. Being the lone male buffet employee present, I felt as if I had to prove myself to the men. More conspicuous than my gender was the fact that I was the only white person in the neighborhood. I could sense that this made the other guys a bit uncomfortable, too.

"Do surfer boys drink Heineken?" Kalia asked as she handed me a beer. She was wearing all black with purple eye shadow.

After a few drinks, we started doing our best Stanley Donovan impersonations. I stopped caring about what the guys thought and how white I was. I waited for Kalia to start organizing and, just as I was about to do some agitating, she asked String if the vacation time she had requested for her wedding had been approved yet.

"Nope," String said. Kalia already knew that. We talked

about how we didn't get auto-gratuity on parties of six or more in the buffet.

"We used to get eighteen percent on private parties, now we get fifteen percent," I said. I knew this issue wouldn't mean much to the other buffet servers as I was given almost every private party in the Tavern. The parties were easy money, too. The hardest part was trying to convince guests to eat the fried mac-and-cheese balls or mini beef wellingtons, which people rarely took the second time I offered. "Also, I know I always get first dibs to work the private parties. You guys should be getting more of those." They seemed pleased by this admission. Kalia suggested that we collectively bring these issues to Donovan. She had met with Alex to plan this part of the barbecue. She was trying to organize a delegation, a common tactic workers use to confront bosses. Everyone agreed. We also agreed not to tell Rita, who had a tendency to brownnose; nobody trusted her not to tip off management.

When I told Alex about how Kalia had agitated and organized a delegation at the barbecue, he stood on his chair, bouncing up and down with excitement.

"She's the real deal, man. We owe it to her to win this thing. She can be a leader in the union, bigger than just this campaign."

At the same time, Alex's apprehension about Erin's leadership was validated when we learned that she had been gossiping about the union. She wasn't the only one; there were other leaks. Word spread quickly. Mysterious union organizers were visiting employees' houses. Dot, a cashier in the concession stand, told managers she had been visited. I knew she hadn't. While smoking cigarettes out back, Debbie, the buffet manager, asked Erika, "How the hell do they know who works here and where they live?" Erika suppressed a giggle. While serving a private party one afternoon, Rita asked me if I had been visited.

"No, why?"

"Two girls in the buffet have."

"Who?"

"Kalia and Erin. And the union's promising the world. Free health care, better wages. Listen, I went to human resources and told them 'cause these union people are telling people not to talk or else they'll get fired." Peggy, the head of human resources, assured Rita that no one would be fired.

I told Rita about a "friend" at Gulfstream, a unionized casino close by, who didn't pay much for health insurance and had better wages.

"Yeah, but how much is he paying in dues? Also, if we want a schedule change there's no goin' off to Jon or Debbie to change it. It's all through the union."

At that point, I had no reason to talk to Rita about the union. It was pointless to tell her that changing schedules would not be as inconvenient as she thought it would and that the guaranteed raises, more affordable health insurance, holiday pay, and other union benefits outweighed the cost of dues. Rita was a quidnunc. There was nothing to stop her from telling Peggy that I had been talking to her about the union.

My interaction with Rita epitomized the pervasive misinformation about unions that circulates throughout workplaces during unionization drives. Far more disturbing was my encounter with another veteran server who, approaching fifty, had been working service jobs her whole working life. She grabbed my arm and pulled me so close I could taste her last cigarette. "Listen, the union is a good thing but don't sign up. You don't have to pay dues. We'll still get it all."

She knew Florida was a right-to-work state, where workers at union shops can decide whether or not they want to pay dues even though they enjoy the benefits.

"That doesn't seem right," I said, equally saddened, disgusted, and impressed. I couldn't blame her for the low-wage gamesmanship; she was playing by the rules.

As a right-to-work state, the union cannot require Florida workers to pay dues. Regardless of whether workers pay dues, they still receive the benefits of the union contract: the same wage increases, cheaper health insurance, holiday pay, and union representation throughout grievance proceedings. In 2014, Florida was home to 115,000 workers who were not union members but were covered by union contracts. Lawmakers market the right-to-work system as a way to promote freedom in the workplace and liberate workers from the chains of labor unions. In practice, right-to-work is the most effective weapon in the fight against organized labor. Unions immediately feel the effects of right-to-work laws. Not only do they lose out on dues in each shop, the law hamstrings their ability to expand because they spend so much time and money maintaining the shops they've already won. Barely more than 50 percent of the workers at Local 355's unionized casinos were dues-paying members, and if that number were to dip below half at a shop, the union would face decertification.

The term "right to work" was first used in 1941 in a editorial that appeared in the *Dallas Morning News*. After reading the editorial, Vance Muse, a political activist, adopted the right-to-work cause. The book *Southern Exposure,* a 1946 exposé on racism in the South—quoted in a 2015 *New York Times Magazine* piece about Governor Scott Walker's fight to make Wisconsin a right-to-work state—quotes Muse as he decried compulsory union dues: "White women and white men will be forced into organizations with black African apes, whom they will have to call 'brother' or lose their jobs." Arkansas became the first right-to-work state in 1944. Today, half of the country's states have right-to-work laws.

In the spring of 2010, Local 355's treasurer, a brawny former New York corrections officer, met with Calder management and said that the union intended to organize Calder employees. Soon after that meeting all employees received a lengthy letter, which explained that "after considerable review from both corporate and outside legal counsel, we firmly believe that the [card-check agreement] of 2004 expired after the failed 2004 slots vote." Calder still believed that the card check was invalid because Miami-Dade voters hadn't passed gaming in 2004. But, of course, Miami-Dade voters did pass gaming in 2008. The union supported both votes and the agreement didn't have any language limiting it to the 2004 vote. Despite their contention, which would eventually be dismissed by an arbiter, the letter went on to share the company's position on the union:

> There were times throughout history when third-party representation provided protection to the general work force . . . However, over time, laws have been passed that protect, support and ensure fairness in the workplace, without third party representation. Our leadership team believes that together we have built a culture of creating WINNING EXPERIENCES for both our Guests and Team Members. The way we have honored our Pledge to Team Members is the cornerstone of why we believe you will reject Union representation. Churchill Downs Incorporated and Calder Casino & Race Course provide team members with equitable wages, good benefits, fair discipline and opportunities for advancement.
>
> Electing to have union representation is a decision made by frontline team members and the decision to do so will place the union representatives between the team members and the Calder Leadership Team.

The letter went on to warn of "high monthly union dues and initiation fees" and reminded employees to think—and think hard—before signing anything.

After reading the letter, Alex told me to prepare myself for a fight. Management would be overly kind and inquisitive. They would likely start holding "captive audience meetings," a common component of any anti-union campaign, when managers and executives round up employees to tell them the truth about unions. Alex was right. On my next shift Jon, the manager, gave me a packet of information that detailed the company's benefits programs. It was like a "best of" orientation packet: 401(k), online classes, health insurance, and dental. Then came the meetings.

One afternoon, as I was about to start a lunch shift in the buffet, Stanley Donovan asked me to join the rest of the staff in the dining area. There, I found about twenty cooks, servers, busers, and dishwashers gathered around a group of executives including Peggy, the head of human resources, who had spoken at orientation, and Austin Miller, the new president of Calder. Tom O'Donnell, the man behind the casino's "Winning Experiences" slogan, had been replaced. Miller would eventually land a job as a Churchill Downs senior executive in Louisville. They were all wearing business suits, a stark contrast to the cooks and dishwashers, who wore white, and my cohort from the front of the house, in our celery-green shirts. It wasn't just the clothing that made the executives stick out in the buffet. Because they worked in another building and rarely visited our corner of the campus, they felt like foreigners. In fact, the only time most people had seen an executive in the buffet was during "Walk a Day in Our Shoes," an event put on by the human resources department meant to boost team morale. A few executives had worked some shifts on the front lines. Ostensibly, the day was a chance for executives to learn more about the jobs and the company's employees, but the curious branding choice, "Walk a Day in Our Shoes," only brought the differences between the lives of executives and front-line employees to the fore. "Why don't you walk a day in my shoes" is most often uttered by someone fed up with a person whose life is measurably easier. "Team Member

Appreciation Day" wasn't much better. The event was held in the employee dining area. Executives and managers served cake to the employees. An iPod was raffled off. Such were the little jackpots Calder offered its employees.

Peggy started the meeting.

"We need to tell you that, legally, it's your choice if you want to join a union or not." I started wringing my hands behind my back. The salt coordinator, Dan Connolly, was the first to warn me about the anti-union buzzwords and catchphrases that management relied on, without fail, during captive-audience meetings. They did three things: 1) Emphasized dues. 2) Claimed that unions were no longer necessary in the United States. 3) Belabored the notion that unions drove a "wedge" between workers and management.

"But we want to tell you," Peggy continued, "that as a company, we don't believe you would benefit from unionization." Peggy went on to list the reasons why. She told us we would likely lose our paid vacation and 401(k). We would lose our relationships with our managers. In order to make any changes we would have to go through the union and a thorny contract that would micromanage every facet of the workplace.

"The Isle employees can't stand the union," Peggy told us, referring to the unionized casino thirty minutes north of Calder. "Apparently, they don't pay much for health care but we hear the coverage is terrible. And the union is starting their campaign here illegally. In order to get a union they are supposed to submit a letter to us and we give them a list of employees and they never did that, which is illegal. This union is doing those kinds of illegal practices."

A dishwasher asked what she should do if the union knocked on her door.

"I'd call the police if I were you," Peggy said. "Seriously, if you don't want them there, they're trespassing. You haven't invited them."

There were no more questions, save for the ones my coworkers kept to themselves. Would we lose our paid time off? Our 401(k)? Our relationship with management? Union member- ship would replace those benefits. Peggy was making it sound as if we wouldn't be receiving any benefits under the union. I had also met plenty of workers from the Isle at the union office who were enthusiastic about the union. In fact, Isle workers would soon ratify their second union contract.

Miller, the new president, continued the meeting. The first thing I noticed about Miller was his great hair, a gray and white coiffure that would have made a Just for Men casting agent swoon.

"I was reading the other day that the union is broke," Miller said as if he had rehearsed the line in front of his bath- room mirror. I'm not sure what publication Miller was read- ing. Unite Here's funds had been frozen during the Raynor/ Wilhelm divorce, but it was temporary. He may have been making a vague reference to the depleted state of unions ev- erywhere. As he was talking the lights went out in the buffet. "That's a sign," he said. There was some nervous laughter. The lights flickered back on.

"Anyway, about thirty years ago there were laws put in place that make unions obsolete. They're broke and they want your money. They *need* money. Look, the union is a business. And businesses sell you something. But the union doesn't sell anything! I mean, what kind of business plan is that? The only thing you'd be paying for is the wedge they will drive between you and management. You won't be able to change your hours. If you want a transfer, you need to go through the union. Why would you want to pay money to basically have them ruin your workplace? They are really like stalkers. Stalkers who will do anything to get you to sign a card. Don't sign anything until you've really thought about it. They will try to intimidate you."

Miller continued to talk about how unions, before child labor laws and the forty-hour workweek were written into law, had been necessary. He told us that while life had been hard for the longshoreman, we had it pretty good at Calder. Miller's argument is a common one. The great American labor cake is done baking. Of course, some twenty-first-century workplaces continue to evolve, with nap nooks, standing desks, and farm-to-table lunches. But Miller believed workers who were looking for a living wage, a retirement plan, and an inch of power in their own workplace were paying dues for services that government taxes already paid for.

A few weeks later, Peggy and Miller returned to the buffet for another meeting. At first they acted as though they were there just to check in. Miller started the meeting with some basic announcements about events going on at the casino.

"Are you guys taking advantage of the 401(k) program?" Miller asked. He was wearing a gray suit and bright blue tie. "I want to make sure you're putting money into that because it is a great part of what Churchill Downs offers. And Churchill Downs will actually match contributions up to a certain amount. It's like free money, guys. It doesn't get much better than that. Keep putting money in that 401(k) and we'll all be sipping tropical drinks on a hammock in the Bahamas when we retire!" Miller brought up the 401(k) at the meeting Colette attended, too. Jon, the manager, was the only employee who said he was enrolled in the program. One cocktail waitress asked, sarcastically, what money did she have to put in the 401(k). Miller demurred and, when he spoke to the slot attendants, altered his retirement fantasy, replacing the hammock with a "yacht."

"Anything else?" Miller continued. "Let's see . . . any unions coming to your houses?"

We shook our heads no.

"Well, that 401(k) I was talking about? You'd lose that if the union came in. In fact, even if the union did come in here and win, we wouldn't have to recognize them." Calder was still fighting the card-check agreement and Miller, apparently, felt confident enough to tell us that if a majority of his employees voted in favor of the union, he would not recognize the vote.

Immediately following these meetings, I stole away to call or text Alex. Though I'd been told to expect a fight, it was hard to imagine a company as large and powerful as Churchill Downs scared enough to send executives into the buffet to quell organizing efforts. Alex calmly told me to document each meeting and, when I got home, to send him an e-mail with everything that was said. Presumably he would send my write-ups to union lawyers so they could be used as evidence if the union were ever to claim that the company violated the card-check agreement. As for how the meetings might influence the campaign, Alex didn't think they would do much.

"Yeah, they can throw a couple of bombs around but they can't really do shit," he assured me. "I mean, that's why the revolutions in Latin America were so successful. Nobody knew who was running them. They can do anti-house-visit campaigns and tell them that the company didn't give out their information and they would advise them not to talk or to call the police. And your response to that needs to be something really American about freedom to open the door to whoever you want, you know? I have Jehovah's Witnesses knock on my door, you know? Or what if someone shows up with one of those Publishers Clearing House checks?"

For the first time ever, because of the captive-audience meetings, I was allowed to start conversations about the union. "What did you think of that?" I would ask. Most people didn't think much of the meetings. Kalia scoffed, "Man, they must think we're dumb." But I wouldn't have blamed some of the quieter, less confident employees for being wary of the union now that they knew the Big Bad Wolf was in the neighborhood. Peggy and Miller had made Alex and the other organizers seem like thugs who had employees' addresses and were coming to knock on their doors to "intimidate" them.

When I asked Priya what she thought of the meeting, she told me about a story she had seen on the news. A woman had posted a picture of her wedding ring on Facebook. A robber, having seen the picture, came to her apartment, beat her up, and stole the ring.

"She was Facebook friends with the robber? How did he get her address?" I asked.

"I don't know," she said. "But you gotta be careful."

For most, work continued as usual. As a salt, I clammed up every time a manager addressed me, ready for an anti-union lecture. All employees were required to sign a paper promising we wouldn't gossip, a kind of workplace gag order. Walking through the kitchen one day I saw an e-mail that Stanley Donovan had sent to all food and beverage managers—one of the kitchen managers had printed it and left it unattended on his workstation. In the e-mail Donovan beseeched his managers to cut hours whenever possible. (Donovan himself would soon be a victim of downsizing. He was fired and replaced by Mike DiStefano.) Donovan also instructed managers to remind their employees—"especially the English challenged"—about the oppressive work environment that unions create with "rigid" work scheduling, high dues payments, and fewer benefits.

After a few weeks the anti-union meetings and conversations died out. Alex's assurances proved true. There was nothing Calder could do to prevent us from organizing.

Our team kept growing, salts beget salts. College grads from Pennsylvania, Alabama, and Massachusetts came to Miami to salt. Outside of work and socials, I just hung out with salts. Early on, Erika made a tremendous effort to prioritize our friendship. Erika had a best-friend boot camp that she put new friends through. Once she had your name, she wanted to know every detail about your upbringing, interests, and relationship status. When you gave her your phone number, you could expect text messages as well as check-in phone calls with no discernible purpose. Erika's blitzkrieg approach to friendship made her a good salt. After boot camp we could communicate as if we were old friends. I found another good friend in Colette. We talked about the social implications of salting, whether we were engaged in low-wage voyeurism, pseudo-solidarity, or motivated by some privilege shame. Other salts didn't think twice about the advantage their backgrounds afforded them. I heard one proudly declare himself a "class traitor" dismantling the system that he had benefited from. For the majority of salts, salting wasn't such a dramatic endeavor. Though they had college degrees, salts came from middle-class families. Graduating with degrees in history, English, and sociology limited their job options. After months of browsing nonprofit job boards, salting started to sound like a good opportunity. And while many, if not most, salts had experience in the service industry, the chance to do a hard day's work was more than a bonus for Colette.

Colette had gone to a private school in Manhattan before Yale. Her parents were both immigrants. Her father was a successful surgeon in New York and her mother came from a prominent Nigerian family. One afternoon we shared a six-pack on the beach and she told me she was tired of trying to prove, both to herself and those around her, that she was "black enough." In high school and college, she rarely attended parties with more than one other black person. The cocktail waitresses were her first group of black girlfriends. When Colette was with them she didn't have to think about where she came from or question whether she was black enough. Colette knew the casino floor was a great equalizer. Her Yale degree didn't matter nearly so much as her hustle. While the other black cocktail waitresses sometimes thought Colette's diction and choice of words were funny, they knew she dealt with the same hostility that they dealt with. One night Colette was running late. She pulled her car up near the loading dock and clocked in before parking. It was against the rules but tolerated once in a blue moon. The electronic punch-in kept an unforgiving attendance record. Colette wasn't the first person to do it. Mark, a white beverage manager, caught Colette. "I thought you were smarter than the rest of them," Mark quipped. Mark had a reputation for making racist comments in what he thought was subtle language. *If you catch my drift,* his eyes would say. To Mark, Colette would always be one of "them." At Calder, Colette realized the pressure she felt, the need to be more black, was coming from white America. Her black coworkers didn't have any expectations of her. People like Mark did.

Often, I would go out with Erika and Colette together. As three confident people, it was easy for us to joke and make fun of each other. We were a good team. At times, this alienated Mary. Both Erika and Colette had better relationships with Mary than I did, but we had all been friends at some point. In many ways, Mary had traveled farther than any of us. She had left a supportive community in Milwaukee, a boyfriend (who then broke up with her), childhood and college friends, coworkers, and family. Her father hadn't approved of her move to Miami, a city as far from Milwaukee in geography as it was in character. Mary hadn't just rejected what was expected of her, she had blown it to bits. I had spent enough time with Mary to know that self-doubt was never far from her thoughts. At work, in her uniform, she said she didn't feel thin enough. When hanging out with Erika, she didn't feel funny enough. Around

Colette, she didn't feel smart enough. Mary's isolation multiplied when Alex, in an attempt to organize leadership among the growing salt team, elected Erika, Colette, and me "salt team captains." To Mary, Alex's passing her over was proof of her inadequacy. Her insecurities were most evident when she drank and it became clear that she derived some measure of confidence by flirting. Erika was the first to notice that Mary had been spending a lot of time with Keon. When, as friends do, Erika asked Mary if there was something going on between them, Mary flatly denied it. Erika believed her. But when another Calder employee started gossiping to Erika about the drama in Mary and Keon's relationship, Erika had no choice but to tell Alex and confront Mary about it. Relationships with coworkers were forbidden in the salt program.

Colette and I joined Erika at Jimmy's Diner and told Mary that we knew. The meeting was poorly planned and painful. Mary pushed her food around her plate, denying before confessing and then repenting. She felt ambushed. I would have protested, as Mary's indiscretion seemed innocent enough, but secretly I knew Mary had done this before with another coworker.

Alex met with Mary and told her she couldn't salt in South Florida anymore. A few months later, her mother drove down from Wisconsin, picked her up, and drove her home. Eventually, she was hired by another union to travel the country and organize workers.

The campaign withered. Erika was pregnant and, preparing to start a family, she took shifts at the shampoo shop where she'd worked before Calder. She didn't tell us, fearing we'd label her Off the Program. At our campaign's peak, we'd had seven salts in Calder and ten committee members. But turnover chipped away. Melanie had been increasingly upset at work. One afternoon I asked her how she was doing. "I'm forty-one, man. I need to be making more than twenty thousand dollars a year." It was the last day I saw her at work. Erika told me Melanie's car had been repossessed and she was moving back to the Northwest, where she had a support system. Erin also stopped showing up for work. Keon was fired because he accumulated too many points. I later found out he was nabbed for possession and driving without a license. More than once. His most recent arrest landed him in prison, again. Other leaders quit, were fired, or just faded away. *On to the next one.* I lost sight of the mission; stopped going on socials; stopped asking new employees for their names. The excitement of the campaign burned out the same way employees' hope in the casino had. Nothing was happening. It was maddening.

Then Alex went on paternity leave. When no staff member was assigned to replace him, it became clear that Calder wasn't a priority for Local 355. The local was spread thin and we had no connection to anyone else on staff. Some staff members didn't even know our names. At best, organizers would ask us to help out with small tasks, like picking up workers for a meeting. Colette went so far as to say that at times, she felt like a "subcontracted" worker at Local 355.

Colette had aspirations to work as a staff member. Yet, there was a sense that Alex, her first boss out of college, felt that after a year of cocktailing she hadn't "struggled" enough. There was no contract for a salt, no end date, and Alex was never willing to discuss life after salting with Colette because, in his mind, if she didn't prove her worth as a salt, how could she help the movement on staff? The union's staff does consist of professions other than organizer. There are political strategists, researchers, accountants, and public relations managers. Alex was ill suited to mentor anyone in those positions because not only had he never done those jobs, he believed they were second class compared with organizing. Why would anyone research if they could organize? Whenever Colette, or other salts, brought up a career beyond the Calder campaign, Alex took the moral line on salting's most sacred tenet: for the movement, not for your career. During the doldrums of our campaign Alex told us that *we* were the campaign. In the old days there weren't any professional staff organizers, he would say. "You don't need me, dude." But in the old days, there weren't card-check agreements and Alex sure as hell didn't want me standing in the middle of the buffet holding a "Union" sign. It would have been impossible to organize a union at Calder without the full-fledged support of Local 355.

By the spring of 2011, Kalia was the only leader still meeting with an organizer. I passed afternoons playing solitaire in the service station. Swiping cards, I enjoyed the fog. Ace of hearts—swipe. Three of clubs—swipe. Sometimes I would fantasize about a casino heist. *Which president's face would be on my mask? And who's gonna drive the getaway car?* One Sunday evening in August, a Calder security guard and a security manager—both acquaintances of mine—actually robbed the casino.

When the Brinks armored truck arrived to pick up the weekend's take, the security manager called the security guard, who had taken the day off, who then called an accomplice waiting outside the casino. The manager escorted the Brinks guard throughout the casino, something managers never did, as the Brinks guard collected the money. According to the prosecutor, the plan called for the accomplice to shoot the Brinks guard, who was wearing a bulletproof vest, and disable him. The plan also called for the accomplice to shoot the security manager in the leg, making him a hero and opening the door to a lucrative lawsuit against Calder. The plan didn't account for a brave Brinks officer making $11 an hour who drew his own pistol. He got a shot off, hitting the accomplice in the leg. The accomplice shot the Brinks officer twice, once in the torso and once in the head. The accomplice then grabbed the bag containing $350,000 and limped away as the twenty-five-year-old Brinks guard choked on his own blood. He was flown to a hospital, where he was pronounced dead. I had been at the scene of the crime only an hour earlier. Five people were eventually convicted in the case. The night of the robbery, the Calder security guard had spent his last bit of freedom using the stolen cash to log some "time on device" playing the slots at the Hard Rock.

Erika was about to go on maternity leave and Colette and I were both making plans to pack up and leave Miami. That's when Colette had an idea. Mardi Gras had just lost its most recent round of card-check litigation and had complied with Local 355's request for an employee list. Wendi did not want the card check to expire at the end of 2011, only five months away, without making an all-out effort to organize the casino. Colette and I told Alex we wanted to transfer to Mardi Gras. We wanted to work on a campaign that had a timeline. Alex agreed.

Within a week of our conversation, I shaved, put on my suit, and started smiling again. I went to Mardi Gras and sat at Louie's Lounge in the casino's poker room, which had a bust of its eponym blowing on a trumpet above the tap handles. A tanned woman in her sixties with a bird's-nest haircut was working behind the bar. Her name was Deirdre. She was from Boston, and despite her having lived in South Florida for decades, her "r"s were nowhere to be found.

"So you're a bahtendah?" she asked me. "We need a real bahtendah, someone who knows what they're doing."

I assured her I knew what I was doing.

"The bah managah, Frank, is around here somewhere." Deirdre and I talked about all the people at Calder who used to work at Mardi Gras until Frank, the bar manager, showed up. He was in his fifties and, with his high-and-tight, looked more like a retired police officer than a bar manager. I gave him my résumé. He was happy that I already worked at a casino so he wouldn't have to wait for the state to approve me.

"Let me talk to the decision-makers," he said.

A week later, I got called for an interview. Frank didn't ask me a single question during the interview; he just told me what I would be doing. It was more like an interview for a roommate than a job. Soon after, someone in human resources called to offer me the position. Forty hours a week, $5 an hour plus tips, and benefits after ninety days. Colette had also gotten an interview and was offered a position as a cocktail waitress. I signed the papers, gave another pee sample, and soon I would start as Mardi Gras's newest bahtendah.

When I went to turn in my badge and uniform at Calder I saw Kalia in the break room. I asked how her boyfriend was doing at his new job.

"Torrance doesn't appreciate his old job. Yeah, he makes ten dollars an hour now, but he doesn't get insurance, vacation, or overtime. And he can't fall back on me. If it doesn't work, he can move back with his mom. What am I going to do? I don't know, maybe I'll go back to Arizona with my mom."

I didn't know what to say.

"I'm out," I told her.

"Cut already? When are you working next?"

"No, no. I'm out for good. Got a job at Mardi Gras as a bartender. Apparently the money is better there. I gotta take it."

She nodded her head; disappointment glazed her eyes. It was time for me to move on, she understood. She gave me a hug. I was happy to leave Calder, but a part of me hated salting, and Alex, and Peggy, and Austin Miller, and myself for failing Kalia.

"This place, man," she said. "We never did that meeting with Stanley. Who am I gonna do that with?"

A few months later I heard Kalia had been fired. Too many points.

Part 3

THE DOG TRACK
CAMPAIGN

◎

My first shift at Mardi Gras was on a Tuesday, September 6, 2011. Guests that day could get their pictures taken with a tiger in the lobby. Lions, a zebra, and monkeys were all scheduled to make appearances in the coming weeks. The casino's concept, "*Laissez les bon temps rouler,*" was refreshing. In this spirit, I was given a glittery, pumpkin-orange vest to wear over a black uniform. I looked like a magician at an eighties bat mitzvah.

I arrived ten minutes early for every shift at Mardi Gras. I would enter through the employee entrance, clock in, and get a walkie-talkie from Bobby, a geriatric security guard with a Christmas-white beard. He usually listened to an oldies station that played songs with beachy harmonies. I would press a blue "Exit" button to the right of the door and proceed onto the casino floor. Immediately, I would feel the machines around me, exploding, quaking, and blinking. *Ding, bling. Ding, ding, bling. Bluuuueooorrrp.* After a few seconds, the commotion receded into my subconscious like traffic on a New York street. They were the same machines that cluttered the floor at Calder. The customers were the same, too. Some came to Mardi Gras because they were tired of Calder, others bounced around from one casino to another. They had the same foggy stares. On weekends, *passistas,* female samba dancers adorned with a preponderance of plumage, would parade through the casino. Some guests seemed to like the entertainment, but most never looked away from their slot machines.

Early casino design gurus hypothesized that gamblers were most comfortable in tight spaces with defined borders that minimized visual intrusions. Bill Friedman, the godfather of casino design, believed that while slot machines should be "boundless" and "never-ending," the space in which the games exist should be narrow and focused. Freidman's model has been considered outdated for some time—most new casinos look more like Calder's open floor plan—but Mardi Gras's low ceilings and confined spaces, with its ubiquitous purple, green, and black color scheme, gave the casino character, something Calder lacked. Mardi Gras hadn't expanded or built new buildings to house its golden geese, it just filled the dog track's grandstand with them.

The walk to the money room was short. I would swipe my badge and enter the first of two mantraps. There was always a moment of claustrophobia, as I couldn't open the next door in the sequence until the door behind me had locked. Sometimes someone in surveillance would chirp through the radio, "One second, someone's coming through." That meant I had to wait for someone on the other side of the door. I was always under surveillance. It only took a couple of shifts to get over that. I had nothing to hide.

Inside the money room an attendant wearing a pocketless jumpsuit would hand me a clear plastic bag through a window. It had $300 in it. The cashier tellers were given much bigger bags containing at least $20,000. They would flip their hands periodically to show the cameras they weren't hiding any money. The quick gesticulation looked like something my grandfather would do while describing good, but not great, spaghetti. Though I was counting only $300, I was required to use a machine for my stacks of one-dollar bills. I had seen such machines in movies alongside piles of cash, kilos of cocaine, and burning cigars. On one of her first shifts, Colette had received a write-up for failing to use the money counter. The machines were fickle and on one of my first shifts my counter wasn't working.

"Try this, *bebe*," said the cage cashier standing next to me as she hit a button on my counter. I knew it was against the rules to make conversation in the money room, but I was happy to have her help. "That one got problems." She had a Haitian Creole accent and a big smile. Her name was Saraphina, and after that first interaction, she would point and wave every time we made eye contact at work. I liked her.

After counting my bag, I would radio surveillance.

"Sierra 1, this is James Walsh going from MR-1 to the main bar."

"Ten-four, you're clear to walk to the main bar."

Using the barnacles on Mardi Gras's ceiling, surveillance watched me as I followed a designated route through the slot machine labyrinth to the main bar. I wasn't allowed to talk to anyone along the way. Depending on the day, I worked the main bar, the sports bar, the French Quarter restaurant bar, the dog-track bar, the VIP bar, or Louie's Lounge in the poker room. A manager would usually be waiting at the bar. He or she would log me into the cash register and I would begin prepping, collecting ice from the ice machine, restocking the beer and mixers, or cutting fruit.

I liked bartending more than serving in the buffet. Earning $1 for pouring a rum and Coke beats earning $1 for scrubbing plates and fetching iced tea for an hour. In addition to the tips, I made 15 percent automatic gratuity at Mardi Gras. Sure, that amounted to $0.15 for every $1 draft beer, but I was told the money added up on busy nights. I could expect to make at least $100 a shift at Mardi Gras and I was working half as hard as the Calder buffet waitresses. Bartenders were slightly higher up in the service caste system than waiters. Maybe it had something to do with the prerequisite knowledge of mixing cocktails, however minimal that was at a place like Mardi Gras—margaritas and Long Island iced teas were pretty much the only drinks people ordered that required more than two ingredients. Or maybe it was because of their close contact with patrons. Diners have a preferred waiter; drinkers have a *favorite* bartender. It wasn't unusual for customers to frequent bars at Mardi Gras based on the a bartender's shift. They would pick up conversations right where they left off the day before. Customers spent even more time saddled up at the casino's main bar because virtual poker machines were built into the bar top. The majority of my job was talking to Louise about her kids, Rick about his new Camaro, or Ben about the Dolphins' backfield.

Because I was the newest bartender, I was given a lot of afternoon shifts that rarely had much business. Those shifts were a great opportunity to talk with cocktail waitresses. Alex had decided that, given our limited time for the campaign, we didn't need to pursue socials as maniacally as we had at Calder. Instead, we would learn as much about the workers as possible while at work. I'm not sure if the job made them tough or if tough people were attracted to the job, but cocktail waitresses were always the grittiest, savviest people in the building. I may have griped about life in the buffet, but after one shift as a cocktail waitress, I would have begged for crab night and iced tea refills. Their entire shifts, six to eight hours, were spent walking, which was fine for spritely twentysomethings but brutal for the older waitresses. They also endured some of the most degrading treatment from customers. There were regular Joes who believed the cocktail waitress's uniform was an invitation to compliment her appearance, or worse. There were people who snapped their fingers for service, or clapped their hands, or whistled. There were drunks, creeps, and men too thick to know when to shut up. There were loathsome customers who would call the waitresses "bitch" and "cunt." Most of the time the women just took it on the chin. It was all part of the hustle.

The cocktail waitresses at Mardi Gras were of the same ilk as the waitresses at Calder. During one of my first shifts, I worked alongside two cocktail waitresses, Elisa and Lena. Elisa couldn't have been older than twenty-five, petite, a blond Cuban-American who lived near Magic City Casino. Lena was forty, and as she liked to say, she looked good for her age. She had dark black hair that she pulled into a ponytail, toned biceps, and a faint Polish accent. She was finishing a graduate degree in interior design. I asked Lena how she could afford it.

"She dances at Scarlett's," Elisa said. Scarlett's was a popular strip club nearby.

"Shut up," Lena said, laughing. "She's joking. I don't know, I keep working."

Lena used the casino floor like a catwalk. She walked with her shoulders back, stiff and upright, her ponytail swinging with each long stride she took. It was as if she knew she was better than the customers she served, and that's probably why they tipped her so well. Lena came to the United States when she was twenty-four. She'd earned a master's degree in physical education in Poland, but she didn't speak a word of English. She got her first job as a waitress at Hooters on Long Island by learning to recognize interview questions and memorizing rote responses. *I vant to make customer happy.* Eventually, she moved to Florida, where she and her boyfriend opened a dirt-bike track. After her boyfriend was in a life-threatening dirt-bike accident, Lena was forced to close the course and nurse him back to health.

"It was really bad. I had to clean him when he shit himself."

Then, when he got his strength back, he started hitting her.

"I told him: after I take care of you, this is how you treat me? No way."

"Now she's with his brother," Elisa chimed in.

"Shut up. No, I'm not. I'm single and happy."

After a few shifts, I started asking Lena about the job. The campaign's timeline meant I had to start pollinating agitation as quickly as possible. Often, workers would brush off my questions by saying this job was a temporary stop between their past and future. Lena believed interior design was her future. She was ready to quit Mardi Gras as soon as she could support herself as a full-time interior decorator, which made it hard to talk to her about her current situation. But when I asked her about the head of the food and beverage department, Sally, Lena lit up. I hadn't met Sally yet but I'd heard she was icy. A customer had complained about Lena's service. Most managers are reasonable people who understand that complaints often come from irritable guests who mistake a waitress's busyness for negligence or a bartender's efficiency for rudeness.

"She calls me to her office," Lena said about Sally, "and she point her finger at me and she says, 'You will not talk until I tell you to talk.' If I didn't need this job, I would have told that bitch off and walked out."

It wasn't much, but I made a note: Lena hates Sally. I asked her about insurance, scheduling, and seniority. It was the work-issue car wash. Then I asked about paid time off.

"You know, they only pay five dollars for vacation pay."

"What? Like you're earning tips on vacation, too?"

I'd had a similar problem with vacation pay at Calder. Vacation time was doled out in eight-hour increments and I had been paid as a tipped employee instead of minimum wage. I told my manager about it and I got the full minimum wage, $7.25, the next time I used vacation time. In Lena's case, it could have been an honest mistake by Mardi Gras, but I figured that in an industry that required employees to flip their hands to show that they weren't holding any money, anything was possible.

On Sunday afternoons I worked with Vanessa. Tall and buxom, Vanessa glided about like there wasn't enough luxury in this hard world. She called customers baby whether they tipped her or not. She confidently strutted around, unhurried, hypnotizing men into ordering drinks. Once I watched her kiss a regular on the cheek ten times in a row, each time he dropped a $10 bill on the bar for her. He was paying her back for past-due tips or a bet she had won; the kisses on the cheek were just her way of sweetening the deal. Colette worked one of her first shifts with Vanessa and we both agreed she would make a great leader. She also happened to be best friends with a Local 355 staff organizer. However, the organizer was hesitant to sully their friendship by pushing Vanessa. Also, Vanessa's brother-in-law was a manager in the food and beverage department, which put her in a precarious position. Still, I liked working with her because she knew everything that was going on at the casino. "See that woman there, the one drunk at the bar? She won ten thousand dollars. Downhill ever since. Every two weeks she spends her entire sixteen-hundred-dollar paycheck here. She was cheating on her husband with tons of guys here and more at Calder and Hard Rock."

Before my afternoon shifts ended, the cocktail waitresses working the afternoon would be relieved by the night shift. More often than not, Grace worked evenings after picking up her two children from school and dropping them off at home. In her forties, Grace was older than most of the other mothers with young kids. She would arrive at work with all the excitement and fatigue of a mother engulfed by her children's schedules. After cleaning and arranging the cocktail waitresses' workstation next to the bar, she would open her compact and use the mirror to fix her eyeliner. She was white with golden-brown hair aided by hair spray. She had the energy and toned figure of someone much younger. Grace patrolled the floor taking care of her customers in her maternal way, bringing bottles of water to customers who hadn't asked for anything and giving advice to the other waitresses and customers seated at the bar.

Like Lena, Grace detested Sally, the head of the food and beverage department, and claimed that the feeling was mutual.

"That woman has it out for me," Grace said. "She feels threatened or something."

Grace had worked in Atlantic City and knew the casino business. Her hope for a better job, she told me, was in the prospect of a bigger casino industry in South Florida.

"I've got one foot out the door. As soon as Caesars comes, I'm out."

There was always talk of the casino industry growing in South Florida, big Vegas-style palaces on Miami Beach. Who would go to the desert if they could do the same thing next to the warm blue waters of Miami Beach? Bigger casinos, better jobs, lights in the fog.

Lena, Vanessa, and Grace seemed to be the strongest candidates among the cocktail waitresses. I barely knew them but all three had followers on their shifts. So, before September was through, I gave Alex their names along with Saraphina's, the smiling cashier who had fixed my money counter. My reasoning was shallow compared to the thorough vetting I had done at Calder but we were in a rush.

Alex had visited a handful of employees at Mardi Gras who already had a connection to the union—people who had been members at previous jobs or had family who were members. While everyone he visited had been receptive to the union, they were also skeptical of the union's chances.

"They know how anti-union this company is," Alex said.

I could tell that he was anxious to start the campaign in full. For Local 355, the Mardi Gras campaign would be a big test that had the potential to set the tone for negotiations at other casinos and hotels. Mardi Gras was the only non-union casino in Broward County, the county just north of Miami-Dade. If Mardi Gras remained union-free throughout its card-check agreement, the casinos in Miami-Dade, which had opened after the casinos in Broward County, would use Mardi Gras's playbook to keep the union out throughout their card-check agreements.

◉

Traveling eight miles from Miami Gardens, where Calder was located, to Hallandale Beach, where Mardi Gras was located, meant going from a city that was 76 percent African-American to a small city that was 74 percent white. Hallandale Beach was only about five square miles, packed with strip malls, houses, a swath of prime beachfront real estate, and two casinos.

Mardi Gras sat in the middle of a large parking lot on the west side of US 1 with businesses lining the roads to the north and east, a quiet neighborhood across train tracks to the west, and a mobile home community to the south. The dog track, a toy-sized horse track, opened in 1934 among farms and dirt roads. Florida has a long history of gambling. Horse racing, dog racing, jai alai, cockfighting, boxing, bingo, and *bolita*. The industry always faced plenty of opposition from church groups and entertainment rivals, namely Disney, which have all sparred with the pro-gaming lobby, not to mention the ire of animal rights advocates. In 1935, a year after the dog track opened in Hallandale Beach, slot machines were legalized in Florida in order to help repair the state's budget, which was limping along after the Great Depression. Hallandale Beach soon became a favorite getaway for mobsters from Chicago and New

York. One of the country's most famous mobsters, Meyer Lansky, would call Hallandale Beach home. The gaming industry thrived even after slot machines were outlawed in 1937, as did the mobsters, who ran their operations with the blessing of a well-liked and well-paid sheriff. Underground gambling got so out of hand that Senator Estes Kefauver, head of a Senate committee charged with investigating organized crime and gambling throughout the fifties, described Hallandale as "the sin city capital of the South, a wide-open den of iniquity."

As part of its investigation the Kefauver Committee accused Florida governor Fuller Warren of neglecting to address the problem of illegal gambling and failing to disclose more than $100,000 in campaign contributions from a Chicago businessman and mob associate who owned four dog tracks in Florida. Political donations from pari-mutuels were illegal at the time for fear of political favoritism.

"The only purpose that this committee can conceive in the making of such contributions by persons engaged in gambling on the scale at which they operated was in the expectation that the contribution might prove an ultimate quid pro quo."

Governor Warren escaped indictment and a subsequent impeachment attempt by Florida's House of Representatives.

Track owners continue to be valued among state lawmakers in Tallahassee. And no pari-mutuel spent as much on lobbying as Mardi Gras. Unlike Calder's parent company, publicly traded Churchill Downs Inc., Mardi Gras's parent company, Detroit-based Hartman & Tyner, was privately owned. In addition to Mardi Gras Casino in Florida, Hartman & Tyner owned and operated Mardi Gras Casino in West Virginia, a horse track just north of Detroit called Hazel Park Raceway, and scads of housing developments around Detroit.

Cousins Bernard Hartman and Herbert Tyner merged their

fathers' contracting businesses to form Hartman & Tyner in 1952. They started in real estate and housing development and purchased Hazel Park Raceway in 1972 when the track's owners—Detroit mobsters—got in trouble with the law. In 1978, the cousins acquired the dog track in Hallandale Beach that would become Mardi Gras Casino. They bought and sold other tracks and properties. In 1990, they purchased Tri-State Racetrack in West Virginia, now also a Mardi Gras Casino.

Business must have been good for the cousins. In 1973, Tyner became a co-owner of the Detroit Pistons. That same year, Tyner offered $30,000 to Secretariat's owners, fresh off the legendary horse's Triple Crown victory, to have the horse jog five-eighths of a mile at Hazel Park. Secretariat's trainer rejected the offer. Twice, Tyner made multimillion-dollar donations to a hospital in Detroit. His donation to a local temple was large enough to name the religious school after him. Around 1989, Tyner purchased oceanfront property forty-five minutes north of Mardi Gras. The eleven-thousand-square-foot house is nestled in a row of mansions owned by people who keep residences around the world. Tyner's most recent neighbor, David Glass, is a former president of Walmart and current owner of the Kansas City Royals.

Bernie Hartman and Herb Tyner were known to be creative businessmen working in highly regulated industries. They knew how to use the system and found loopholes to get what they wanted. Their cleverness earned them both praise and ire in the industry.

By the time I was hired at Mardi Gras, Bernie and Herb were in their early eighties. (Tyner died in August 2015.) As they got older, the cousins handed their operations, at least publicly, off to Dan Adkins. I had heard former Mardi Gras employees at Calder say Adkins made things "fun" at Mardi Gras by encouraging quirky giveaways and live entertainment. Two Calder employees who used to work at Mardi Gras also told me about his temper. He was the face of pari-mutuel gambling in Florida. Adkins was the star of Mardi Gras's commercials. He gave plenty of interviews to reporters, appeared on an "interview show" paid for by Mardi Gras, wrote a blog called "Mardi Gras Boss," and was active on Twitter using the handle @mardigrasboss. But even without the visibility, Adkins was known as one of the most strident forces for gambling in Florida.

According to interviews with the *Sun-Sentinel,* Adkins grew up in a Mormon family in Ohio. As a teenager, Adkins would accompany his father, a police officer by day, while he fixed betting machines at the local track at night. After his father died of cancer, Adkins started working for the same betting machine company as his father. Soon Adkins was traveling around the country for the company. He met his wife at Flagler Dog Track (now Magic City Casino), where she was a cashier, and settled in South Florida. In the late 1980s, he started working at Hollywood Greyhound Track, now Mardi Gras Casino. Eventually Adkins was promoted to vice president of Hartman & Tyner. The *Sun-Sentinel* quoted the mayor of Hallandale Beach who described Adkins as philanthropic and someone who "exemplifies a gentleman." Conversely, one lobbyist for Florida's greyhound industry called him "the most despicable human being I've ever met."

A decade after Adkins took the helm at Hartman & Tyner, Florida's pari-mutuel industry faced more competition than ever. The Florida state lottery gained in popularity, the Miccosukee and Seminole tribes opened casinos, and "cruises to nowhere" started ferrying locals and tourists out to sea. Greyhound racing's popularity, already on the decline, plummeted. State legislatures across the country were considering legalizing slot machines to generate tax revenue and shrink budget deficits. Hartman & Tyner had already rescued its dog track in West Virginia with slot machines; Adkins led the way in Florida. He made it rain on the Sunshine State's legislature. Whether through Hartman & Tyner or one of its many shell companies, Adkins, like the rest of the pari-mutuel industry, found ways to give money in Tallahassee. In 2004, he served as the chairman of Floridians for a Level Playing Field, a political action committee formed by Hartman & Tyner, Calder, Magic City, and a handful of other pari-mutuels that spent more than $15 million to legalize Vegas-style slot machines at tracks and jai alai frontons in Miami-Dade and Broward Counties. The committee proposed a statewide ballot measure that amended Florida's constitution to allow Miami-Dade and Broward voters to decide whether the two counties would legalize slot machines. Marketing for the statewide vote was intense. Commercials urged Floridians to vote yes on Amendment 4. My favorite was set in a kindergarten classroom.

REDHEADED FIVE-YEAR-OLD BOY:

When I grow up I want to be a fireman.

Shots of teacher singing along with her students and students working at their desks.

VOICE-OVER:

Life's about decisions and Amendment 4 lets voters in Miami-Dade and Broward Counties decide whether to regulate and tax slot machines at existing facilities. That could generate $500 million a year for all Florida's schools, and unlike the lottery, the money is guaranteed to supplement, not replace, current school funding. Help all our children realize their dreams: vote yes on 4. It's our decision . . .

The redheaded boy from the beginning puts on a firefighter's helmet.

```
            VOICE-OVER (cont):
 . . . it's their future.
```

The casinos hired top lobbyists in Tallahassee, got the support of the teachers' unions, and hired a former head of Florida's Department of Education to be their spokesperson. In addition to citing the potential $500 million annually for schools—for various reasons, the first five years *combined* generated about $500 million for schools—the political action committee's top lobbyist said casinos in Broward and Miami-Dade would bring 18,200 new jobs. Adkins himself told the media that he expected Mardi Gras to employ five hundred people. "And these are not minimum-wage jobs," he told the *Sun-Sentinel*. In 2006, he speculated that tipped employees would be making $30,000 a year. As if to signal to lawmakers that these would be quality jobs, Adkins, along with the rest of the pari-mutuels in Broward and Miami-Dade Counties, entered card-check and neutrality agreements with Local 355. Florida voted yes, which cleared the way for county voters to approve gambling in Broward in 2005 and Miami-Dade in 2008.

The pari-mutuel industry's campaign to expand gambling in Florida epitomized the kind of influence money can have on a state legislature. In 2009, Hartman & Tyner bought a $5,000 candle for Governor Charlie Crist's birthday cake at a GOP fundraiser. Adkins enlisted political operatives, of which there are many in Florida. One lobbyist instructed Adkins to make a donation to a private school, which the lobbyist then exchanged for free tuition for his children. Through it all, neither Adkins nor his counterparts at other pari-mutuels have ever been charged with any wrongdoing.

After the pari-mutuels renovated and opened as full-fledged casinos, almost all of them tried to sidle their way out of the card-check agreements. Mardi Gras was the most determined of them all. In 2008, two years after Mardi Gras opened its doors and the card-check agreement took effect, Local 355 made its first attempt at organizing the casino's workers. This was before Wendi's arrival in South Florida, and an entirely different group of Local 355 organizers ran the kind of slipshod campaign that made Wendi cringe. The leadership at the local sent a notice to Mardi Gras's management announcing its intent to organize, something Wendi wouldn't have done until she had some sort of a committee inside the casino. Soon after, the company reinstated a 15 percent automatic gratuity for waiters (it's illegal to offer benefits as an incentive not to support the union) and distributed a series of "educational" flyers to employees. One such flyer compared pay between employees at the Isle Casino and Mardi Gras. A table showed that many jobs at Mardi Gras offered higher hourly wages than unionized jobs at the Isle. But while the flyer noted that the wages shown didn't include monthly union dues, it didn't mention guaranteed raises, lower health insurance rates, and the fact that the Isle was the first union contract negotiated at a casino in South Florida, thus making it difficult for the union to negotiate much more. Another flyer had a watermark of stacks of cash and urged employees to challenge union organizers by asking them how Unite Here spent member dues. The numbers looked bad: "$3,302,442 on hotel stays; including dozens of luxury hotels such as the MGM Grand in Las Vegas" and "$7,024,025 in political activities and lobbying." Sure, the union needed to cut back, but running any organization that represents hundreds of thousands of workers is always going to cost millions. "If you join Unite Here you too can contribute to all of these excesses," the flyer finished. In response to the flyer, Unite Here's counsel sent this to Mardi Gras's attorneys:

> This flier is misleading in innumerable ways, including the fact that UNITE HERE is different in key ways now from in 2006: for example, the flier talks about two presidents but now there is only one. The flier is misleading by omitting

material information such as the [Bureau of Labor Statistics] data showing that unionized employees make so much more than non-union employees on average that the cost of union dues is dwarfed by the value of higher wages and benefits. The flier fails to mention that union officials are paid on average a mere fraction of their management counterparts, including the labor relations counsel and consultants who engage in anti-union campaigns. Please provide us a copy from 1/1/06 to present of all documents showing the salaries, hourly rates, benefits and other compensation of the employer's top five executives, the amounts paid to its owners, and the amounts hourly and monthly paid its labor relations counsel and its labor relations consultants, so that the union may provide employees with information responsive to this hit piece.

The company never complied with the requests. The casino distributed articles from a business journal about infighting among Unite Here's top brass and past Unite Here labor violations. Years passed. Local 355 changed. Finally, Adkins sent a notice to Wendi that said the company would not be complying with the neutrality agreement because it "was illegal and unenforceable." Wendi had seen these tactics before from feisty companies in other cities. Arbiters repeatedly sided with Local 355 when the union accused Mardi Gras of violating the neutrality agreement. But arbitration was slow and put any organizing efforts on hold. Now that Local 355 and Mardi Gras were out of arbitration, Wendi wanted to win and send a message to the other casinos and hotels in South Florida: there was no detour around the union.

"They're all going to be looking to see what happens at Mardi Gras," Wendi said about the casinos and hotels. "We need the wind at our back for this one because right now we're losing in South Florida. It's black or white. Win or lose. We can't talk a big game if we're not growing our numbers."

Because of the importance of the campaign, Wendi dedicated more resources to four months of Mardi Gras organizing than had been used over the previous year and a half at Calder. Alex would be working full-time on Mardi Gras along with two other Local 355 organizers.

Alex and his wife, Jill, purchased their first home in North Miami, where the majority of Local 355's membership resided. The house was a charming ranch with a royal palm tree in the yard. Their son was less than a year old. It was heartening to see Alex, the militant radical, taken by fatherhood. He beamed when he got the chance to bring "the boy" to the office dressed in a "Union Thug" onesie. He gave us updates on his son's triumphs: when he slept three straight hours, flipped himself on his back, and made noises that almost sounded like words. During campaigns, organizers are sometimes expected to work eighty-hour weeks, which makes family life difficult. After his paternity leave, Alex had taken a few minibreaks from work to spend more time with his young family. He promised Jill that he wouldn't work on Sundays and was trying to take phone calls only if there was an emergency. But the beginning of the Mardi Gras campaign meant that Alex would need to be working full throttle again.

Alex was so buoyed by the prospect of the Mardi Gras campaign that his energy seemed to be back at its baseline, quiddities intact, profanity gushing. He had already been visiting workers. While at work, I would receive text messages from Alex about people I'd met only once or never knew existed.

Just saw Kurt. Good visit
Got Harriet on committee!
Just recruited Sergio!! Si se puede!

In early October, Wendi requested the employee list from Mardi Gras. Ten days later, the company complied and sent a full list of employees' names and addresses, including mine. Alex and Wendi wanted to make sure management didn't know which employees were being visited. As a precaution, organizers would sometimes present themselves as members of the Florida Freedom Charter, an organization of community groups that Local 355 had assembled. Alex wanted to eliminate the stigma of the word "union" and, should the meeting go poorly, workers wouldn't be able to tell management that the union had come to their front door. It was a clever strategy that had been used successfully in other campaigns and one that Alex and another organizer, Pilar, used when they visited Lena for the first time.

Though Lena never let them into her apartment, she talked to Alex and Pilar for forty-five minutes while standing in her doorway. Alex liked those kinds of visits, the ones that left room for progress. He wasn't looking to collect cards at this early stage, just leaders. First visits were rarely an indication of whether a worker would become a leader. Alex wouldn't discount anyone on account of wariness.

Five days after Alex and Pilar visited Lena, I began a shift with her at the main bar. Frank, the bar manager, checked me into my cash register and called Lena to the bar.

"It's come to the attention of management that employees are being visited by someone."

"Who?" I asked.

"We don't know. Deirdre and Sarah were visited. It's not us, we wouldn't visit you at your homes." Alex's visit with Deirdre, much like the visit with Lena, hadn't gone well.

"Oh! They came to my house!" Lena said.

"Oh, really?"

"Yeah, it was really weird." Frank wrote Lena's name down on a piece of paper next to Deirdre's and Sarah's.

"You're the third person we know about. What did they look like? What did you talk about?"

"The guy was tall, bald. The girl was Spanish or something. They were young, probably younger than me, but I look good. They just talked about how to improve the community and stuff. They were nice, but it was weird. I'm not going to talk to them."

Frank wasn't listening closely. He didn't seem to care about the details. "Be smart. Be careful. I've heard about robbers knocking on doors, visiting people, pretending to be somebody else just to case the apartment. It's Florida, you never know."

Someone I had identified as a leader was snitching. I fought off an urge to squeeze two limes into my eyeballs. More concerning was the fact that management knew about the campaign. I frantically texted Alex, leaving out the fact that Lena had described him as bald. "Document everything," he told me, same as Calder.

David, a bartender, stopped by to gossip. "I know who they are," he said. "The union." Lena didn't seem to care. I wondered if Frank actually didn't know who was knocking on employees' doors. Management wouldn't have been so concerned if Girl Scouts had been showing up at employees' homes peddling Thin Mints. Yet, Frank hadn't used the U-word. The neutrality agreement prohibited managers from talking to employees about the union, but Mardi Gras was challenging the agreement in court, so would managers still abide by it? Any doubts about whether Frank knew the visitors were from the union were assuaged when he returned a few hours later. He said that he'd been in meetings with management about the visitors and he wanted us to notify him if we were visited in the future. He also took the opportunity to remind Lena of how good she had it at Mardi Gras.

"You know, if you ever need anything, you can come right to me. It's easy. Like, remember when you started school again and I fixed your schedule? No problem, right?"

Lena nodded her head in agreement.

"Really, I can't believe they visited *you*," Frank said, chuckling, the implication being that Lena would never need a union. Frank didn't know he was throwing salt on a salt's wounds.

At about four p.m., Debbie, the chatty food and beverage manager from Calder, sat down at my bar. Debbie had worked at Mardi Gras before Calder and liked to come back and visit from time to time. She loved to gamble. Debbie was kindhearted, one of my favorite managers at Calder. She told me about a new young white guy in the buffet who looked just like me. "We call him the 'new James.'" Unbeknownst to Debbie, I knew the "new James." I had helped him put together his résumé. He was a salt. Debbie was filling me in on all the gossip at Calder when suddenly, without warning, Dan Adkins was standing next to me. So were Frank and Sally, the director of food and beverage.

Adkins was wearing a cream-colored oxford without a tie. He was shorter than I pictured, thin, with a helmet of salt and pepper hair, and a flat, wide nose. Frank didn't introduce us. Adkins's attention was on Lena.

"I heard you had some visitors?" Adkins casually asked Lena, careful not to spook her. His voice was nasally and he spoke slowly, in control.

"Yeah, they were really weird," Lena said.

"What kinds of questions did they ask you?" Adkins asked. He was leaning against the bar, relaxed, holding his glasses in his hand.

"Oh, you know, about the job. How do I like Mardi Gras. They asked what I make for vacation, I don't know why. I told them five dollars . . ." Dan and Sally looked surprised. "I'm happy with it!" Lena backtracked. "I've never had a job that paid me while I'm not working!"

"I know what they're talking about," Debbie said to me. I was trying to focus on what Adkins was saying. "And it's gonna happen at Calder soon; you know how unhappy people are there."

"Did you ask for identification?" Adkins asked.

"No."

"Well, they're lying to you. They're not telling you who they really are. Ask for identification next time. Don't let them in," Adkins warned her in a fatherly way. "If they come back, please come right to me. You know where my office is, right?"

"Yes, third floor," Lena assured him.

When Grace relieved Lena that afternoon, Frank gave her the same pre-shift talk. I knew that Pilar had visited Grace that afternoon. Grace just smiled and nodded to Frank. Her silence elated me.

"Oh, they're scared," Grace said once Frank walked away. "They know the union's coming. They were at my house today." After a stressful day, my grin must have given me away. She gave me a high five and hit the floor. "Drinks! Cocktails!"

Organizers spent the next two weeks trying to recruit committee members. Close to half of the workers eligible for unionization at Mardi Gras were Haitian, and Alex was confident that almost all of them would join. As at Calder, the housekeeping department at the casino was almost entirely Haitian, and before long, five housekeepers had committed to leading. Unsurprisingly, the first worker to join the committee was a housekeeper, Benita. Meanwhile, there were rumors of anti-union meetings on the third floor and managers who would confront employees about the union. Someone claimed managers had orchestrated meetings in which workers could "ask" Adkins for a raise. In late October, I found a letter attached to my pay stub:

Please be advised that we have been informed that our employees have been receiving unsolicited strangers knocking at their doors.

These individuals have identified themselves as working for the "community" or for "Mardi Gras Casino." In some cases, they have not wanted to identify themselves at all.

Please know that Management at Mardi Gras would NOT visit your home. We are doing everything we can to protect your privacy.

If you have any questions or concerns—or have had a similar experience—PLEASE let us know!

Once again, the U-word was nowhere to be found. Given the fact that Wendi had already requested the employee list—and that the casino had complied by sending it—there was little doubt Mardi Gras knew exactly who the "unsolicited strangers" were. As to the company's assertion that organizers were claiming to be "working for Mardi Gras Casino," that simply wasn't true.

As the committee grew, I wondered how far the company would go to stop the union. In my first month at Mardi Gras, I had witnessed more organizing, both in favor of and against the union, than I had in almost two years of employment at Calder. I asked Alex what Mardi Gras would do next.

"We don't know, dude," he said. "It all depends on how dumb they are. They might start slitting throats."

The first Mardi Gras committee meeting was on October 28, 2011. Walking into Local 355's office that day, I needed to treat the people I knew (Wendi, Alex, and the other union organizers) like strangers, even though I had spent more time with them than any of the committee members. As soon as I entered the conference room I saw Saraphina, the Haitian cage cashier who had helped me in the money room. She walked across the room and gave me a warm hug that immediately made me feel welcome.

"I'm so glad you're here," she said. She didn't remember my name but I didn't care.

I took a seat next to Colette. Just as Erika and I had staggered our arrivals to Calder's orientation, Colette had arrived early to the committee meeting so we wouldn't be connected. But I knew all of that salt stuff didn't matter anymore. Soon, we would all be out of the shadows and the rest of the committee members would be asked to do the same things salts did. Ten Mardi Gras employees were in attendance along with Alex, Wendi, two other union organizers, and two workers from a unionized hotel a few miles from Mardi Gras there to cheer us on. A second group of Mardi Gras leaders would meet later that day.

Everyone was quiet and anxious. Wendi started the meeting by introducing herself. Going around the room, we each said our name, our job, and why we believed Mardi Gras employees needed a union. At first, people were sheepish and awkward. Then Benita spoke. She started slowly, in Creole. Then, her pace quickened. Rozaline, a Haitian Local 355 organizer, tried to slow her down to translate, but Benita was getting agitated. She got louder. Everyone began to nod along with her, even those of us who didn't speak a word of Creole. When Benita stopped, everyone clapped and cheered.

"She says that this company don't treat anyone with respect," Rozaline translated. "She says sometimes customers treat her bad but if Mardi Gras don't respect her, customers won't. She says the money is bad, the insurance is bad, the supervisors are bad."

Benita spoke again.

"She says, 'They don't listen, and I just want to be heard.' "

Everyone clapped again.

"I'm Saraphina but people call me Big Mouth. We need the union at Mardi Gras because we need respect."

"It *is* about respect," Harriet, a middle-aged slot attendant, said. "I mean, this company doesn't do anything for you. I work really hard for them. I don't just pay out jackpots, I clean up garbage. I literally take elderly and handicapped people to the bathroom. The company never does anything for us."

Rozaline wanted people to talk about specific issues more. "James, what are your issues at work?"

I was apprehensive about exaggerating any of my issues at work. I was still in my honeymoon period at Mardi Gras, happy to be out of the buffet. I didn't have the stress of kids, debt, or ailments. I had a college degree and parents who could help me out when I needed something. The stakes weren't high for me.

"*Bonjour*," I said jokingly. The Haitian women laughed. Colette rolled her eyes. "I haven't been at Mardi Gras too long but I worked at Calder for a while and it's similar. I know that there is favoritism," I said. "I know that I benefit from that favoritism. I'm white and I know that my black and Haitian coworkers don't get the same shifts at the same bars or the same chances that I do. And that's bullshit." A few people nodded their heads; everyone else looked unsure if they had heard me correctly. Later on, a few people would tell me that they were really happy to hear me admit this. Rozaline asked everyone about health insurance.

"I can't afford twenty-five dollars a week for health insurance. And then they switch up the type of insurance every year so I never know what's covered," Alexis, a slot attendant, said.

"Twenty-five dollars a week? I can't afford the family plan, which is way more," someone else added.

"How much more?" Alex asked.

"About a hundred fifty dollars to add one person."

"Some people pay more than three hundred dollars for the family."

"I got a five-cent raise," Harriet said. She had a scratchy voice with a Long Island accent. "How insulting is that? Well actually, they cut all the slot attendants' pay 'cause they thought we were making too much. Then I got a five-cent raise. I mean, we're out there hustlin' for you. How could you do that to us?"

"They cut your pay?" Alex asked.

"Yeah," Alexis said. "We started at ten dollars an hour and they thought we were making too much so it got cut to eight dollars."

"I get all of this," Wendi said. She had been quiet for much of the meeting. "But why be a leader?"

"We're a family," Harriet responded. "Some of us have been together since day one. Like five years? We spend more time with each other than we do with our real families. We look out for each other."

"We need this," Alexis said.

No one was asked to sign a card that day. Instead, Alex explained the importance of a strong leadership committee. Over the next week, he told us, we needed to recruit more leaders. He put a schedule on the wall. He wanted people to sign up for times to join staff organizers on house visits. No one volunteered.

"Winning is not inevitable," Wendi said.

"This is it, guys," Alex said. "It's a matter of weeks. If we put the work in now we will win the union for a long time. If we don't put the work in, we will just sign cards and get forty-one percent and we *will* lose."

Just like that, all of the time slots were filled. Before the end of the meeting, Wendi, Alex, and Rozaline reminded us to keep quiet. "Absolutely no talking about the union at work. The company is definitely going to retaliate. We don't know how yet, but it's not worth the risk."

I could sense this was the beginning of a real campaign, one that I wished I had experienced at Calder. I imagined the room filled with Melanie, Kalia, Priya, and Vidya. I wanted to know my Mardi Gras committee the way I knew the women in the Calder buffet. My work at the two casinos represented two different kinds of salting. At Calder, I would have been a valuable member of the committee. At Mardi Gras, I felt like a plant, there to boost the numbers and, ever so delicately, help shape the committee's approach.

Everyone at the committee meeting radiated a timid excitement; there was a sisterhood in the room. While each of them had been told about the potential risks and rewards of unionization, they didn't know the history of organized labor, the good or the bad. They didn't know how the Mardi Gras campaign fit into Local 355's strategy. Some still didn't even know the name of the union—was it Unite? Or Here? Or United Here?—but they were tired of waiting. The union wasn't a solution; it was a chance to quit the waiting.

Grace, the cocktail waitress who had worked in Atlantic City, was enthusiastic about the union, but she had told Pilar and Alex that she didn't want to join the committee. Alex badly wanted to recruit her and thought she might be more inclined to join if she saw a friendly face. Pilar and I visited Grace's home. It was a modest bungalow just around the corner from Mardi Gras. Her husband's sleek black Dodge Challenger was parked out front. Four kids answered the door and stared at us for a minute before Grace appeared wearing a colorful silk slip. She rolled her eyes and screamed sarcastically. "Okay! Okay! Okay! Come on in."

The house was cluttered with toys. The kids, two of them hers, sat on the floor and worked on a school project. Pilar and I sat on her leather couch and Grace sat in a lawn chair across from us. Her muscular husband walked through the kitchen in a bath towel.

"This is the busiest time of year for me and the kids. We're getting ready to go to Spook Fest tonight."

I asked Grace about the difference between Mardi Gras and the casino she had worked at in Atlantic City.

"Night and day," she said without missing a beat. "Atlantic City was a well-oiled machine. We had everything figured out. Better money. Better insurance. This is like a long nightmare."

"That union was built. It didn't just come into existence," Pilar said.

Her husband reappeared dressed like a sailor for Halloween. He was on his way to his weekend job at a restaurant.

Grace embodied the great challenge of union organizing. Local 355's contracts provided better benefits than non-unionized casinos, but not by much. The potential to be ostracized by management, or fired, trumped any short-term gains Grace would get from unionization. So how do you ask hardworking, low-wage mothers to sacrifice time with their children for something as abstract as a better South Florida through incremental gains? Alex believed most organizers didn't put enough faith in workers' ability to handle the "big ask." "The push on Grace is too small," he told me. "It shouldn't be 'You should be on the committee.' We'll never win the fight between kids and a committee meeting. We need to say, 'This is *for* your kids.'" I tried to express that to her.

"I get it. I know what's going on," she said. "I'm pro-union. I'll sign a card. But I can't be on this committee, or whatever, right now."

She never joined.

Pilar and I kept knocking on doors. Some people never answered, others were happy to see us. A twenty-seven-year-old money room attendant was frightened when she answered the door but thrilled when we told her we were with the union.

She agreed to a second meeting. We visited a money sweeper, Alice, who went to work at four thirty a.m. to empty the slot machines. She had a Monroe piercing above her lip. Her voice was deep and raspy. Sitting in her dark living room, curtains drawn, she told us that when she started at Mardi Gras she was working thirty-six hours. Then she was knocked down to thirty hours. She was officially listed as part-time and as such she was ineligible for benefits. She didn't have health insurance and her three kids were on KidCare, the state-subsidized insurance for children. It wasn't like she was about to visit any doctors, she told us. "I can't afford a sick day," she said, snickering at her own glum humor. Alice agreed to join the organizing committee.

We recruited Rosalie at her apartment in Miramar. She answered the door in a bathrobe and we waited for her to change. She welcomed us into her dimly lit living room. She told us that she'd decided to send money to her mother in Haiti instead of paying her electric bill.

"She wouldn't ask for it if she didn't need it," Rosalie said.

Rosalie was a cage cashier making $10.79 an hour. She had been working at Mardi Gras for five years. She mentioned that the company had always promised raises, especially when Adkins was working to get the slot machine state tax rate cut from 50 to 35 percent. (A successful effort.) But, aside from one small raise, the company never kept its promises. She was on Mardi Gras's health insurance plan and her sons were on KidCare. She wanted to put them on her own plan, but it would have cost more than $100 a week, and that was more than she had left after paying her bills.

"I am a strong woman and a good mother," she told us. "I buy my sons the nice sneakers even though I can't afford it. I don't want them thinking they have to go looking other places for money. That is dangerous."

When Pilar told her how little workers at the Isle and Gulfstream paid for family insurance, Rosalie put her hand over her mouth and gasped. Pilar didn't need to go into the higher pay, guaranteed raises, guaranteed bonuses, or uniform allowances. Rosalie said she needed some time to think about whether she would join the committee. A day later, she agreed.

By the end of two weeks we had fifteen committee members. Women of color are much more likely to join unions and it came as no surprise that twelve committee members were Haitian, Haitian-American, or African-American women.

A bartender, Brett, told Colette that he had been in a union and believed Mardi Gras would benefit from one. So, the day after the first committee meeting, Colette and Pilar went to Brett's house. They knocked on his door and waited. Colette thought she saw the curtains in his window ripple but no one came to the door. That night Colette was scheduled to work the VIP lounge, a private open bar exclusively for customers who spent enough money in the casino. Frank signed Colette into a register without saying a word to her. This made Colette nervous, as Frank was usually animated and chipper. Colette chalked it up to paranoia. A little while after her shift started, Frank returned to the VIP bar.

"Have you been visited?" he asked her.

Colette, caught off guard, jammed up. "No. Well, what are you talking about? Here? Or at Calder?" Frank looked at her dubiously. "No," she said.

It was too late.

"These people are dangerous," Frank said. "They're lying. Violine was visited and came to us about it. She was very scared." Colette knew about the Violine incident. She also knew that Violine, unaware that management was at odds with the union, had naïvely asked a manager about the visitors because she wanted to know more about the union, not because she felt threatened. The head of security scared Violine when he interrogated her in a back room, even recording the conversation. When Violine eventually did sign a union card, she was terrified and made Alex promise that no one would find out.

"Are you sure you're not with the union?" Frank asked Colette.

"I don't know what you're talking about," Colette said, still unsure of how to respond.

A short while later, Marat, another food and beverage manager, visited Colette at the VIP bar. "Do you like your job?" he asked her. "Do you like your managers?" Colette fought back tears. She knew she was in trouble. She confronted Brett.

"Did you tell Frank I was at your house today?"

"Yes."

"Why?"

"I don't know. He was the first person I saw when I came to work. I just thought it was weird that you were with those people."

"Were you home? Why didn't you answer?"

"I don't know. I'm pissed at Mardi Gras but I'm on the fence about the union. I don't think they'll win here. Why were you with them?"

"I had met with them and thought you'd want to hear about it. You said you had been in a union."

"I'm pro-union but just not here. It seems too shady here."

Brett agreed to have coffee with Colette so she could answer any questions he had about the union. That never happened. Colette started to worry for her job.

Two days later, I worked the main bar with Vanessa. Since the first shift we'd worked together, Vanessa had freely brought up the union at work, saying that she was "in good with the union people." I encouraged her to get more involved but she was hesitant. That Sunday, she told me that she would join the organizing committee and come to the next meeting. I wasn't sure if she was hustling me the way she hustled customers but I hoped for the best. Frank came to the bar toward the end of Vanessa's shift.

"I might need to move the schedule around, and I might need you to cover a few shifts. You okay with that?" he asked her.

"Sure, I'm fine with that. Whatever you need," Vanessa said.

"Yeah, someone's gonna be fired," he said, keeping his voice down. "It probably won't be tomorrow or anything. I have a meeting with Mr. Adkins about it; I'm pretty sure it will happen soon." Vanessa knew better than to ask. I already knew.

I texted Alex:

> They wouldn't be that dumb, right?
> Who knows. We'll find out.

Alex was hounding me to talk to Deirdre, the Boston bahtendah, about the union. He had met with her once, and though the meeting had not gone well, Alex believed she was the lynchpin in the beverage department. She could wrangle Brett, David, and Jenny, bartenders who were friendly with the cocktail waitresses. Pilar and I went to Deirdre's apartment. To avoid being compromised like Colette, I waited in the car for the all-clear from Pilar. Deirdre slammed the door in Pilar's face. I was safe. To Alex, Deirdre's refusal to talk to Pilar meant that she was scared or misinformed. He was convinced that I needed to have a conversation with her. So after my shift one night, I approached Deirdre while she was working Louie's Lounge.

"What did you think of that memo that came with our pay stubs?" I asked her, referring to the memo about the "unsolicited strangers." She was serving a Coors to a guy with an unkempt beard wearing a camo trucker's hat. He didn't tip.

"Where'd you work tonight?" she asked me.

"French Quarter. Made two fifty," I said, meaning two dollars and fifty cents. Everyone knew the French Quarter bar was the worst shift.

"Two hundred fifty dollahs? Not bad," she said sarcastically.

"So what'd you think of the memo?" I asked again.

"I plead the fifth," she said without making eye contact. I walked away.

Later that night I got a text message from Colette:

> Deirdre told the managers that you and I are talking about the union. She told [two cocktail waitresses] to avoid us.

Things were normal when Colette arrived at work on November 3. Frank and the other beverage managers had been particularly courteous to her the past few days, and she hoped it was just their way of killing the union with kindness. An hour into her shift Nydia, a food and beverage manager, told Colette she needed to fill out some paperwork in the human resources office. Colette, well aware of the fact that it was too late for human resources to be open, followed Nydia through the slot machine maze, up two flights of stairs to the third floor, and down a hallway. Human resources was closed, but its director, Steven Feinberg, was waiting for her in a small room across the hall along with a security guard, Sally, and Jay, the assistant food and beverage director. Colette sat down at the table across from them.

"I'm sorry, but we're not happy with your performance," Sally told Colette. Despite all of the signs, Colette couldn't believe this was happening. She collected herself. She wanted to make the most of this meeting.

"Let's be adults here. This is not about my job performance. Just last week my manager told me he was happy to have me back." (Colette had worked at Mardi Gras before Calder.)

Sally told Colette that she had been late for work too many times. Colette asked to see the record. Sally, holding a piece of paper in her hands, said she didn't have a record.

"Surveillance also caught you loitering in the poker kitchen two nights ago," Jay said.

"I went to the kitchen to get a meal during my break. I got someone to cover for me."

"It was an unauthorized break," Jay said. "If you want to eat something you need to eat and go back to the floor."

"You are still under your three-month probationary period. We've decided to terminate you," Sally said.

"This is ridiculous. I know it's because of my union activity. It's shameful that in 2011 you think you can get away with firing me for this. It's illegal."

They sat in silence.

"Is this because I'm a member of the union committee?"

"You can think whatever you want," Jay said as he shrugged. "We're going to need your ID badge."

A security guard escorted Colette to the bar so she could close out her open tabs.

"What happened?" a bartender asked Colette.

"I'm being fired for supporting the union."

Grace was standing next to Colette, visibly shocked. She started to tear up.

"They can't fucking do that," the bartender, Deirdre's best friend, said.

Colette closed her tabs and collected her things. The secu-

rity guard walked her across the casino floor, out the door, all
the way to her car.

Fourteen committee members remained.

I was on my way to work when Colette called me sobbing.
"What the fuck just happened to me?" It didn't matter that
she knew losing her job was a possibility or that I'd heard
Frank talking about it. Termination, even when expected, is
sharp-toothed and humiliating. Colette drove straight to Local
355. Despite having been in hundreds of campaigns, Wendi
and Alex were equally shocked. We had known the company
would fight the union; now we knew they would slit throats.

The next day the committee met at Local 355. Colette was
there. Everyone gave her hugs. Despite the blow of losing a committee member, the unionization drive marched on. Large pieces
of paper with every worker's name lined the walls of the conference room. Next to the list was a giant thermometer that would
measure how many members signed cards along the way. We, the
committee, were the first to sign up. Alex handed out the cards.

> I hereby authorize UNITE HERE! to be my collective bar-
> gaining representative in all matters relating to my wages,
> hours, and terms and conditions of employment, and request
> and accept membership in UNITE HERE!

As I read the card, it occurred to me that the employer, legally,
had nothing to do with the agreement. It was a contract between
the union and me. After almost two years of salting, I finally
signed a card. I found my name on the wall—there was already
a check mark next to it, meaning a union organizer had visited
me—and highlighted it in pink to indicate that I had signed.

Wendi explained how Colette's termination fit into the
broader context of the company's tactics. They had fired Co-

lette not simply because she was pro-union, but because it sent a message to everyone else.

"Fear is the only weapon this company has to use on workers. If we eliminate fear, we can do anything," she said.

Alex was big on fear. He said he wanted to write a book about it one day. He once told me that if "someone says they can't meet with us because they're sick, it's fear, not apathy. And if they are actually physically ill, it could be from fear. Fear will do that. Everything comes from fear."

Wendi passed around sheets of blank paper. "Here's what I want you to do," she said. "If the company came out and said: 'It's completely up to you if you want to join the union. We are going to let you do whatever you want and no matter what we won't interfere.' If they said that, what percentage of your coworkers would join? Write down that percentage."

The committee thought about it and wrote down their answers.

"Ninety-five percent."

"One hundred percent."

"Eighty-eight percent."

"And why wouldn't everyone join?"

"Because some people would be scared the company was lying."

All of the committee members present signed cards, including Colette. Someone started a small red pool at the bottom of the thermometer to signify the seven of us who had just signed. We needed a minimum of 111 cards to win, one more than half of the bargaining unit. But anti-union campaigns usually include an effort by the company to encourage workers to exercise their right to revoke their cards. Therefore, 111 was not going to be enough.

That afternoon we each grabbed a stack of cards, split off with organizers, and started knocking on doors. Over the weekend, despite the story of Colette's termination circulating, people signed up. The thermometer started to fill quickly. We collected nearly sixty signatures in two days, more than 25 percent of the workforce eligible for unionization. As time passed and the red on our thermometer climbed, so too did our hopes. Haitian employees, 44 percent of the workforce, were signing up at a blistering rate. "Haitian people know what's up," Alex said. "These people left a fucked-up dictator in Haiti; they're not afraid of Dan Adkins." Everything was going right. I started to wonder if Colette was just a sacrificial lamb. Colette asked me, "Are we really gonna win without Mardi Gras putting up more of a fight?"

A few nights after she was fired, Colette drove me to work. A mile away from the casino, and ten minutes before I was scheduled to clock in, I realized I had forgotten my all-black sneakers, a uniform requirement. Colette pulled her recently retired work shoes from the backseat of the car. They were Coach, four sizes too small, and had little Cs embroidered on the sides. But I wasn't about to let the company burn me for a uniform violation. I stuffed my feet into the sneakers, stretching the fabric as far as it could go. Once behind the bar, I pulled my heels out and wore them like slippers.

The VIP bar was painfully slow that night. The VIP room shared its storage closet with a small concession stand. I struck up a conversation with Tina, who was working the stand. She was young. So young that she had been assigned to that concession stand at the entrance of the casino because she wasn't old enough to walk across the casino floor. She was shy, with a cherub face, and made eye contact with me only for the first few words of each sentence. She might have been shy because I was wearing women's shoes. Tina told me that she didn't mind making $7.50 an hour, but she was frustrated with the way Frank messed with her schedule. Most of all, she was upset with Mardi Gras because a technical glitch in payroll meant she'd unknowingly missed months of health insurance payments and now she was stuck paying $350 in back payments, which she couldn't afford.

"A group of us are getting together to talk about these kinds of things," I told her. "Wanna meet up and talk about it?" She agreed without hesitation and gave me her phone number. A part of me knew that Tina wouldn't have agreed to meet up had she known what had happened to Colette. I would explain what happened to Colette during our first meeting, I told myself.

◎

The committee spent the following weekend knocking on doors and signing people up. I went to Grace's house, and as promised, she signed while standing at her front door. I got two more bartenders to sign up, then visited two wrong addresses, one cynic—*job's gonna suck with or without a union*—and two people who were home but wouldn't come to the door. I called Tina a few times but she never picked up. I looked up her address on the list the company had provided and went to her house. After a few knocks, her mother answered and said that Tina was taking a nap and wouldn't be coming to the door. I had the sickening feeling that Tina had put the pieces together and hadn't liked the idea of jeopardizing her job. Vanessa had also given me her phone number so that we could arrange to meet and she could sign a card. She never picked up.

I saw Vanessa at work on Sunday. When I got to the bar there was an untouched croissant sitting by the cash register. I hadn't had breakfast that morning and looking at the doughy crescent made my mouth water. While I've never been someone prone to paranoia, I didn't touch it in case management had placed it there in an attempt to catch me stealing. Sierra 1, the all seeing eye in the sky, was always watching. Vanessa had a different theory.

"They're trying to poison us," she said when she saw me staring longingly at the croissant. She told me that she had been at the house of her brother-in-law, the manager, so she couldn't pick up when I called her over the weekend.

"You know they got all our names on a blackboard upstairs?" she said.

"Whose names?" I asked her.

"All the people who are with the union."

I wasn't sure what to tell her. *Under the National Labor Relations Act they can't fire you for being pro-union, so just be sure not to loiter on your shift?* It was the same conundrum Alex, Wendi, and union organizers everywhere faced: how to encourage legally protected union activity that might get workers fired. Vanessa agreed to meet on Tuesday to sign a card.

When Saraphina reported for work on Monday she was told to go to human resources. Feinberg, the head of the department, was waiting for her.

"I'm sorry, we have to let you go."

They told her the decision had come from above them. She asked why. She was being terminated because of an incident during her shift Saturday afternoon. Saraphina had upset a customer by following a meaningless protocol. A customer had come to Saraphina with $0.15 and a ticket worth $59.85. He asked for three $20 bills. Saraphina told him this was against the rules and gave him $59.85 for the value of the ticket. The customer then gave Saraphina all of the change, $0.85 plus $0.15, and she gave him a $1 bill. Then the customer gave Saraphina all of the money and said he wanted three $20 bills. Cage cashiers were allowed to carry out a maximum of two consecutive transactions for each customer. Saraphina, likely taking the customer's rude tone into consideration, informed him of the policy. The customer then told Saraphina that he knew the general manager of the casino and that he was going to get her fired. Saraphina's manager was called and everything was resolved. The altercation could have been avoided. But it was the kind of incident that happened all the time in casinos. In fact, Saraphina's manager told her she had nothing to worry about. Saraphina asked Feinberg the same question Colette had asked.

"Am I fired because I'm with the union?"

He didn't answer her.

Thirteen committee members remained.

That night, Alex called and told me about Saraphina. Her firing hit harder than Colette's. Saraphina had been working at Mardi Gras since the day it opened in 2006. She was a single mother with two diabetic daughters. And while it had taken Colette only a few hours to get over her firing, Saraphina hid from the union at her sister's house. Though I hadn't recruited Saraphina, I remembered mentioning her name to Alex after she had helped me in the money room. I wondered if she would blame the union.

The next day, I woke up to a text message from Vanessa:

> I'm not going to join just yet surrounding the circumstances so there's no need to come today ttyl.

Later that day, I joined Colette and Bridget, a union organizer, on house visits. Dante, a server in the French Quarter restaurant on the third floor of the casino, was the last person we visited that day. He was walking his lapdog when we pulled up to his mobile home. When Dante saw Colette in the passenger seat he started power-walking toward his front door. Colette jumped out of the car and ran after him. By the time I arrived, Dante's hands, steady when I loaded his tray with cocktails, were shaking. Kind and jovial at work, standing outside of his home, Dante was a portrait of fear.

"The company knows you're here," he said, his voice crack-ing. Behind his glasses, Dante's eyes looked past us, scouting the horizon. "They know you're at my house right now, these people . . . they know everything." He was wearing his black work slacks and a black T-shirt. His hair was gelled.

"The company doesn't know we're here," Colette assured him.

Dante inched toward his screen door. On the other side was a porch, bare except for a few tropical plants. There was a long pause. Bridget stood quietly between Colette and me.

"It's important that we talk," Colette pleaded. "You know I was fired last week, right? That's why you're scared?"

"I heard about that. I'm sorry but I can't lose my job right now, I have bills." His Argentine accent swelled as he became more agitated. "I know the union is a good thing *pero* you have no shot. Life is no good at Mardi Gras but if they know you are here, I'm done. They fucking do not care about us, any day at that place could be your last."

It was the first time I saw the kind of fear that Alex and Wendi had warned us about.

Bridget took a shot. She had been an organizer for a few years and had dealt with far more workers than Colette and me. She was in her late twenties. Her biting humor was en-livened by a home-cooked Chicago accent that could sound exaggerated when she delivered punch lines, but while talking to Dante it was subdued, even delicate. Being the only one of us who hadn't met Dante, she was trying to connect with him. Bridget had worked at a hotel in Chicago and told Dante about a housekeeper that management was out to get. The housekeeper's coworkers had rallied around her and manage-ment had eventually eased up on her.

"The same thing goes for you and your coworkers at Mardi Gras. You're right, any day could be your last day, and without you, we have no shot. Without your help we are going to lose at Mardi Gras, and you know what? Chances are things aren't going to change. More people are going to get fired; who's to say that they won't fire anybody for a stupid reason after the union leaves? And you think you can go on just paying your bills? Without affordable health insurance? Without more respect? Life is not going to get easier if you don't take a stand and this is your chance."

Over the past few weeks, I'd begun to get frustrated by workers' hesitance to join the fight for the union—*Don't you understand? This is your chance for a better life!* Seeing the fear in Dante was sobering. I knew about roller-coaster fear. I'd watched *Scream, Scream 2,* and *Scream 3.* When I got my driver's license, I'd felt my heart jump when my car hydroplaned. But I'd never experienced the kind of fear that Dante exhibited. I'd never seen it up close. It was unbridled and could rear its head at any time. Each time he swiped his credit card at the grocery store. Or when he felt a scratch at the back of his throat and worried about taking a sick day. Or when his engine made that ripping and banging sound. That fear could make him run, hide, or do something stupid. He might tell the company I was there, in the hope of currying favor. We were counting on the fear to make him do something bold.

Dante nodded in reluctant agreement with Bridget. He turned to me. "You still working there?"

"Yeah. Why? Do you know something I don't?" Colette, Bridget, and I laughed.

"No, just wondering."

Bridget told Dante a Peruvian folktale about Pepito, a fisherman who went overboard at sea. Another ship was close by and offered to help Pepito but he refused, saying God had a plan for him. More sailors offered to help him, but still, he refused and said God would straighten everything out. Bits of flotsam that could be used as a raft went by but Pepito clung to his faith in the Lord. Then Pepito drowned. Once in heaven, Pepito asked God why he hadn't saved him. "I tried, Pepito!" God said.

Dante didn't react to Bridget's story. Distracted, he told us he would think about the union and sent us on our way. He had to get to work.

Before I went to work that night I stopped by the union hall. There was a group of unionized workers there for a meeting. Wendi had me stand at the front of the room and talk about the Mardi Gras campaign. The conversation with Dante had left me dispirited. Up until that point, I had been hopeful. I had thought of the anti-union meetings and Colette and Saraphina's firings as casualties that we could overcome. But now I was thinking about Vanessa, Tina, and, most of all, Dante. He looked like he had seen a ghost.

Of course, he had.

"I think I'm going to be fired tonight," I told the crowd. I left for work.

I arrived at work that night just as the gloaming set in. It was the end of hurricane season and South Florida was beginning to feel less like a swamp and more like a tourist destination. I changed into my uniform, grabbed my bottle opener out of the glove compartment, and, for the first time in two years of salting, slipped a voice recorder into my back pocket.

Like at the start of any other night, I clocked in and got a walkie-talkie from Bobby. I picked up my bank in the money room.

"Sierra 1, this is James Walsh going from MR-1 to the sports bar."

There wasn't a manager waiting for me at the sports bar.

"Can I get a manager to the sports bar?" I called into the radio.

"On my way," Jay said.

Jay, the second in command of food and beverage, came to the sports bar a short while later. Jay was quiet and stern. He was Jordanian, with a cleanly shaven scalp that reflected the ceiling's lights. When he didn't wear a business suit, he would at least wear suit pants with a maroon or white button-down business shirt, ever ready for a promotion. He went to Louisiana State University and was a Tigers football fanatic. His office was floor-to-ceiling in the Tigers' purple and gold with plaques and pictures.

"You must have enjoyed the game on Saturday," I said to him while he logged me in to the cash register. LSU had beaten the top-ranked team in the country, Alabama, in a wacky 9–6 game. I always tried to talk sports with managers—it wasn't too personal.

"I did. That's why my voice is so scratchy. You went to Boston College, right?" It was the first time Jay had ever asked me anything about my life, which was unnerving.

Jay left and I opened the sports bar like I would any other shift. I turned on the fifteen TVs that got me through comically slow nights, stocked the coolers with beers that wouldn't sell, wiped down the bar top, and filled the well with ice. I had just finished a double check on the beer inventory in the cooler behind the bar when I almost bumped into Sally, the director of the food and beverage department.

"James." She messed with the overhead projector's remote, trying to turn the volume down. I showed her how to do it. She took a deep breath and started over. "Okay now, James, I need you to come with me."

The moment Sally opened her mouth everything stopped. My relationship with management—rather, management's relationship with me—had been shed of agenda and pretense. What remained was unambiguous: I was a cancer, and amputation would be necessary. I let out a sigh of relief. Sally led me through the sports bar and onto the escalator up to

the third floor. Walking down the hall toward the human resources office felt like walking on the ocean floor. The weeks of
certainty leading up to this moment didn't make the situation
any less surreal. *Is this really happening?* I reached into my
back pocket and fumbled with the voice recorder. In Florida
it's illegal to record a conversation without the other party's
consent but I didn't care. (I hit the wrong button and didn't
record a thing.)

Sally led me to an office barely big enough for a small
table. She left me with Jay, who was sitting at the table, and
a large security guard leaning against the wall behind Jay.
Steven Feinberg, the head of human resources, was the last to
arrive. Colette had described him as "meek" and "puny." He
was a twiggish ball of nerves. I don't know how many people
Feinberg had sacked but he was shaking as if the ghosts of
employees past had taken over his central nervous system. He
didn't look at me. Out of nervousness, and an overwhelming
desire to make Feinberg even more uncomfortable, I stood up,
smiled, and held my hand out to him.

"Hi, I'm James, I don't believe we've met."

He shook my hand, dropped some papers, and made eye
contact for a half second. Jay started the meeting. "James,
you've been with us for two months now, right?"

"That's right."

"As you know we have a ninety-day probationary period
and . . . we've decided we no longer want to keep you on . . .
so we are terminating you, your employment."

Silence.

"Okay, what's the reason?"

"We don't need a reason with the probationary period,
it's under ninety days, so it's just that we're not going to keep
you on."

Sam, a researcher at Local 355, would tell me later that the
"no reason" excuse was probably advice from Mardi Gras's
lawyers. Fabricating a reason—"loitering," for instance—

would require proof in court. The ninety-day probationary period was a free pass.

"I know I've done a good job, Frank has told me so. And I know at least one casino host has told Sally about my strong job performance." Both facts were true. I'm not a tremendously confident person. I wasn't a good buffet server. But I knew I had done a good job at Mardi Gras. I made sure I did a good job at Mardi Gras. I wasn't pleading. I was trying to catch them and I was failing. Feinberg chimed in.

"The company's policy is to do an evaluation within ninety days and—"

"Can I see the evaluation?" I said. He looked at his papers.

"It was an observed evaluation, and it wasn't satisfactory."

The tall security guard standing behind Jay and Steven never took his eyes off his feet. I took a deep breath, desperate to trap them in their lie. Logic had been swallowed by outrage. *Why didn't I plan the perfect response? Why didn't I talk to a lawyer? Or consult a comedian so I could go out with a really good burn?*

"Jay, I like you," I said.

"I like you," he said, surprised by my flattery.

"It's over, right? I mean, I don't work here anymore. So I have to ask you, is this about my involvement with the union?"

Jay looked to Steven. "No, this was an upper-management decision."

"Steven, is this based on my union involvement?" Steven looked away. His lack of eye contact was agonizing and felt incriminating. He was like an executioner who took his eyes off the target as he brought the ax down, making everything bloodier.

"No, we're not even allowed to talk about that. It's just a decision that was made."

The silence and blank stares were an open invitation to ask more questions. But I had nothing.

The guard took my ID. In an effort to buy time so I could

think of another question, I asked when I should return my uniform.

"You can return it whenever you have time. Be sure to call ahead though." (Despite receiving two letters from the company, I still haven't returned my uniform. Sometimes, I wear the glittery vest when I drink.)

The security guard escorted me down the long hallway, past the French Quarter restaurant, where Dante was working, and onto the escalator. I knew Dante didn't have to see me paraded through the casino to find out what had happened. It wouldn't take long for word to spread. Disappeared man walking. I remembered Colette had called her own firing despicable.

"This is despicable," I said to the guard.

"Hey, man, I have nothing to do with . . . you know."

When we reached the ground floor, the security guard said I could walk out of any exit I wanted. I chose the exit at the far end of the casino, hoping we would pass someone I knew. I wanted my own Colette moment. I wanted to stand on the bar with a cardboard sign that said "Union." I wanted to shout "Organize! Organize! Organize!" I wanted it to echo long after I walked out the door. But the only employees I saw were on the other side of the casino floor, and even if I had shouted, they wouldn't have heard me over the slot machines' bells and whistles. *Ding, ding, bling, ding, ding.*

Twelve committee members remained.

Since requesting the employee list at the beginning of October, Wendi had corresponded with Adkins on a few occasions. After the memo about "unsolicited strangers" was attached to our pay stubs, she sent a letter to Adkins accusing Mardi Gras managers of violating the neutrality agreement when they interrogated employees, telling them not to let organizers into their homes. This was only a few days after Colette had been confronted by Frank. Alex sincerely thought Wendi's letter might save Colette's job. He didn't think Adkins would fire Colette if the letter made a subtle connection between Colette's interrogation and Local 355's knowledge of the questioning. Wendi asked that Mardi Gras managers be informed of the rules of the neutrality agreement. She also requested a meeting with Adkins. Most of the correspondence between Wendi and Adkins was formal, obviously shaped and approved by lawyers. It wasn't a surprise that Adkins's response, sent the same day as Wendi's letter, flatly denied any violation of the card check. But I was surprised by how Adkins went on the offensive.

> . . . please be advised that your allegations are false. Quite to the contrary, we have several statements from employees regarding the manner, in some cases very disrespectful manner, in which they have been approached at their homes. The complaints are specific and range from the hours of the visits to being visited under false pretenses and demeaning the manner in which they live.
>
> Many of these employees are insulted and frightened by your disrespectful and devious behavior and have asked that we contact you to ask that you not re-visit them . . .
>
> . . . In light of your abhorrent approach to the employees of Mardi Gras, we will respectfully decline your request to meet. And, in addition, we would ask that you refrain from the devious behavior and tactics utilized to gain access to these employees.
>
> I will continue to listen and document these actions and will take whatever steps are necessary based on each individual complaint to protect the employees of Mardi Gras.

Two days later, Wendi sent another letter to Adkins informing him of the union's plan to talk with workers on Mardi Gras's property, which was the union's right under the card-check agreement. Wendi requested a meeting to figure out the details.

> Perhaps at the time of this meeting, we could discuss our letter of October 31 which detailed our concerns about the behavior of some managers that we believe violates the Agreement.
>
> We wish to reiterate that we have every hope that we can move forward in a mutually cooperative and respectful manner.

Adkins didn't respond to Wendi's letter, which wasn't a surprise. It seemed as though Adkins would rather burn Mardi Gras down than allow Unite Here organizers to talk to employees in his break room. Wendi was creating a paper trail, hoping each exchange might come in handy in court one day.

While also running an effective campaign, Wendi needed a strategy that protected the committee members who hadn't been terminated. But to make committee members' jobs the priority would have been to tiptoe around the dragon, an approach that most certainly would have ended in defeat. Instead she and Alex chose to match Adkins, push back, show some audacity, and make an all-out attempt at unionizing the casino. Of course, this required the committee to expose themselves even more than they already had. Ultimately, the union needed to have one of two things when the card-check agreement expired at the end of the year: 111 union cards signed or proof that Mardi Gras had mounted an illegal anti-union campaign.

But workers weren't answering their doors anymore. After I was fired, the doors went cold. The campaign started averaging one new card a day. One afternoon I visited a cocktail waitress, Lynne. About a month earlier, Lynne had invited me to have drinks with a few coworkers. We'd had a good time and became friends at work. The day I visited Lynne a relative, probably her mother or an aunt, answered the door. I told her who I was and asked for Lynne. The woman went to the back of the house to get Lynne, only to return to say that she didn't want to come to the door. I would have pinned Lynne's skepticism on the fact that she was close with a manager, but Dante's chalk-white face was singed in my memory. Fear—the almighty weapon.

"Dan Adkins wants us to violate the agreement," Wendi told the committee the day after I was fired. If the union violated the agreement with Mardi Gras, all bets would be off and management would have carte blanche to run an anti-union campaign without consequence. "So we're going to figure out ways to organize in a public way without breaking the agreement."

Two days after I was fired, Fabiola, a young Haitian housekeeper, was summoned to meet the head of housekeeping and Steven Feinberg. Fabiola suspected that an anti-union coworker told management that she had been visiting housekeepers. Fabiola liked to have dinner at the concession stand during her break. Ten days earlier, she had left her post five minutes early to order so that the food would be ready when her break started. Her manager had caught her. She apologized and promised not to do it again. Now, she was told that she was being fired for "gross misconduct."

Eleven committee members.

After the first committee meeting, each member had his or her picture taken. We'd been told that one day, when we all felt comfortable enough, the pictures would be assembled on a flyer that would be distributed to everyone at the casino. The flyer, which was a cornerstone of Unite Here campaigns, was intended to not only be informational, in that it directed all workers to union leaders, but also inspirational, because it licensed workers to be publicly pro-union without fear of retribution. Just as important, the pictures solidified a commitment between committee members and the union. Wendi and Alex hadn't released the flyer yet because they didn't want Mardi Gras committee members walking around with targets on their backs. Now they believed the flyer might actually protect the committee. Without the flyer, Adkins could continue to fire the committee members while claiming he didn't know their union affiliation.

After Fabiola was fired, Wendi and Alex assembled the committee and suggested that we go public by releasing the flyer. By stepping out from the shadows the remaining committee members would go from guerrilla insurgency to legitimate political party with the protection of the National Labor Relations Board. The committee agreed. If four people had been fired for union activity, no one knew how many more Adkins would knock off to stop the campaign. We signed release agreements that gave the union permission to use our pictures on the flyer.

Wendi and Alex timed the release of the flyer with another aggressive maneuver. The neutrality agreement stated that the union had the right to access certain employee-only spaces in the casino. In addition to taking this access, they decided it was time to introduce the union committee to Adkins in person.

On the morning of November 17, Wendi sent the flyer to Adkins. Just before eleven a.m., Alex, three other union organizers, an Episcopal priest, a community activist, the four of us who had been fired, and four of the eleven committee members still working at Mardi Gras met in a small parking lot across the street from the casino. Alex told us the plan. We would enter the lobby calmly and request a meeting with Adkins. It was important, Alex said, that we not wander from the group or bother any of our coworkers. We weren't there to cause a disturbance. Unite Here uses delegations in many union campaigns. I'd seen union-produced videos of worker delegations in which housekeepers marched to the offices of hotel general managers, confronting them about anti-union bullying, unjust firings, or contract negotiations. Almost all of them ended anticlimactically as executives rarely emerged from their offices. Though we wanted to introduce ourselves to Adkins, everyone knew getting past his assistant in the front office was unlikely. Reverend Aguilar led us in a prayer before we set out: " . . . We are instruments of your justice." Followed by a quick union *clap . . . clap . . . clap . . . clap, clap, clap, clap, clap, clap.*

We were wearing our Sunday best. I wore a tweed jacket, a hand-me-down ill suited for South Florida's heat. I could feel sweat dribbling down my back. No one spoke as we walked across the vast parking lot. The only sound was the clicking of heels on pavement. Delegations were standard union work for Alex. He was comfortable with conflict, even good at it. Everyone else carried their butterflies in silence. I've always avoided conflict, and a few months earlier, my coworkers wouldn't have dreamed of demanding a meeting with Dan Adkins.

I hadn't entered the casino's main entrance since my job interview and was happy to feel a tempest of cold air-conditioning as I walked through the sliding doors. Alex and Aguilar approached the reception desk. Alex told the two receptionists behind the desk that we were there to meet with Dan Adkins. The receptionist called upstairs to Adkins's office and told someone that there was a group there to meet with Adkins. "Mhm, unhha, okay." She hung up and said Adkins was on a conference call, and would we mind waiting a few minutes? We waited in near silence. A few morning gamblers walked past us, offering little more than a second glance before making their way to the slot machines. At eleven thirty on a Thursday morning most of the customers were retirees. A housekeeper waved to us. We waved back.

Less than two minutes after we'd entered the lobby, a Mardi Gras employee sent from upstairs corralled our amoebic group. We complied, still quiet and nervous. Suddenly, a man with the body of a retired WWF wrestler came barreling out of a doorway next to the reception desk, flinging the door open as if it were a piece of cardboard. Dick Trotter, the head of security at Mardi Gras, was flanked by a few grimacing deputies who, like me, seemed to be there just for effect.

"On behalf of management, you need to leave," Trotter told Alex. At six foot two, Alex was tall and lanky. Trotter was about the same height but much thicker. Alex introduced himself in a matter-of-fact way. He was holding a manila folder containing a letter to Adkins, a committee flyer, and a copy of the card-check agreement.

"We're not here to cause problems," Alex said. "We're just here to introduce ourselves to Mr. Adkins and take access to the break room, which is the agreement we have with Mardi Gras."

"There's no meeting. That's not going to happen. There is no agreement," Trotter replied.

"Yes there is," Alex said.

"With who?"

"With the union."

"And who?"

"The company, Mardi Gras. Signed by Dan Adkins," Alex said.

That seemed to trip Trotter up. He paused for a moment. He didn't like being uninformed. "I don't know what you're talking about."

"Are you speaking on behalf of the company?" Alex asked him.

"As far as I know, there is no agreement. You're being asked to leave. If you guys don't leave, you're going to be arrested." Trotter was a former captain in the Hallandale Beach police department. "Leave through here," he said, pointing to the door. Alex nodded at the group. We stepped outside and waited in the shade of the casino's portico.

"We're not here to cause any trouble," Alex repeated as he offered the folder to Trotter, who refused to take it. Alex tried to hand the folder to one of Trotter's deputies. Trotter instructed him not to take it. Alex placed the folder on the reception desk. Trotter knocked it off the desk onto the floor. One of his deputies stepped on it. We retreated across the parking lot, just as silently as we had come.

"We are in the right," Alex said when we got back to our cars. "We have the law and justice on our side. We're coming back tomorrow."

That night, Maya, a guest service representative who had come with the delegation, worked her shift without hearing a manager mention the delegation or, worse, being summoned to human resources. Alex hoped that after the delegation Adkins had talked to his lawyers and decided against firing union leadership. So, the next day, the group met at the same parking lot to do it again.

"I want them to call the cops today," Alex said. "I want to organize the cops."

It was drizzling and a few people opened umbrellas as we walked across the parking lot toward the casino. My tweed jacket hadn't had much of an impact on the first delegation so I didn't wear it on the second. This time, there were ten of us: Alex, three organizers, three current employees, and three ghosts. Alex approached the same receptionist he had talked to the day before. He asked her to call Dan Adkins. She kindly asked him to wait a second while she made the call. Alex, wearing a white guayabera, held his hands behind his back, cooperative and confident. We waited to the side, neatly corralling ourselves this time. Just over a minute after we entered the lobby, Dick Trotter came out of the same door he had the day before. He was calm this time. He wore a white polo shirt tucked into dress slacks. He asked us to step outside.

"How often are we going to do this? Every day?" he asked Alex once we were all outside.

"We're here because we intend to abide by our agreement," Alex said.

"I'm being told there is no agreement," Trotter said. Alex opened the folder and produced the contract. He showed Trotter where Adkins had signed his name.

"Whose signature is that?"

"Mr. Dan Adkins," Alex said.

Trotter paused for a moment, stunned. "The company is telling me that there is no agreement. I work for the company. Therefore, I need to ask you guys to leave."

There was more back-and-forth about the agreement until finally, Trotter made the call. When the police arrived, they talked to Trotter. I don't know what they said but surely, as a retired officer, Trotter knew the drill. Then the officers talked to Alex, who tried to tell them about the neutrality agreement and our right to be there.

"I'm sure you guys have lawyers to figure that stuff out," the officer said. He started taking names and addresses so that he could issue trespassing warnings.

"Look," Alex said to the officer. "There are current employees here right now who have to come back here to work. I don't want them trespassed. We are going to ask them to leave. If they come back here are they going to be in trouble?" The officer walked over to ask Trotter, who nodded his head.

"Yes, if they come back to work they're going to be arrested," the officer said. Alex went to Trotter.

"These are employees who need to work. We are here peacefully. We are just trying to meet with the owner. We're not doing anything bad. They need to be able to come back and work." Alex was pleading, genuinely concerned about the predicament.

Trotter shrugged his shoulders.

While Alex was talking to Trotter, the police officers were

taking the names and addresses of the organizers and the workers who had been fired.

"I need to come back to work," Alice, one of the committee members, told an organizer. "I can't give him my name." Alice, Alexis, and Harriet slipped away and started walking back across the parking lot.

"They're going to be fired," Rozaline, an organizer, whispered to me, her face stuck between woe and disgust. She said what everyone already knew. Harriet had a lump in her throat as she walked across the parking lot that afternoon. It was like walking across a blacktop desert and all she could think about was her car payment at the end of the month.

I was worried the whole ordeal would spook the committee members. When we made it back to the safety of the parking lot across the street, everyone was smiling.

"Never, ever, would I have thought they would treat us like that. They were so scared!" Harriet said, shaking her head. Alexis did a little boogie.

Despite her uneventful shift after the delegation on Thursday, when Maya, the guest services representative, arrived at work on Friday she was sent to human resources, where Feinberg gave her the news.

"What's the reason?" she asked.

"Violating company policy," he told her.

"What policy? Can I see it in writing?"

"You know what you did," Feinberg said.

"No, I don't."

"You know what you did."

"Does this have anything to do with the union?"

"I'm not allowed to answer that."

"Whose decision was this?"

"It's an executive decision."
Ten committee members.

Early that evening, Alexis, Alice, and Harriet received phone calls from their supervisors instructing them not to report to work over the weekend. Instead, they were to go straight to human resources Monday morning. About the same time they received their phone calls, Rosalie, the cage cashier who had gone on the first delegation, was finishing up her shift at work. Her manager told her to go to human resources. Before making the trip to the third floor, Rosalie cleaned her locker out. "I didn't want to do the walk of shame," she said later. "I just didn't want the whole casino to see me being escorted out." While she was cleaning her locker out she saw Maya cleaning her own locker. When Rosalie got to the third floor, they told her what she already knew. She asked why she had been fired.

"You know what you did," Feinberg said. Like the other firings, he told her that it was "an executive decision." He said she had violated company rules. He handed her a note with a phone number on it. He said she could call and "appeal" the decision. No one was sure what that meant. How does one appeal an "executive decision" at a privately held company?

Nine committee members.

Monday morning came and Alexis and Harriet met Alex, Reverend Aguilar, and Jeanette, a community activist, in the small parking lot across the street from the casino. Alex had recommended that Reverend Aguilar and Jeanette join Alexis and Harriet for their termination meetings. Reverend Aguilar, in particular, had taken a strong interest in our campaign. He wanted his own meeting with Adkins. Aguilar was soft-spoken, genial, and humble. He always made a point of using people's names when he talked to them: "And how are you today, Colette?" He knew about our personal lives. "How are your kids, Saraphina?" "James, where are you bartending these days, I want to come have a drink." It was no surprise that he was happy to accompany Alexis and Harriet on their walk to the gallows. Alex, having been issued a trespassing warning a few days earlier, waited in his car across the street.

Once inside the casino, Alexis and Harriet approached the receptionist. They were told they needed to be escorted to the human resources office and should wait on the couch in the lobby. As they were waiting, Trotter appeared and told Aguilar and Jeanette they needed to leave the building. Once outside, Trotter told them to wait for the police to issue them trespassing warnings. While they stood waiting, a man in his midfifties with grayish hair approached them. Suddenly, the man was uncomfortably close.

"Who are you representing?" the man shouted.

"I'm a priest with the Episcopal Church," Aguilar said.

"I didn't ask who the fuck you are, I asked who you're representing," the man said, getting angrier. He was inches from Aguilar's face, pointing his finger at the collar around Aguilar's neck.

At that point, Aguilar pointed to the Unite Here button on his lapel. "As you can see right here, we are in support of the union. Who are you?"

"I'm Dan Adkins."

"Oh! We're here to talk to you about the agreement," Aguilar said.

"There's no damn agreement. You're not a priest; you're a con man. You should be ashamed of yourself. You're deceiving these workers, trying to get them to join this union. Go to hell."

Both Adkins and Aguilar would later recall different versions of what happened, but only small details, like exactly how far away Adkins was from Aguilar when he was yelling at him. Aguilar would say that he hadn't felt such aggression since he was a kid growing up in a tough Texas neighborhood thirty-five years ago. Adkins walked away in fury and sat down on a bench outside of the casino. "You're a disgrace, not a man of the cloth."

Aguilar and Jeanette decided against waiting for the police and started walking back across the parking lot. "You need to wait," Trotter said.

They kept walking. As they neared the edge of the property, they noticed a golf cart following them. Aguilar thought he saw Adkins in the cart but he didn't want to look back.

Inside the casino, Alexis was escorted to human resources. Once there she announced that she planned on recording the conversation on her phone. Feinberg told her she couldn't record. She placed her cell phone on the table. "I won't record," she said.

"I don't believe a word you're saying. This meeting is over," Feinberg said.

Eight committee members.

Harriet was next. She also said she wanted to record the conversation. "This meeting is over," Feinberg said.

Seven committee members.

A little while later, Alice showed up for her meeting with human resources. Alice had signed up her entire department, fifteen people. Over the weekend, she had received calls from three supervisors, each of them telling her not to come to work and to report to human resources on Monday.

"It's an executive decision," Feinberg told her, one day after her five-year anniversary at Mardi Gras. He gave her a note with a phone number for her to appeal the decision. She called and was granted a meeting with Dan Adkins. In early December, Alice met Adkins in his office on the third floor. A 2006 *Sun-Sentinel* article described Adkins's office as being filled with porcelain plates commemorating Marilyn Monroe. "Her looks were average," Adkins said of the starlet. "She didn't come from anywhere. She was an average person who took the world by storm. You have to respect that."

Adkins asked Alice why she was there.

"Because I never got a reason why I was fired. A letter, a paper, or anything."

"You came with a group of people and you were being disruptive."

"I was never disruptive."

"You came with a group of people, right?"

"But I wasn't being disruptive."

"That's not the way you come to meet with me."

"I thought we had permission to be in the break rooms, to speak with the workers."

"This meeting is over now," Adkins said.

Six committee members.

On November 21, Adkins sent a letter to all employees reminding them that the mysterious visitors were not from Mardi Gras and that the casino did "not support this activity." Michael, a committee member and saucier in the French Quarter restaurant, received the letter. Other than me, Michael was the only white person on the committee. Colette was the first to tell me about Michael and how enthusiastic he was, not just about the union, but also about the fight for human rights and ending poverty. His Toyota's bumper was adorned with stickers decrying the death penalty, torture, and the war in Iraq. He was one of the most active members in the Amnesty International Miami chapter and regularly attended rallies. When he protested the detention center at Guantánamo Bay he dressed in the orange jumpsuit worn by the base's detainees.

Michael had worked as a cook at a few hotels in the Miami area. Before Mardi Gras he had worked as a cook on Fisher Island, a private residential island off the southern tip of South Beach accessible only by ferry. With a population of about 130 people, Fisher Island has the highest income per capita in America. The island's beaches are covered with sand imported from the Bahamas. Michael had been part of a semisuccessful effort by SEIU to unionize the workers there. While some employees unionized, the cooks did not and Michael was laid off in 2009, "because of the recession," he was told. Michael knew that the recession hadn't depleted Fisher Island's bank accounts enough to necessitate his firing, but he couldn't do anything about it. *On to the next one.*

The Mardi Gras campaign held more promise for Michael. As such, it made Michael furious when, after nine of his fellow committee members had been fired, Adkins held a meeting in the French Quarter and declared that the union couldn't deliver on its promises. There was no agreement between the company and the union, Adkins said. Before leaving, Adkins told the assembled staff that he "loved" his employees.

Michael was friendly, he was devoted to the union, and his view of the big picture was wider than most. Yet, it became clear early on that he didn't have many followers in the French Quarter kitchen. Still, he tried. Two days after he received the second letter warning about "visitors . . . making promises that sound too good to be true," Michael was in the commissary, gathering the food he needed to prep for the day ahead. While he collected his ingredients, he tried to talk to a young porter, Sean, about the union. It was hard for Michael to get Sean to talk. Michael was a middle-aged white guy who was a bit awkward. Sean was a young, shy black guy who stuck to his own crew of friends. Michael had been at Mardi Gras less than a year and the two hadn't worked together very much.

"Some of us are organizing a union. I think we can do better with a union," Michael told him. He asked Sean if they could meet up outside of work to talk.

"I'm busy with school," Sean said. Michael asked for his number. To which Sean said, "My cell phone is off, sorry." That was the end of the conversation.

Michael didn't know that Sean's mother, Tammy, was a security supervisor. Later that day, Jay, the manager who had fired me, sought out Michael in the French Quarter kitchen and escorted him to human resources, where Feinberg was waiting.

"Why?" Michael asked when Feinberg told him that he had been fired.

"You interfered with the work of an employee who told you that he was busy," Feinberg said.

"Who?" Michael asked.

"Sean."

"No, I didn't interfere with him in any way. This is about the union."

"No, it's not," Feinberg said.

"This is illegal. I have the right to engage in legal union activity." On his way out Michael couldn't help himself. "I'll see everyone when we win a union contract and I've been reinstated." It was the day before Thanksgiving 2011.

Five of the original fifteen committee members were left.

Each time Mardi Gras fired a committee member, it created a ghost. Untethered by any corporeal obligation, the ghost passed freely through the vault and the money room, stalked the aisles of slot machines, sat behind the glass of the cashier cages, and roamed aimlessly through the French Quarter's kitchen. In each of these places, the ghost reminded its former coworkers, whose bank accounts still had a pulse, to avoid the union. The company liked the ghost.

Mardi Gras's committee members were the kind of responsible people who *want* to work. For all its trouble, work was more than just a paycheck; it was a daily affirmation of movement in the right direction. For a short time, Local 355 had helped the committee channel these inclinations into something more fulfilling than their jobs: the campaign. But without jobs, there were no coworkers. And without coworkers, there was no campaign. The campaign was dead. They were ghosts.

The anti-union campaign continued. Supervisors hassled the five remaining committee members. There were rumors the company had begun firing people indiscriminately, as if trying to hide the truth under a pile of corpses. (In court, the company would, in fact, point to their record of seventy-five involuntary terminations in 2011 as evidence of how unremarkable our firings were.) One day, Adkins gathered all of the employees and claimed that the union was making false promises, that the employees who had been fired were just a bunch of people trying to cause trouble and tear the business apart. Management said raises were coming. Workers at Mardi Gras talked about the disappeared in hushed tones. After Saraphina was fired there was a rumor that cage cashiers weren't allowed to say her name.

Ten committee members had gone from low-wage to no-wage in less than three weeks. For Thanksgiving, the union collected money and gave grocery store gift certificates worth $100 to eight of the fired committee members. (Colette and I were given $15 gift certificates to Starbucks.) It was more than the company had ever given them for Thanksgiving. Harriet cried when she opened her card. Everyone helped the fired committee members create résumés and fill out unemployment claims. Unemployment didn't amount to much, $150 to $160 a week. Sometimes less. Food stamps helped. Salts and organizers gave the committee members rides to job fairs and interviews. The local established a "heroes fund" to help committee members pay their bills. The rudderless hum of unemployment left hours for idle wonder and panic.

The job search epitomized the divide between the salts and the rest of the committee. For me, unemployment was just a hassle. Before long I was bartending at a dimly lit cocktail bar in downtown Miami. While I wasn't working for some greater purpose than making money, I enjoyed my new job. My dog sat behind the bar and I played my own music. I spent my nights off drinking at that bar, too. It helped that I made more money on a Saturday night than I did in an entire week at Mardi Gras or Calder.

Colette moved back to Connecticut, where she could be with her fiancé. Unite Here hired her to work as a political organizer in New Haven. Michael, the saucier at Mardi Gras, got a seasonal job as a cook at Gulfstream, the union casino down the street from Mardi Gras. Fabiola was hired at Whole Foods on South Beach. Alexis was eventually hired as a mail carrier. I figured the rest of the committee would find work soon. I was wrong.

"I dropped off my application *everywhere*," Harriet told me, her voice hot like an engine after a long day on the road. "I don't know if people weren't hiring, or not hiring people like me, or if I was blackballed or something at the other casinos."

I wondered if some of the committee members resented Local 355. One afternoon I drove Rosalie to a few businesses where she dropped off job applications. She was dressed in heels and her short hair was sharply parted to one side. We went to a job fair at Gulfstream. She came out with a part-time seasonal job for $8.50 an hour without benefits. "Last time I worked for eight fifty was 1990," she said after I congratulated her on the new job. On the car ride home she got a phone call. There was a man on the other end. He was talking loud enough for me to hear his Haitian Creole from the driver's seat. She let him talk a bit and then countered, also in Creole. It sounded like they were talking about the union. We were driving west on one of those big Florida roads lined with strip malls and dirt lots. It was sunset. Bathed in pink, even the most unnatural landscapes inspire awe. After ten minutes, Rosalie hung up. She was angry. Or exercised. I asked if everything was okay.

"He told me, 'You should have never gotten involved with the union. That is why you are fired.'" She was looking at the pink sky. "He thinks he knows, but he doesn't know why I joined. He thinks I didn't know what I was getting into. But I know. I'd do it again. I did the right thing. I have two children, I'm a single mom, and I am scared. I'd be lying if I said otherwise. But I'm not going to have anyone else fight my battles for me."

Part 4

THE TRIAL

◎

T he first few firings had motivated us. We needed to work faster, knock on more doors, and be more mind-ful of our conversations. But by the time Michael, the cook, was fired, the effort had flatlined. The enthusiasm at the beginning of our campaign took a nosedive, taking with it everyone's will to go on house visits. The thermometer on the conference room's wall stopped at ninety-two, below half of the workers eligible to join the union. Mardi Gras had won, Dan Adkins had succeeded, and the casino would not be unionized before the card-check agreement expired at the end of 2011.

The campaign, as we knew it, was over. The new campaign would focus on achieving some measure of justice for the fired committee members while publicizing the ordeal in a way that would make other casinos scared to use the same union-busting tactics at their properties. If Mardi Gras had intended to make examples of the committee, then the union was going to make an example of Mardi Gras.

I'd heard of locals abandoning campaigns after they had been decimated. Local 355 had neutrality agreements at other casinos and hotels that would expire, places that weren't run by Dan Adkins and where the union had more leverage. With only a few thousand members, Local 355 needed to grow fast and digging in for a long, expensive fight with Mardi Gras wasn't necessarily the quickest way to add numbers. But Unite Here's strength, what the union is best known for, is its willingness to fight.

"The strength of the union is based on what we do in fights like this," Wendi said. "As tough as it is to have workers lose their jobs, it is the kind of fight that can send a very, very, very clear message across South Florida—that you don't mess with the union."

First, the local would file charges with the National Labor Relations Board. If the NLRB were to prove that we had been fired because of our union activity, there was a chance that Mardi Gras would be forced to reinstate us. We could go back to work and organize the union. The NLRB is an independent arm of the government set up to enforce the National Labor Relations Act. Unlike other forms of civil law, we, as the charging party, could not file our own suits against the casino. If Colette had been fired for being black, or Rosalie had been fired for being Haitian, or Saraphina had been fired for being a mother, they would have been able to hire their own lawyers to file charges against the casino in addition to any charges the Equal Employment Opportunity Commission might have brought. Not so with charges filed with the NLRB. When someone is fired for exercising his or her right to unionize as provided under the act, the only legal recourse is through the NLRB process.

Alex collected our stories in short unofficial affidavits and submitted them to the board. The board opened an investigation to decide whether or not it would file charges against the casino. All we could do was wait.

After reading our stories, the board decided to collect official affidavits. In January 2012, each of us got a chance to tell our story to a board agent. That afternoon I met Alex at a Starbucks in downtown Miami to prepare. I knew the important parts of my story, the events that had led to my termination and the termination of my coworkers. What I didn't know was whether I needed to tell the board agent that I had been a salt.

"You tell them whatever you want," Alex said. "But I'm just not sure that it matters. How is it relevant?"

We walked across the street to the Claude Pepper Federal Building, named after one of Florida's most famed politicians. In 1947, Senator Claude Pepper led a losing opposition vote against the Taft-Hartley Act, widely considered the most extreme curtailing of union power since the National Labor Relations Act had been passed. "The common man is on the march . . . [The Taft-Hartley Act] shall not endure," Pepper said at the time. The Taft-Hartley Act has very much endured.

The sixteen-story edifice, paneled with large slabs of concrete and thin rectangular windows, was home to the NLRB's Miami branch office as well as a buffet of other federal agencies. The office had a small lobby with a reception desk behind a sliding glass window and chairs arranged against light blue walls. Save for the large American flag and the framed photos of the NLRB's higher-ups, it was exactly like the waiting room of any doctor's office, replete with obscure magazines published for people trying to save battery life on their phones.

Not long after I had arrived a lawyer in her early forties brought me to her office. Her name was Susy Kucera. She was petite with brown hair and glasses. Her office was sparsely decorated. A law diploma from the University of Miami hung on the wall. Kucera sipped water from a canteen and spoke with a professionalism that was nowhere to be found at the casino or the union hall. She explained that she was there as an agent of the government, not as my lawyer. I was to treat her office like a courtroom—I needed to tell the truth.

I didn't tell the truth, or at least not the whole truth. I decided against cluttering my narrative with the salt thing. The casino hadn't known I was a salt when it hired me, while I was working there, or when it fired me. (To fire me because I was a salt would have been illegal.) I didn't want the other committee members to discover that I was a salt. Most of all, I didn't want to give the defense an undeserved foothold. From day one, I'd been told to safeguard my secret from the company, so why stop now? My plan was simple: tell the truth, just not all of it. Sure, I wasn't a labor lawyer, and it wasn't up to me to decide what was relevant and what wasn't, but it was my story. I was going to tell the truth, and the truth was that I'd been fired for having conversations about the union, plain and simple.

Kucera swore me in and asked some basic questions about my employment. Then the questions got tricky. Rather, answering truthfully got tricky.

"When did you first become aware of the union?" Kucera asked.

"I've been aware of the union for a few years." I went on to explain that I'd worked with the union at Calder, which was true.

"How did the union know that you were at Mardi Gras?"

"I guess that the union saw my name was on the list of employees and that is how they got in touch with me." It was true that the company provided a list of employees to the union. I saw it. And it was true that the union saw my name on that list. I watched Alex literally point to it. But there was no way around it. The union knew I was working at Mardi Gras because I was a salt. I hadn't told the whole truth.

Some mistakes take time and distance for you to realize how dumb they were. Lying to a federal agent was not one of those mistakes. I knew instantly how dumb it was. I could have stopped her. "Listen, Susy, I believe it was Nietzsche who said, 'There are no facts, only interpretations . . .'" But I didn't.

Or I could have told her the plain truth, all of it. But I didn't. The interview continued. I told the straight story throughout the rest of my affidavit. But I would lose sleep over that one line, and for good reason.

In early March, after collecting affidavits, the NLRB filed a host of charges against Mardi Gras. The charges included, among other things, interrogating employees, making coercive statements, and firing ten workers because of their protected union activity. After months of uncertainty, we had something to look forward to: a court date in June.

While we waited for our day in court, Wendi considered different tactics the local could use to publicly shame Mardi Gras. If we made Dan Adkins a target of criticism from the community, Hartman & Tyner might try to distance itself from Adkins and install an executive who knew how to work with unions. We launched a social media campaign that barraged @mardigrasboss on Twitter. We created a Facebook page and reached out to bloggers, but we knew that the likelihood of our story going viral was low. What Wendi really wanted was a protest at Mardi Gras's front gates, bigger than anything Local 355 had ever done before. The only way a protest would be worth the time and resources was if people were willing to be arrested. Local 355 had done rallies before, between twenty and one hundred people holding signs and chanting outside hotels and airports, but nothing like the big civil disobediences Unite Here organized in Chicago, San Francisco, and Los Angeles.

Wendi was frank with Local 355's staff; she didn't think the local was ready to put on the kind of civil disobedience that would make an impact in South Florida. It wasn't only that Local 355's membership was small, but her staff was also relatively inexperienced. At the time, Local 355 had ten full-time staff organizers and none of them had been with the local for more than a couple of years. A few had come from other locals around the country and others had experience as political organizers in Haiti before fleeing after the 2004 coup. Wendi's concern about the civil disobedience was that most of the staff hadn't been exposed to a fight like Mardi Gras. Compared with Mardi Gras, campaigns and negotiations at the other casinos and hotels had been easy. Yet, when she posed the possibility of a civil disobedience to the staff, everyone agreed that it was time for a large-scale action. The date was set for May 8.

As May 8 drew near, Local 355 was full of nervous tension. Wendi decided the civil disobedience wouldn't be newsworthy if fewer than twenty people were arrested. A piece of butcher paper at the front of the local's conference room listed the names of people who planned on being arrested. It was short. Wendi, Alex, Colette, James, Michael, Bridget, John. Wendi knew Local 355 organizers couldn't ask workers, members of the community, or Mardi Gras committee members to get arrested if the union organizers themselves weren't being arrested. For me, arrest at a civil disobedience meant a cool story and the chance to use my mug shot as a Facebook profile picture. Arrest, even if it was an act of civil disobedience, was a lot scarier for parents who needed to look after their kids, immigrants who believed arrest meant surrendering some of the freedom they had come to the United States for, or black or brown people with plenty of reasons to be distrustful of law enforcement. Each volunteer would be vetted by a union lawyer to measure the risk. Yet many staff members remained unwilling.

"The only way we're going to make progress is by confronting our fears," Wendi said. "As a local we haven't earned anything we have in Miami. It was earned by New York and Chicago and Boston. We haven't won yet. This is what makes us a fighting union."

Eventually, twenty-seven community activists, workers, and organizers agreed to be arrested. We invited every television station, newspaper, blogger, and independent reporter in South Florida. A marching route was mapped. The details of the protest were given to the Hallandale Beach police department. (The chief was not pleased.) Posters were printed with the slogans "Bring Back the Mardi Gras 10" and "Freedom, Not Fear."

Throughout hurricane season you could sit in the union's office and watch storms gather and float around the county. Such was the weather on May 8. Thunder crashed. Apocalyptic downpours slowed to drizzles, then poured again. Urban flood advisories were issued. Wendi checked the radar. The thick of the storm was set to hit Hallandale Beach at six p.m., just as the rally was scheduled to start.

"You know it's supposed to be perfect and sunny the rest of the week," Wendi said to me as she looked out from the office into the dark middle distance.

Sam, the local's researcher, bought as many ponchos as he could find. Clueless as to how many people would come to the rally, I bought plastic garbage bags, hoping there would be more people than ponchos. Late in the afternoon I headed to the rally's starting point, St. Anne's Church, stopping at the pharmacy to pick up batteries for bullhorns.

Cars arrived first. Two, three, four people. Groups of workers from Orlando. Then buses, chartered by Local 355, came directly from the union shops. Soon, St. Anne's Church, its walls lined and pews packed with people in ponchos, was overflowing. After a few speeches, Harriet, the slot attendant, took to the podium. She was in a giant blue poncho and her glasses rested on her nose. I knew Harriet a little more than the other committee members. She'd taken to me—and my dog. She was born in Harlem, grew up on Long Island, and settled in New Jersey. Surgery for cancer had left her unable to shovel snow back in New Jersey, so she took an opportunity to move to Florida with her boyfriend. He was locked up after he started beating her. Standing at the podium, Harriet wasn't a slot attendant, a victim of domestic violence, or a committee member. She was a poet.

"Hello," she began, "my name is Harriet Oliver. I am a product of slave sharecroppers, revolutionaries, visionaries, and I was told that this is the place to be.

"I worked at Mardi Gras Casino for five years and I was told that this was the place to be. They took two dollars away from me, gave me fifteen cents back, and told me that this was the place to be.

"I worked my hands to the bone, my feet 'til they were raw, my mind and body 'til they were both limp, and I was still told that this was the place to be.

"I lined your pockets with silver and gold, housed you, fed you, provided for your wife and your children, and I was told that this was the place to be.

"You turned your back. I kissed your ass. You slapped my face. You fired me. And I was still told that this was the place to be.

"I will not cry. I will not hide. Hand in hand, arm in arm, we will stand tall and fight you all. And we will win. And then, this will be *the place to be*."

The church erupted.

Reverend Aguilar spoke. "We have a message for Dan Adkins tonight: let my people go! Tonight we say this to all the pharaohs of South Florida . . . choose freedom, not fear! Amen, and God bless you!"

The crowd filed out of the church and onto the street, and as if at the signal of a Hollywood director, the rain stopped, leaving a cinematic shine on the pavement. We marched a mile, a long jubilant parade of service workers. There were close to three hundred protesters, a pittance compared to similar rallies in other cities but more than anyone could remember in South Florida. People were clad in Unite Here red holding "Freedom, Not Fear" pickets. Wendi and the other organizers wore the biggest smiles. They had been working toward this moment years before the Mardi Gras campaign had even started. Mardi Gras was a symbol of all service workers' frustrations in South Florida. Somewhere in the crowd a protester was holding a poster with my face on it, and there were nine other posters for the other fired committee members. *Vuvuzelas* blasted. Housekeepers, fresh off their shifts in Miami Beach hotels, chanted in their work uniforms. There were community members, college activists, and even a few people from SEIU, Unite Here's service union nemesis, wearing their signature purple T-shirts. Marchers chanted call-and-response classics: "Show me what democracy looks like!" *"This is what democracy looks like!"* And a clunky new one: "Bring! Back!" *"The Mardi Gras Ten!"* "Bring! Back!" *"The Mardi Gras Ten!"* There were clouds overhead but to the west the sky was pink and gold. Wendi, in a red dress and heels, was jumping up and down as she led the crowd: "What do we want?" *"Justice!"* "When do we want it?" *"Now!"*

When we arrived at the entrance to the casino, the group split in half and lined both sides of the road. Mardi Gras's entrance was a short road that emptied into a large parking lot where most of the Hallandale Beach police force stood on guard. The twenty-seven of us who planned on getting arrested walked to the middle of the road, placed plastic bags on the ground in a futile attempt to keep our butts dry, and sat down. The crowd cheered and, beneath Mardi Gras's giant billboard advertising car giveaways, began singing the anthem of the civil rights movement, "We Shall Overcome."

"I don't think they're going to arrest you there," Andy, the treasurer of Local 355, said. Andy had been a prison guard and NYPD officer in New York and had a tough, lunch-pail comportment. He had been enlisted to communicate with the police. "I asked him what we needed to do to get arrested," Andy said, looking at one of the officers. "He nodded toward the casino."

We stood up and marched closer to the casino. Fifty yards later we were standing directly in front of the chief of the Hallandale Beach police department. Dick Trotter, the head of Mardi Gras's security, stood nearby with a few other Mardi Gras employees. All of them had their arms crossed like awkward husbands at their spouses' office party. Thirty yards behind them, twenty police officers in riot gear waited in the parking lot. A caravan of police vehicles, including a black armored truck, surrounded them. The officers stood in front of a purple mural of maniacal laughing jesters. The western sky was still pink and purple and the parking lot's spotlights reflected off the puddles around us.

The show of force seemed a bit excessive as the protesters looked more like the picnic type than the riot type. In fact, union members took pictures of menacing-looking men in the crowd because they so obviously looked like undercover members of Mardi Gras security or the Hallandale police force, Pinkertons peppering the union.

The chief hushed the crowd with his hands because he didn't have a bullhorn. Strangely, the crowd acquiesced; the singing stopped.

"You're on Mardi Gras's property, so someone from the casino will address you and ask you to leave. If you refuse, you will be arrested."

Standing next to the chief, Trotter spoke to the crowd. He was wearing a maroon button-down shirt and black dress pants. "At this time we are asking you to leave the property. If you refuse, the Hallandale Beach police department will arrest you for trespassing. Are you willing to leave the—"

We sat down before he could finish. The crowd resumed

singing. A few protesters started their own chants. *Hell no, we won't go!* As encouraging as the chants were, Wendi had been right; it was the people sitting around me who were making the most powerful statement. There were workers from the airport, a buffet server from the Isle Casino wearing his apron, a cook from the Westin Diplomat hotel wearing his full white uniform. There were workers from Disney World who had driven down from Orlando, prepared to spend the night in a Fort Lauderdale jail. There was a student from the University of Miami, community activists dressed in their Sunday bests, and two Episcopal priests kneeling in their heavenly white vestments. I had wanted to wear my sparkly orange vest but the union lawyer had advised against it because legally it was still the company's property. I wore a shirt and tie instead.

The Isle buffet server was the first to be arrested. The crowd went wild. "*Bring. Back. The Mardi Gras Ten!*" Camera flashes popped. "*Bring. Back. The Mardi Gras Ten!*" Up until that moment, I hadn't thought much about what it would be like to get arrested. I had prepared, leaving my phone and wallet in my car and stowing my license in my pocket. But I hadn't considered what might happen if a surly cop thought he heard me talk back, or if I got separated from the group, or if they forgot about me in a cell. Those were the kinds of news stories that came out of Florida, right?

"*Bring. Back. The Mardi Gras Ten!*"

Wendi turned to me. "I don't think you should do this," she said.

"What?"

"I don't think you should get arrested because of the case." She saw the confusion and disappointment flooding my face.

"*Bring. Back. The Mardi Gras Ten!*"

"I know. It would have been fine to get arrested over there where we were just blocking the road, but here, on the property, it will be trespassing, and that might jeopardize your chances of going back to work. It's completely your decision. I just don't think it's a good idea."

I needed to make a quick decision. I hadn't expected the civil disobedience to rouse such energy in me. Participating in it was my chance to be a part of a long tradition. I wasn't in a classroom looking at black and white photos of civil rights protesters. The colors and sounds were as real as the adrenaline charging through my body. I wasn't surrounded by a homogeneous lump of college students intoxicated by the romance of activism. I was sitting next to workers and community members. And yet, the chance to participate in the trial was more important. I wanted the system to work. Colette, Michael, and I—the committee members who had planned on participating in the civil disobedience—stepped away from the group. "*Bring. Back. The Mardi Gras Ten!*"

Twenty-four people were arrested and spent a long night in a Fort Lauderdale jail.

There would be two trials over a two-week period in June. The first, called a 10(j), would determine whether or not our terminations had iced the unionization campaign. If the judge ruled that the firings influenced the campaign, the company would be forced to temporarily reinstate us while the second, more important, trial would decide if the company had fired us because of our union affiliation.

As the 10(j) approached, the fact that I'd withheld information from Kucera nagged at my conscience. I felt guilty for lying to her, but I also worried that my omission might hurt the case. I couldn't keep my secret under the floorboards any longer. I met Kucera in her drab office a week before the 10(j) court date. She was preparing each of us for the witness stand. Before we started I closed her office door.

"I've known about the union a long time," I said. "I got hired at Mardi Gras with the intention of organizing it."

"So, you're talking about salting?"

"Exactly." I listened for the footsteps of federal agents coming to arrest me for perjury.

But Kucera didn't react. "That's not a problem. Salting is legal. What do you even think salting means?" I wasn't sure what she meant by the question. I explained that I had tried to identify leaders.

"You haven't done anything wrong," Kucera said. "Again, salting is perfectly legal." I was surprised by how easily she dismissed my fear. I was relieved. But two days later, less than a week before the 10(j) trial, Kucera called me. She was angry.

"James, you weren't truthful in your affidavit. How could you have lied to me? Did the union tell you to lie?" It was as if our last conversation hadn't happened. My confession hadn't conveyed the message I was trying to deliver—that I had lied in my affidavit. I apologized. I apologized, again. I told her that lying had been my decision; Alex hadn't pressured me. I told her that I had tried to stick to the truth but I knew there was one line in the affidavit that wasn't true. And wasn't salting irrelevant? I explained that I had been conditioned never to talk about salting.

"Even under oath? With the penalty of perjury? And omission can be a violation of that oath so it's not just that one line." There was silence. She was distraught. "The company has filed their evidence. They know you're a salt," she said.

"How? What have they said?"

I could hear her shuffling papers. "Something about college and grad school. It doesn't really matter. James, they are going to crush you as a witness."

On the phone with Colette, Kucera was caustic. She said that she didn't trust Colette, Alex, or me. She referred to salting as a "conspiracy." While I was paralyzed by remorse and self-indignation, Colette and Alex were coolheaded and chalked it up to Kucera's pretrial jitters.

"She told me this is her first 10(j) and she really wants to win," Colette said.

"The NLRB is just scared and is really sketched out by the whole salting thing," Alex said.

Later that weekend, days before the 10(j), Kucera called again to tell me that the NLRB had decided against including Colette and me in the 10(j). "I've been repeatedly misled and compromised as a government agent. The union did not respect the process and I can't take these risks when your credibility is in question." Another wave of disappointment knocked me over. First, I had missed out on the civil disobedience; now I was missing out on my first chance in court. Colette and I weren't the only ones left out of the 10(j). The board decided that Saraphina's and Fabiola's disciplinary records at Mardi Gras complicated their 10(j) argument too much. The NLRB would argue that the firing of six committee members had iced the union campaign.

"That's the difference," Alex said. "This is why we don't want it to come to this, because the NLRB are not on our side. They aren't labor lawyers." I remembered my first conversation with Alex at Jimmy's Diner. He wanted to make sure I didn't get my throat slit. The lawyers at the NLRB were duty-bound to enforce the act; they weren't representing workers. When I'd shown Local 355's lawyer—a man who once described NLRB lawyers as "good people who are stuck enforcing bad laws"—the omission in my affidavit, he shrugged it off.

"So? Who gives a shit? You were fired because of union activity, which is illegal."

The 10(j) was argued in front of United States District Judge William Zloch. A former Notre Dame starting quarterback and Vietnam veteran, Zloch was a Reagan appointee known for his short temper. The first item before Judge Zloch was Kucera's request to remove Colette and me from the case because of "late developments." Robert Norton, a partner at one of South Florida's top company-side labor law firms, represented Mardi Gras. (Norton's wife, and fellow partner at the firm, represented Calder when the horse track was trying to get out of its neutrality agreement.) Norton jumped at the chance to use the "late developments" to characterize the union as nefarious.

"We believe [the removal] relates to the fact that some of these alleged terminations were from salt—Yale graduates, Columbia graduates—that were put in there as a fix and an attempt to manipulate this court. And, I don't know, but when I read Mr. Walsh's affidavit in my office I got a red pen out and wrote 'salt' across it because it was so obviously connived, and manipulating, and insincere, disingenuous."

Norton went on to claim that Alex, Colette, and I had "assault[ed] these employees in their homes in the night . . . they took the behavior designed to get those employees terminated. . . it is all orchestrated."

Zloch didn't seem to react to Norton's assertions and he agreed to remove Colette and me from the case. After hearing both sides' arguments and testimony from nine witnesses (six fired committee members, Reverend Aguilar, Alex, and Adkins), Zloch ruled against the NLRB, saying that for every piece of evidence supporting the assertion that the firings had a "chilling" effect, there was evidence that suggested the campaign had been dead before committee members were fired. I was astonished. How could anyone reasonably conclude that the committee members' terminations hadn't influenced the unionization campaign? After I read the transcripts, I understood how Zloch came to his conclusion. The four committee members who had been removed from the case—Colette, Saraphina, Fabiola, and me—were the first four people to be fired. By the time we went on the delegations, and six other committee members were fired, the campaign had already chilled. Thus, to Zloch, these firings had been inconsequential to the overall campaign.

Neither Alex nor Kucera seemed surprised by the 10(j) ruling—judges rarely rule in favor of putting employees back to work temporarily. Rather than dwell on the 10(j), they focused on the second, more important, trial that would determine whether Mardi Gras had committed any unfair labor practices during our campaign. Colette, Saraphina, Fabiola, and I would be included in this case.

Language in the National Labor Relations Act is famously imprecise, leaving plenty of room for interpretation. Most of the NLRB's complaints against Mardi Gras concerned section 8(a)(3), which makes it illegal for an employer to discriminate "in regard to hire or tenure of employment or any term or condition of employment to encourage or discourage membership in any labor organization." In 1961, Supreme Court justice Felix Frankfurter said such arguments relied on the "drawing of lines more nice than obvious." In other words, there's wiggle room.

The second trial, a week after the 10(j) trial, was held in an NLRB courtroom attached to the board's offices in downtown Miami. We met in the waiting room Monday morning. The day's gravity fully set in when I saw Alex, never one to dress up, wearing a shiny gold tie. Committee members were still arriving when I got there. Colette had flown down from New Haven. I heard Saraphina in the hallway before she entered the lobby.

"I'm so happy," Saraphina said, smiling as she opened the door. "Today's the day!" She had a new hairdo, poufy curls, and wore a colorful pastel-striped shirt. She took a seat in one of the chairs. "That man is the devil," she continued. "I'm for real, he's a very bad man."

"Who?" I asked.

"Mr. Adkins! He's in the hallway."

I wanted to see for myself. It had been about nine months since I'd last seen Adkins in the flesh, standing at the bar interrogating Lena. I walked out of the waiting room and there he was, dressed in a tame business suit, leaning against the wall. My pulse spiked.

"Hi," Norton, the lawyer, said cheerily as I walked past them toward the bathroom.

"How's it going?" I said without making eye contact.

Alex and Adkins were the only witnesses allowed to sit in on the entire proceedings. The rest of us were sequestered in a small conference room. Time passed slowly. People talked at first, in English and Creole, but by lunch everyone had retreated into their phones and magazines. After lunch, there was more waiting.

Meanwhile, unbeknownst to us, Adkins was the first witness to testify. One of Kucera's first questions was whether Mardi Gras Casino was located in Hallandale Beach.

"It's actually a racetrack," Adkins responded. "And yes, it's located in Hallandale Beach."

Historically, the NLRB hasn't had jurisdiction over dog and horse tracks and Adkins and his lawyers were laying the groundwork to argue that Mardi Gras was more dog track than casino. Thus, it was up to Kucera to prove that a business legally registered under the name Mardi Gras Casino was, in fact, a casino. She was prepared.

"Would you agree with me you make way more money off the casino operation than the pari-mutuel operations?" she asked.

"Absolutely not. I would not agree with that at all."

Adkins explained that the slot machines have a much higher operating cost.

"So you're telling me you make more money off the pari-mutuel activity than the casino operation?"

"We actually look at our operation as a whole."

"All right, but that's not my question."

"If I were just now, if nobody in this market area had slot machines or casinos, because it's a very competitive market, if we strictly had pari-mutuels, I would make more money than I do . . . off that money than I do on slots."

"But I'm looking at the hearing now. What's going on right now?"

"Well, you asked me. Look, Palm Beach Dog Track up in Palm Beach County—"

"Well, I'm not asking about that operation. I'm asking about your operation. Are you telling me you make more money off of the pari-mutuel activity than the slot machines and the casino outfit?"

"When you look at the operations as a whole, okay—"

"Okay, but you have numbers."

This squirrelly runaround went on for some time. Adkins kept making room for himself by saying, "It's a very complicated matter." The back-and-forth must have been agonizing for Kucera because Adkins had been publicly pushing Florida's legislature to authorize "de-coupling," a measure that would have allowed Mardi Gras to get rid of its dog track and continue to operate its slot machines. In February 2011, Adkins told a reporter from CBS that the dog track was losing $2.5 million a year. "I've been in the business my entire life," he said. "And it's dead." When Kucera asked him about the quote he ducked and dodged. Kucera failed to ask him about what he told a reporter from the *Sun-Sentinel* five months before the NLRB trial. Adkins had lamented the fact that the state required him to keep the dog track open: "For me to be forced to operate something that's a loss to me doesn't seem fair." In 2014, Adkins went so far as to coauthor an op-ed with the president of the Humane Society—an organization he had been at odds with previously—in which he argued that the lack of revenue from greyhound racing was jeopardizing the safety of the dogs. The industry in Florida was "on life support." Yet, when Kucera asked Adkins about the dog track in court, he said, "In the past year or so we've seen a resurgence in pari-mutuel wagering."

When asked why Mardi Gras hadn't provided documents that could furnish numbers on slot profits and dog profits, Adkins blamed Kucera and the NLRB for not being specific enough in its subpoena.

Back in the conference room, by late afternoon only Patricia, a Haitian dishwasher who was still employed at Mardi Gras, had been called as a witness. The board had dismissed everyone but Colette, Saraphina, and me. Saraphina was called as the last witness of the day.

The next day, Tuesday, I showed up at nine a.m. At nine twenty, I was told to go home and come back on Wednesday. Rosalie, Michael, Fabiola, Harriet, Alexis, Maya, and Alice all testified on Tuesday but the sequester forbade the witnesses from talking to each other about their testimonies. I had no idea how the case was unfolding.

On Wednesday morning, I sat alone in the waiting room. While waiting, I heard someone, who sounded a lot like Norton, talking through a door that connected the waiting room to some other room. "Now this fucker's over here," the man said. I think he was describing surveillance footage from the delegation and Alex seemed to be the "fucker." Or was I the fucker? A few minutes later, someone from the NLRB opened the door and peeked his head in.

"Mr. Walsh?" he called, like a nurse summoning a patient.

The judge was taking care of some housekeeping when I entered. I slipped into one of two rows of benches directly behind Alex, Kucera, and another NLRB lawyer. The courtroom was miniature, about the size of a classroom, and lacked the pomp television had conditioned me to expect. There were no finely detailed mahogany banisters or brass sconces. With standard office furniture and fluorescent lights in the ceiling panels, the courtroom was built for business, not entertainment. Adkins sat across from me on the defense's side. In front of him were Norton and his co-counsel, Peter Sampo. What felt like an extraordinary morning for me, one that made puddles in my palms, was another day at the office for everyone else in the room.

"General counsel calls James Walsh," Kucera said. Walking up to the witness booth felt just as surreal as walking to human resources with Sally, the food and beverage director, the day I was fired. I was bouncing along the ocean floor.

"Okay. Mr. Walsh, come around, please. Raise your right hand," Judge George Carson said. Carson had once been an attorney for the NLRB. The trace of a Southern drawl in Carson's voice added Grisham gravitas to the proceeding and made up for his not wearing a robe. Carson swore me in and Kucera asked basic questions: name, occupation, bosses' names, details of the job, termination date. Before the trial Kucera had told me to come clean to the judge. I had to confess that I had lied under oath. "Once you make that clear, they don't really have anything and testimony on the stand means more than the testimony given in your affidavit."

"Why did you contact [the union]?" Kucera asked.

"Because I wanted to volunteer and salt for them."

Sensing something was up, Judge Carson interjected. "Counsel?"

"This is showing the genesis of how he began organizing activities at Mardi Gras. It's not going to take too long, Your Honor."

"But the question—"

"And [the defense is] going to bring it up too, so . . ."

"—is whether he was discharged for union activity . . . I think you're giving the [defense] meat to chew on that is not necessary." Carson, more than anyone, seemed to understand that salting was irrelevant to the case.

Eventually, Kucera got to my involvement in the campaign.

With Adkins sitting ten feet away, I told the story of his visit to my bar to question Lena. I told the judge about Colette's firing, how scared Dante had been when we visited him, how Vanessa had decided not to join the union, and how I had been fired. I felt like I was testifying at my own murderer's trial. Kucera gave me a chance to talk myself up as a bartender: how much Frank liked me before he knew that I was pro-union, how I'd never been reprimanded, how I was given some good shifts, and how a casino host had once told me that he had sung my praises to Sally. Then Kucera was done. It was time for cross.

During the case, Peter Sampo questioned all of the Labor Relations Board's witnesses except three. Robert Norton questioned Alex, Colette, and me. Norton had salt-and-pepper hair and a finely groomed goatee to match. He was tall and relatively fit for a man in his sixties. As much as Kucera had prepared me, I knew Norton was an experienced labor lawyer and I was on his turf.

"Mr. Walsh, you made reference several times in your direct testimony to an individual named Nwachukwu, am I saying that correctly?" (The pronunciation of Colette's last name was a topic visited and revisited throughout the trial. To avoid the ignominy—or trouble—people often referred to her as Ms. Colette.)

"That's right," I said.

"And she was a salt hired on the same day as you, September 6?"

"That sounds about right, yes."

"And did you have a personal relationship with her?"

"Prior to being hired?"

"No, period."

"Oh, yes."

"Have you had a personal relationship? Were you dating each other?"

"Dating, no."

"Just friends?"

"Just friends, yeah." Of all the questions I expected Norton to ask, juicy details about my relationship with Colette hadn't been one. Wasn't this the sort of irrelevant question that Kucera was supposed to object to? Was he trying to throw me off? Maybe he was clueless. Or maybe he just wanted me to think he was clueless?

Norton asked if I knew Colette had been late clocking in eight times or that once she hadn't shown up for work. A scheduling error, I assumed. Norton asked me about my education and why I hadn't included graduate school on my job application.

"And when you were terminated and you came to the NLRB in January, you gave a fairly lengthy affidavit to the National Labor Relations Board, did you not?"

"I did."

"And in that affidavit that statement was taken by Ms. Kucera, who's sitting here in the room, correct?"

"That's right."

"And did you share with her that you were a salt?"

"No, not at the time."

"So your statement was taken by her without her, to your knowledge, having knowledge that you were, in fact, a salt?"

"Yes."

"As a salt, do you consider it one of the strategies to go in and try to bait managers into making statements that might be inappropriate? You wouldn't do anything like that?"

"No."

"And to be very cognizant in the workplace, ever aware of anybody in management making any kind of what you deem is inappropriate statements?"

"That's sort of secondary to organizing the workers. We focus on the workers. If a manager says something, we always document it, yes."

Norton began asking me questions about where I lived. Unwilling to sign a yearlong lease in Miami, I had bounced around over the past seven months. The only address Norton had was my parents' mailing address in Connecticut. This frustrated him because "the company was desperately trying to serve" me during the 10(j) hearing. In fact, I had been waiting for a subpoena. I had even told the bosses of the bar I was working at to look out for one. I wasn't hiding. But Norton was trying to implicate the union and the Labor Relations Board as conspirators who had tried to keep me from taking the stand at the 10(j). To that, Kucera objected.

"Well, that's neither here nor there," the judge said. "As I say, this isn't going to help me decide the case."

"We would hope it would, Your Honor," Norton said. "Because this whole thing is about quite a bit of a conspiracy and quite a bit of misrepresentations made and—"

"I'm hearing that all along, but . . ."

Kucera defended the Labor Relations Board against Norton's implication that she was part of a conspiracy. I sat and waited. ("Conspiracy" is a buzzword in labor cases. In 1806, in one of the earliest courtroom conflicts between striking workers and their employer, unionized boot makers were accused of having "conspired" to "raise their wages." The charges were based on English common law, which considered organizing efforts to raise wages or reduce working hours an act of criminal conspiracy. Eight boot makers were found guilty.)

Norton finally went for my jugular. He pointed out the inconsistencies in my affidavit. Specifically, he referred to the line about the union seeing my name on a list while I was at Mardi Gras.

"That was a bit insincere, was it not, since you had been previously trained in that regard when you were a salt at Calder?"

"Yes."

"I mean, was it a strategy of the union not to let the National Labor Relations Board know you were a salt?"

"No, that was my own mistake."

"Alex didn't tell you—"

Judge Carson interrupted Norton. "Did you not hear the answer?"

"He said, 'It was my own mistake,' " Norton said.

"There, right," the judge said. I was surprised by how forcefully the judge put a stop to Norton's line of questioning. Norton had employed the same argument during Alex's testimony to get him to admit he hadn't shared the fact that Colette and I were salts. But Alex had no qualms about his omissions and Judge Carson didn't seem to care, either.

"You are aware, of course, that salts are protected by the act?" the judge asked Norton.

"Of course, of course," Norton responded.

"Good."

"I'm also aware that candor is something that a judge should take into account when he's judging credibility."

"I understand."

"But yes, I'm very familiar with it."

"Fine."

"I think it's a tool that's utilized very successfully by Unite," Norton added.

My testimony went exactly as Kucera had said it would. Once I confessed, Norton didn't have much to go on. The rest of his questions were about my interactions with other employees. He tried to imply that I might have neglected my bartending duties or interfered with my coworkers' jobs. Kucera clarified that on redirect. She asked me to describe how many people I worked with throughout my shift. I listed all of the employees a bartender might come in contact with.

"Now, during a regular workday, would you hear those employees speaking about things other than work?"

"Absolutely, yes."

"What kind of subjects?"

"Family, sports, love, everything, everything."

"And did you speak to your coworkers about non- . . . other

than organizing activities, did you speak to them about other subjects?"

"Yes."

"What kind of subjects?"

"Family, sports, love, everything."

"Were there ever supervisors in the area watching these conversations?"

"Sure."

"And did you ever speak with them about non-work-related subjects?"

"Yes."

"What kind of subjects?"

I resisted the urge to repeat "family, sports, and love." "The same subjects."

"Were you ever aware of any rule prohibiting you from speaking about family, sports, the weather . . . ?"

"No."

With that, my time on the stand was over. It had lasted about an hour. The experience left me wanting; I hadn't been given a chance to characterize how emotionally invested I was in the campaign. But, as in the workplace, it was best to leave emotion at home.

Later that day, Jay, the food and beverage manager who fired me, testified. Jay said that I was terminated because I had "harassed" two employees while they were trying to work. Jay claimed that Elisa, the cocktail waitress who worked alongside Lena, and Tina, the young concession attendant, had made the complaints.

"I have two different employees who came to me and complained that Steve [he meant James]—one of them was really upset that he asked her . . . the same thing, asked her for her cell number, he asked her for her address to meet with her and, you know. And the other employee, she app—he approached another employee as well, but she said she told him . . . he asked a couple of questions about how does she like working for Mardi Gras, and she just told him she was happy and she asked him to leave her alone. But Ms. Tina Rich, she was absolutely bothered by it. And my job as an assistant director, any time any employee approaches me with any problem, is to report it to HR. And I do not sweep anything under the carpet. I have to represent any issue that is brought to me."

"And would you characterize their demeanor as being upset with their interaction with Mr. Walsh?" Sampo asked Jay.

"Yes, sir, they were."

"Okay. And what did you do with that information?"

"I took their statement and passed it on to HR and my director and from there we took action."

"And what action was taken?"

"It was determined he has been . . . to be terminated for his action, for . . . he has been working for the company less than ninety days and his behavior was not acceptable."

If I had been guilty of insincerity in my affidavit, Jay was guilty of making stuff up. Tina, the concession attendant, had freely given me her number the first time I'd asked for it. The story about Elisa baffled me because she had quit before the campaign was fully underway. I couldn't remember asking for her phone number. I was especially careful around women my age. I only would have asked Tina and Elisa personal questions if I'd thought they were comfortable enough to know that I wasn't being a creep. Creeps make bad organizers. I don't know if Jay canvassed the food and beverage department, asking employees if there had been anything strange about me, but if Tina and Elisa had given statements about my alleged inappropriate behavior, I wondered why the statements weren't submitted as evidence.

Kucera killed Jay's story. "Did you ask Mr. Walsh about their complaints?" she asked.

"Did I ask him? I did not ask him, no," Jay said.

"Did you conduct any kind of investigation other than these two ladies complaining to you about that?"

"With James, no."

"And who did you report that exactly, those two complaints, to?"

"To my director and to the human resource director, Steve Feinberg."

"So would it have been the same protocol in your experience to have asked Mr. Walsh to write his side of the story, give him that opportunity before he was fired?"

"He was in his probationary period, and I don't have to."

I wondered why Kucera couldn't subpoena the company's e-mails. Surely communications between Jay, Feinberg, Sally, and Adkins would have given the judge a better sense of what had happened on the third floor. But hearings before the National Labor Relations Board aren't subject to the same rules of discovery that other cases are. Instead, they are almost entirely based on witness testimony, publicly available documents, and whatever the company chooses to provide. It was our word against theirs. My word against Jay's.

Save for those employees fired as a result of their participation in the delegation, Mardi Gras's lawyers needed to justify specific instances of wrongdoing for four other committee members.

Saraphina and Fabiola
Demonstrating gross misconduct.

The company cited both Saraphina's and Fabiola's rap sheets as the reasons for their terminations. Saraphina's temper had earned her plenty of write-ups over five years at Mardi Gras and ultimately, the defense argued, it was what got her fired on November 7, when she refused to carry out a transaction for a petulant customer, claiming that his request was against the rules. The interaction was the sort of five-minute night-mare that everyone in the service industry goes through from time to time, but while some people suck up their pride and acquiesce through gritted teeth, Saraphina had a more con-frontational style. For the defense, that style was gold. Sampo pelted Saraphina, asking her to explain thirteen different write-ups, which included failure to clear hands (the hand gesture that proved tellers weren't stealing), talking back to managers, chewing gum in the cage, playing with another cashier's hair on duty, tardiness, and variances in her bank. There were jus-tifications for some of Saraphina's violations—who isn't going to have write-ups over a five-year period?—but she would have dug herself in a hole if she had tried to justify each individual write-up. If Saraphina was embarrassed, it didn't show in the transcript. She responded to a few of Sampo's questions but for most she claimed she didn't remember the write-ups.

Fabiola was about my age. She was tall, graceful, and beau-tiful. She had been working in housekeeping for four years before she was fired and was responsible for getting fifteen people, nearly half of her department, to sign union cards.

Fabiola testified on the second day. Her English wasn't bad but an interpreter helped when she had trouble. In her tes-timony, Fabiola gave a different reason for her termination than the reason her supervisors cited in their testimonies. At her dismissal, Fabiola was told that she'd been seen taking a break ten minutes early. Her supervisors testified that Fabiola was fired for insubordination. She had been summoned to her direct supervisor's office for a meeting but never showed up. Fabiola had been written up for insubordination before. Similar to Saraphina's testimony, Sampo listed four previous write-ups in Fabiola's file. She flat-out denied each one. Fa-biola's manager described her as "a handful" and "hard to manage." She was a troublemaker, which was what made her such a good committee member.

Colette
Failure to pass probationary period.

Colette testified shortly after me. Just as Sally and Jay had at her termination, Norton aimed to prove that Colette had been fired for her attendance record and for "loitering" on her shift. Since firing Colette, the company had taken the time to review its security footage. She had spent a total of twenty-one minutes in the poker kitchen, nine minutes less than the thirty-minute break cocktail waitresses were allowed. As she had every other break she took, Colette had told another cocktail waitress as she would be the one responsible for covering Colette's section of the floor. Colette hadn't told Tim, the only manager on duty that night, that she was taking a break, which, as Mardi Gras pointed out, made it an unauthorized break. But also visible on the security footage was Tim mingling with Colette throughout her break.

Norton invoked Colette's "horrendous attendance at Calder"—which Calder must have provided—and claimed that she would have been fired from Calder after one more tardy, which was news to Colette. Like they had done with Saraphina and Fabiola, the defense belabored the details of Colette's attendance record, claiming she had been late eight times in her short employment. Colette admitted she had been tardy two or three times, but she knew the real reason she had been fired and she countered with logic and precision.

"Yeah. Well, we have a system, right," Colette explained to Norton. "So if you are absent or late a certain number of times, there's a procedure. They call it progressive discipline. I never even had the first incident of progressive discipline, which is if you've been late three times you get a first write-up.

Another two times, you get a second write-up. So I never had been disciplined even for the first step of that."

"You know the company doesn't apply that for people in their probationary period, ma'am," Norton said. "Do you know that too when you're reading the rules?"

Of course, Norton brought up Colette's big omission—the fact that she left Yale off her résumé. Also, Colette hadn't mentioned to Kucera the fact that she'd gone to college. While I'd gone through similar questions, with Colette, Norton seemed to take it a step further.

"You didn't think it was a bit disingenuous to portray yourself as a four-dollars-and-twenty-three-cents-an-hour-plus-tip cocktail waitress?"

Norton didn't know how often Colette had asked herself that very question. Were three years of her life nothing but a portrayal? The implication was that economic class was immovable, and Colette had been playing dress-up; her corset and overnight shifts were just parts of a low-wage costume. Yale graduates and cocktail waitresses, never the twain shall meet. Colette had a different understanding of her employment.

"That is, in fact, exactly what I was," she told Norton.

Michael
```
Disrupting the workplace by interfering
with another employee's ability to work.
```

Michael's testimony was short compared with the other committee members, mostly because the facts surrounding his firing were so inarguably preposterous. Sampo's line of questioning sought to portray Michael as a madman for thinking that he had the right to talk to Sean, the young porter Michael had approached about the union.

"What did Sean ever do or say to you that made you think he might be interested in the union?" Sampo asked. Michael didn't take the bait. Sampo went on to imply that mentioning the union was inappropriate because it was a "hot-button topic."

"What do you mean by 'hot button,' sir?" Michael asked.

"Well, certain controversial issues, maybe animal rights in the context of the racetrack or religious issues . . . Well, you know, there are certain topics that if you bring up with certain people are likely to evoke some kind of a reaction with that person?"

"Well, I think that is true . . . about speaking about the union because people are very afraid to speak about the union because they know the management doesn't want them."

"And you know . . . you knew when you first interacted with Sean and he turned down your request to meet outside of work, that he probably did not consider this to be an appropriate conversation topic in the workplace?"

Kucera objected. Judge Carson sustained.

"Let me ask you this," Sampo continued. "Did you not consider it to be discourteous to continue asking Sean to facilitate a conversation with you about the union when he already told you he wasn't interested?"

"He didn't tell me he wasn't interested. He said that he had school. And I asked one further question, and I certainly didn't feel that to be discourteous."

"That was perfectly okay with you?"

"I did not feel it to be discourteous."

Jay's testimony about Sean's reaction to the incident sounded a lot like his testimony about Tina and Elisa's reaction to my harassment. Jay said that Sean had come to his office "upset" and "bothered" by his conversation with Michael. Sampo asked Jay why such an offense would constitute termination.

"Well, he was out of line. Apparently, my other coworker was upset by his approach. And Mr. Michael, his record during the year he worked for us, he . . . you know, he had several bad incidents that he should have been fired prior to that."

"Explain exactly what you're talking about?"

"What has happened, he was caught double dipping a couple of times . . . He should have been fired right away," Jay said.

Sampo didn't ask Michael about his double dipping during the case. (He did during the 10[j].) But Kucera grilled Jay about Michael's double dipping infractions. In fact, finding more mentions of double dipping in a court transcript would be impossible. Michael wasn't ashamed of the fact that he'd been written up for double dipping. "I was tasting something at a boil. I'm the saucier, it happens. Bacteria kills at one hundred forty and these things are at two hundred twelve," he told me after the case.

Rosalie, Harriet, Alexis, Maya, Alice
Disrupting the workplace, violating
company work rules.

More testimony was given about the efforts to get a meeting with Adkins than any other event. When he questioned the committee members about the delegations, Sampo used words like "descend" and "invade" to describe the manner with which we had walked through the casino doors. I liked to picture such an invasion, Rosalie swinging a mace to lop off the head of the plaster Rex sitting in Mardi Gras's lobby, Saraphina dropping her shoulder into a security guard's chest while Alex manically shouts, "Bring us to your leader!"

In his 10(j) testimony, Adkins described the security footage he reviewed before deciding to terminate the employees who had gone on the delegations. "There was a customer at the desk at the time they approached who was actually pushed aside by Alex to approach the receptionist. They stood there for many, many minutes, five, six, seven, eight minutes while customers came in the front door. It was very disruptive." Norton described the customer that Alex "pushed" as "an elderly-looking gentleman, kind of gray, balding." Adkins later admitted, "I did not see Alex put his hands on the gentleman," but he wouldn't go so far as to say "that there was no pushing."

Most importantly, Adkins and his lawyers argued that the delegation had made a "show" and purposefully blocked the entrance to create a disturbance at the workplace. The main entrance to the casino, where we were, offered multiple wide automatic sliding doors through which patrons could enter. Intentionally blocking customers from entering the casino would've surely been legitimate grounds for termination, but we prevented guests from gambling the way trees prevent people from walking through a forest. Kucera knew that.

"But isn't it true that any customer that walked through was able to walk through the group? I mean they didn't stand there locking arms preventing any customer from walking through?"

"They didn't move either."

"So it's your testimony that they stopped a customer from getting through to the casino?"

"Yes."

"And the customer was not able to get through the group?"

"He eventually got through, but he had to work his way through. These employees did not move. They purposely stood their ground."

"And what did that take, a minute for the customer to get through?"

"Oh, no. There was a couple of cases . . . I even had an employee, other employees that couldn't get through."

"All right. So are you telling me that employees and customers were just standing there unable to get through that group?"

"They eventually got through, but they had to work their way through. No one volunteered to move out of the way or say excuse me or moved. The intent was to block that entrance. That's what they did."

Kucera used time, an objective metric available in the security footage entered into evidence, to reel in Adkins's hyperbole. "But would you agree with me that that was less than a minute's worth of delay of their time?"

"The entire time the employees were in that entryway was more than just a minute."

"Right, but you're not answering my question. The delay for the employee or the customer to get through, are you saying that that took more than a minute from the time they got through the doors of the casino to the time they got to their destination?"

"You know what? Even if it was one minute, that's a long time."

"That's not my question."

"It was disruptive to my customers. And the answer is it did not take more than a minute."

By contrast, Alex's testimony was surprisingly dispassionate. He didn't use descriptors. He told his story like a boring dinner guest. "We did not intentionally block anything."

"So you may have done it unintentionally?" Norton asked.

"Sure. I mean, I suppose. We were not trying to block anything. We were sitting there waiting for Mr. Dan Adkins to get the message."

While I knew that the delegations weren't the suicide missions Norton and Sampo made them out to be, my understanding of the union's strategy was complicated by a letter Mardi Gras's defense team entered into evidence. Adkins had faxed the letter to Wendi after the first delegation. In it, Adkins wrote, "Any employees engaging in these actions during working hours and on these premises will be terminated immediately." Had Alice, Alexis, and Harriet known with certainty that they would be fired, I doubt they would have gone on the second delegation. (Rosalie and Maya, who'd gone on the first delegation, weren't fired until after Friday's delegation.) Alex testified that he hadn't seen Adkins's letter until after the delegation on Friday. Alex had pleaded with the police officer and Trotter, telling them the committee members needed to come back to work, which made me think that he honestly hadn't seen it. If anyone had seen the letter, it would have been Wendi. If Wendi knew the workers would be fired, she would've had to choose between submitting to Adkins's unabashed, illegal, anti-union tactics and slowing the campaign or continuing the fight and sending more employees to the slaughter. Whether intentionally or not, the decision not to tell Alice, Alexis, and Harriet about Adkins's threat was a good one, because had they known they would face termination and still gone on the delegation, the company might have been able to justify their firings in court.

Testifying is difficult. Memories are fickle and curated. Reading the transcripts, I had to discount Adkins's hyperbole simply because I found instances of hyperbole from my coworkers. Rosalie testified that Trotter was "screaming get out, get out, get out" at the delegation. If anything, Trotter had hidden his anger below a calm voice. Rosalie wasn't lying. She had seen how angry Trotter was—everyone had—and his body language had dictated her memory and influenced her testimony.

In court, Adkins and his legal team had a clear message: Dan Adkins isn't anti-union; he is anti-disruption. To prove this, Mardi Gras's lawyers submitted letters in support of Adkins from Lawrence Brennan, then-president of Teamsters Local 337, which represented workers at Hartman &

Tyner's horse track in Detroit, and Randall Moore, a director at United Steelworkers, which represented workers at the Mardi Gras in West Virginia. "In over twenty years, I have never heard or seen anything from Hartman & Tyner or Dan Adkins that would even suggest that they would engage in any unlawful anti-union misconduct," Brennan wrote. (The son of Bert Brennan, one of Jimmy Hoffa's closest confidants, Lawrence was very much of the old union guard.) In court, Adkins described his relationship with "Larry" and "Randy" and their unions as a "partnership." Adkins testified that his managers were constantly reminded that "the right to organize was the employees' rights and it had nothing to do with our supervisors."

I think Adkins truly believed the delegations were an assault on his business. Hartman & Tyner was his kingdom and fifteen pro-union workers had blocked the gate of a beloved castle. To Adkins, the employees who went on the delegation were fired because they had declared war, not because they were pro-union. The delegations were probably unlike anything Adkins had ever experienced. Unite Here was unlike any union Adkins had ever dealt with. Wendi wasn't Larry or Randy. I'm sure Adkins believed, after consulting with his lawyers, that he had the right to fire everyone who had, for less than a minute, made him feel like he'd lost control of his kingdom.

Our trial lasted four days. "I swear to God, man, if that judge wasn't there watching, there is no way I would have shaken his hand," Alex said about Adkins that night. The end of the trial meant the beginning of another waiting game.

Without a protest or court dates to keep me in Miami, I moved back to Connecticut while the case played out. Leaving

Local 355 wasn't easy. I told Alex, Wendi, and the other salts that I was leaving to pursue a career as a writer. Sitting in her office, Wendi asked me what I wanted out of life.

"Fulfillment?" I said.

She smiled. "It's been so long since I've heard anyone answer that question like that. I don't mean that in a bad way at all. But mostly workers are like, 'I want to own a house' or 'I want to put my kids through college' or 'I just want to be happy.'"

Wendi, assuming "fulfillment" meant making the world a more just place, challenged me to think of a job at which I could accomplish that goal in the sustainable, broad-sweeping way union organizing could. I left the office that day wondering if Wendi could have been right; was there any other job at which I could have as big an impact? And if the answer was no, was I morally obliged to continue working for the union?

Alex threw a farewell party for me at his house. He presented me with a framed copy of the Mardi Gras committee flyer and my union authorization card. The card was just a copy; he needed to keep the real one to count when we won at Mardi Gras.

On September 18, 2012, Judge Carson issued his decision. Three months seemed remarkably quick. I rushed to the NLRB's website and read the decision as if it were a courtroom thriller, skimming the legalese to get to the juicy parts. First, Carson addressed the company's attempts to get out of the card-check agreement, including the curious case of Martin Mulhall, the Mardi Gras landscaper who was the sole plaintiff in the case brought by the National Right to Work Legal Defense Foundation.

The Mulhall case, Carson wrote, suggested "animus towards the Union." Carson went on to examine the letters submitted by the representatives of the Teamsters and Steelworkers that attempted to clear Adkins of any anti-union disposition. "The letters do not establish the absence of anti-union animus with respect to this employer . . . the letters establish that Adkins is a businessman and when business demands that he deal with a union, he does so. If business does not demand that he do so, he seeks to avoid doing so."

I felt a shot of dopamine and I wanted more.

Next, Carson listed the allegations against the company. The first was that when the chief operating executive, second in command under Adkins, sent out a memo about mysterious visitors, she "created an impression among employees that their union activities and protected concerted activities were under surveillance . . . and asked employees to report the union activities . . . of other employees." Carson dismissed the complaint. The company had chosen its words well in the memo, never using the U-word.

The next complaint alleged that Adkins "interrogated employees about their union membership, activities, and sympathies." The allegation stemmed from my testimony about Adkins's interaction with Lena at the bar. Again, Carson dismissed the charge, writing, "The report of Walsh regarding [Lena's] conversation with Adkins contains no reference to the Union or any statement by Lena relating to the Union."

Third was the allegation that stemmed from my description of Frank's conversation with Lena. Though Carson found my testimony to be "credible," and he did "not credit Frank's denial that he interrogated employees," Carson dismissed this allegation because Frank hadn't used the U-word.

But Frank wasn't in the clear yet. The next paragraph alleged that Frank had interrogated Colette about the union the night she worked the VIP bar, just before she was fired. Carson credited Colette's testimony and did not credit Frank's. Carson concluded, "By interrogating an employee with regard to her union sympathies the Respondent violated" the act.

Carson ruled that, yes, one of Alexis's supervisors had interrogated her.

Then came the delegation. The judge's job was to determine whether Trotter's reaction, calling the police, constituted a threat of "discharge and arrest because they engaged in union activities." Carson described the delegation in neutral language and concluded, "Employees who are not on duty are permitted to return to the casino. Threatening off-duty employees with arrest, a citation for trespassing, because they engaged in protected concerted union activity" violated the act. Carson affirmed another charge stemming from the delegation: Adkins had violated the act when he told Alice at her "appeal" meeting that she had been fired for her union activity.

Did Sally, the food and beverage director, interrogate workers about the union? No.

Did the manager in charge of housekeeping interrogate workers about the union? Yes.

Next came the allegations of wrongful termination. I skipped straight to mine. Because of how I'd grown up—privileged and very white—I had been preconditioned to believe that the law would protect my rights, which included union activity. Alongside my low-wage coworkers—African-American, Haitian, and Haitian-American women without college degrees—my faith in the law had wavered.

First, Carson reviewed the details of my case. He addressed the company's assertion that I had harassed Tina and Elisa. The company "did not obtain written statements from Tina or Elisa. There is no explanation regarding why Tina reported that she was 'bothered.' There is no evidence following her request that Walsh did not leave Elisa alone. Jay did not consult with Frank, who testified to no shortcomings by Walsh regarding his work as a bartender. The company never gave Walsh an opportunity to address the situation and did not, at the time of the discharge, even inform him of the 'complaints.'" Carson went on to rule that "by discharging Walsh because of his union activity" the company had violated the act.

Of course, out of all the allegations, this was the one I was most sure of. I'd been there every step of the way and knew the company had no good reason to fire me. And still, I felt vindicated by Judge Carson's ruling. In no uncertain terms, his voice, impartial and dispassionate, had countered each of the company's phony claims and arrived at the naked truth: I'd been fired because I had tried to organize a union.

Colette

Judge Carson never mentioned salting other than to say that the company hadn't learned Colette and I were salts until after we were fired. Carson found that Colette had never been informed of her supposed poor attendance, that she did nothing wrong when she took her break and "loitered" in the kitchen, that the company knew she was pro-union and that they were unhappy about it. "Probationary employees and salts are protected by the Act . . . the reason for a discharge is either false or does not exist . . . by discharging Nwachukwu because of her union activity" the company violated the act.

Saraphina

Carson did a full autopsy on the incident that got Saraphina fired and found that she had been wrong. He also carefully weighed her disciplinary record. Finally, there was no evidence that the company knew Saraphina had been a member of the organizing committee or that she was even pro-union. The allegation was dismissed.

Fabiola

Like Saraphina, Fabiola's rap sheet hurt her case. Judge Carson concluded that her "gross misconduct" discharge was within reason. The allegation was dismissed.

Michael

Like my case, Carson found that no one had asked Michael for his side of the story before he was fired and that he hadn't interfered with Sean's work. On this subject, Carson wrote my favorite line in the ruling: "People can still talk while sorting cans or lifting boxes." There was no documentation of Michael's infamous double dipping. By discharging Michael, the company violated the act.

Rosalie, Maya, Alice, Alexis, and Harriet

Reading Judge Carson's ruling on the delegation was my only opportunity to get a sense of what the surveillance footage revealed about the delegation. "Multiple customers . . . walked through or around the delegation," Carson wrote. "There was no purposeful impeding of access, and any delay was incidental." The footage of the second delegation showed that we were in the lobby of the casino for one minute and ten seconds before we were ushered outside.

> Contrary to the testimony of Adkins, review of the surveillance videos establishes that the delegation did not "completely" block "the entrance for several minutes." The surveillance videos show patrons moving around and through the delegation and entering the casino. The longest it took anyone observed on the surveillance video of November 17 to do so was 10 seconds, far less than a stop at a traffic light. There was no chanting or locked arms blocking

access. There was no disruption. The video of November 18 reflects no disruption.

For good measure, Judge Carson cleared Alex's name, observing that "the video does not reveal any shoving."

Was the company's termination of Rosalie, Maya, Alice, Alexis, and Harriet a violation of the act? Yes.

The National Labor Relations Board had triumphed. Eight out of ten. Less than what we wanted, but about what we had expected. In the last passage of his ruling, Carson set forth the remedies. He ordered the company to offer us our jobs back, provide back pay for the time we had missed, remove any mention of our termination from its files, and, through mail and workplace postings, notify all employees of its wrongdoing.

Unsure of why I had ever doubted the system, I imagined the committee's triumphant return to the casino. We would be symbols of an almighty and just system, labor's Lazarus. I was ready to return to South Florida, take my job back at Mardi Gras, and begin organizing the union, again. Sure, I wished our campaign had been protected from the jump, but the system had been surprisingly efficient. Given how quickly things had moved once the trial began, I figured there was a chance I'd be back at work less than a year after my firing. Maybe our campaign hadn't died at the end of 2011; maybe it had been deferred.

Part 5

THE WAIT

◎

W e still don't know how long it's gonna take," Alex
told me over the phone shortly after I read Judge
Carson's ruling. "Could be a few months, could
be another year." He was talking about the appeals process.
But Alex had given me a similar time frame for the judge's
decision, and that had only taken a few months. Judge Carson's swift and sensible ruling encouraged my trust in the
system.

Mardi Gras appealed just about every decision Carson
made in favor of the NLRB, which was expected. There wasn't
a high enough burden of proof here; the judge erred there.
The judge hadn't adequately weighed the seriousness of Michael's "double dipping" or my "repeated harassment" of Tina
and Elisa. Colette and I were "*completely* disingenuous" and
deserved "little, if any, credibility." Our testimonies were to
be "irrefutably discredited." They argued that Colette and I
didn't deserve back pay or reinstatement because educational
omissions on our job applications were offenses worthy of
termination, even if the company hadn't discovered the omissions until after it had fired us. Taking these accusations in

237

stride was easy. Lawyers will be lawyers; their language will always be calculated.

The company appealed to the highest authority in the NLRB. Three of five presidentially appointed board members reviewed the case. Six months after Judge Carson issued his ruling, the panel affirmed it. Once again, I thought the end might be near. Once again, I was wrong.

One month after the board affirmed Judge Carson's ruling, a case between a Pepsi bottling company and the Teamsters challenged the validity of three recess appointments President Obama made to the NLRB in 2012. Among the appointments challenged were two of the three judges who had affirmed Carson's decision. The case made its way to the United States Supreme Court. The scope of the case, an attempt to limit a president's ability to make recess appointments, was far bigger than its immediate effects on the NLRB. But all I could think about was that anti-union groups were making an argument in front of the Supreme Court that had the potential to impact Mardi Gras employees. A year later, in June 2014, the Supreme Court unanimously voted that Obama's recess nominations were unlawful, thereby invalidating a few hundred cases. New NLRB appointments were made and cases needed to be reviewed, including ours.

On September 30, 2014, more than two years after Judge Carson issued his ruling, the board once again affirmed the judge's decision. After Carson's initial ruling, committee members and organizers had exchanged celebratory text messages and phone calls. There was no celebration this time. Our skepticism was practiced; the company's ability to extend the timeline seemed limitless.

Two months later, I received a text message from Harriet. It was a picture taken by a current Mardi Gras employee. The picture showed an official-looking memo that had been posted in employee-only areas around Mardi Gras.

NOTICE TO EMPLOYEES

POSTED BY ORDER OF THE NATIONAL LABOR
RELATIONS BOARD AN AGENCY OF THE
UNITED STATES GOVERNMENT

WE WILL compensate COLETTE NWACHUKWU,
JAMES WALSH, ROSALIE DAMAS, MAYA FOS-
TER, HARRIET WILLIAMS, ALEXIS BOYD, ALICE
BROWN, and MICHAEL LEVINE for adverse
tax consequences, if any, of receiving a
lump-sum backpay award, and **WE WILL** file
a report with the Social Security Administration allocating the backpay award to
the appropriate calendar quarters.
   WE WILL, within 14 days from the date
of the Board's Order, remove from our
files any reference to unlawful suspensions and discharges of HARRIET WILLIAMS,
ALEXIS BOYD, ALICE BROWN and the unlawful
discharges of COLETTE NWACHUKWU, JAMES
WALSH, ROSALIE DAMAS, MAYA FOSTER, and
MICHAEL LEVINE, and **WE WILL**, within 3
days thereafter, notify each of them in
writing that this has been done and that
the suspensions and discharges will not
be used against them in any way.

Alexis called me when she saw the memo. "I'm just so
happy," she repeated, over and over. She was overjoyed and
excited; most of all, she was relieved. In the memo, Alexis and
Harriet had found more closure than they'd ever expected.
In fact, the notice was the first time the company had ever
admitted any wrongdoing.

About a week after the notice was posted, an envelope addressed to Alexis arrived through certified mail. There were two pieces of paper in the envelope. The first told her what she had already read on the notice—the company had cleared any mention of her termination from its records. The second was a bit more surprising. "The purpose of this letter is to notify you that Mardi Gras Casino and Hollywood Concessions Inc., is offering you unconditional full and immediate reinstatement of employment." Alexis, who had barely worked since being fired, was apprehensive about going back to Mardi Gras. "They're gonna respect you now, they don't want to bring attention to themselves," Harriet told her.

Alexis went to human resources and filled out the forms. She applied for a new state gaming license because hers had expired after she was fired. She waited two weeks. Then, on January 19, 2015, 1,160 days since her last shift, Alexis returned to work at Mardi Gras. After a day of orientation, she hit the floor.

"It was a little weird. Some people didn't know what happened to me. I told them that I'd been on a long vacation," she said. Other coworkers knew exactly what had happened to Alexis. "People were running up to me asking about the union and I'm like, 'You're the people who wouldn't come to the door when we were organizing the union and now you wanna know?'" Alexis didn't have any information about the union. She had been to only one union meeting since returning to Mardi Gras and there weren't any plans to start a new campaign. One coworker walked up to Alexis and said, "This is the woman we should all be thanking. We got a raise after she left and now we got a raise when she came back." But Alexis hadn't gotten a raise. She was put back to work at $8.15 an hour, the same as when she'd been fired, and $2 less than what she made when she had started at Mardi Gras in 2007.

Alexis hadn't seen Adkins at work yet. The afternoon of her second shift, Adkins was in Tallahassee, along with the heads of six other pari-mutuels in South Florida, in a private meeting with Governor Rick Scott. The meeting wasn't listed on the governor's public schedule for the day.

Michael, the cook, also got a letter offering him his job back. He was working at Gulfstream, the unionized casino down the street from Mardi Gras. He made less than $1 an hour more at Gulfstream than he did at Mardi Gras. But the insurance was cheaper.

"It's not a vast difference," he said. "It amounts to a few hundred a year." But he was happier at Gulfstream and he was quick to point out that, in addition to the extra money and cheaper health insurance, he would have union representation if he were to get in trouble at work. Most of all, Michael expressed his deep frustration with his coworkers' apathy toward the union. "It's not like people are left wing or right wing, they're just unconcerned," he said. While he understood the need for union leadership at Mardi Gras, Michael had no desire to go back to work there. "I'm better off where I am. Mardi Gras would be a step back."

I also received an envelope in December. I wasn't home when it came. My dad signed for it. My mom called me immediately. "Dad wants to know if he can open it," she said, using the same tone she had used when letters came from colleges my senior year of high school. Unlike Alexis and Michael's envelopes, there was only one piece of paper in mine. "[Mardi Gras] has removed from its files any references to your prior discharge." There was no job offer. The company had filed another appeal in early December 2014 that focused primarily on Colette and me. Mardi Gras didn't want to reinstate or award back pay to either of us. I'd had an idea that this was coming. A few months earlier, an NLRB officer had called me and asked, should the company offer me a job, would I go back? I was perturbed by the question. Why should my intentions have any bearing on the case? I told her that I wasn't sure. In March 2015, the NLRB and Mardi Gras agreed to resolve back pay through a compliance proceeding. Without court enforcement, we had no idea how long we'd be waiting. As of December 1, 2015, the company hasn't offered Colette or me our jobs back, and not one committee member has received a dime.

Four years—and counting—of waiting for some meaningful remedy have all but killed my hopefulness. Deconstructing the campaign, and all that happened in the fall of 2011, it is clear to see how easily Mardi Gras escaped the union. Fire. Fight. Appeal. Delay. Delay. Delay.

With the company's strategy in retrospect, I wondered if we'd ever had a chance. Other than the collapsed time frame (we wanted to win before the card-check agreement expired at the end of 2011), the Mardi Gras campaign seemed ripe for the picking. The timing was right: post-recession protests like Occupy Wall Street had catapulted the issue of income inequality to the fore. At the time, Mardi Gras was the only non-Indian casino in Broward County that was union-free and it was a relatively small shop. We needed just 111 signatures. Twelfth graders need more than 111 votes to win prom royalty. Still, even with the support of a local, two committed salts, and the backing of a well-heeled international, our unionization campaign was obliterated.

When I began salting, I spent a lot of time considering the 7 percent of the private-sector jobs that were unionized. How small but proud the number was and how surely it would grow. Now, after only a few years, I thought more about the 93 percent of union-free jobs in the private sector. How companies, and the anti-union lobby, had worked so diligently to grow that number. Union busting was no longer a bloody business; lawyers like Norton and Sampo, and groups like the National Right to Work Legal Defense Foundation, were sure to keep labor conflicts off the streets, out of the news, and in the courtroom. I began to grasp how utterly unremarkable our case was. Even by conservative estimates, almost one in five committee members faces termination during union election campaigns. Given the choice between a unionized workforce and litigation with the NLRB, management all too often chooses litigation. Companies can afford the legal costs and the NLRB's remedies, which lawyers can delay almost indefinitely (in 2009, the average wait between an NLRB judge's decision and enforcement of some sort of remedy was 963 days), are trivial. After subtracting any earnings and unemployment payments we collected after our terminations, the back pay Mardi Gras needed to dole out would be paltry compared to the cost of a unionized workforce. Mardi Gras had offered six committee members their jobs back and just two had accepted, only Alexis stayed longer than a month. If Local 355 were to start a new unionization campaign, it would have a long way to go to get back to where it started in 2011.

Changes can be made to deter companies from breaking the law during unionization campaigns. Steeper monetary penalties against companies that commit unfair labor practices—such as a $20,000 repeat offender's fee or tripling back pay—might disincentivize union busting enough to spur union growth. One popular suggestion is to protect the right to unionize under the Civil Rights Act. In doing so, companies that commit unfair labor practices would risk more. Fired committee members would be able to hire their own lawyers and the rules of discovery during court cases would broaden; company records (including e-mails) would be fair game.

Some people, when I tell them about the campaign, paint the whole ordeal as an example of capitalism's most powerful currents colliding to create a healthy vortex that spins our country's economy. Out of the chaos of the vortex, they say, comes the order of the free market. But to oversimplify such conflicts is to think of my coworkers as flotsam, necessary casualties in the service industry's fight to keep prices low.

I waited out the appeals and the Supreme Court case at my parents' house, sleeping in my childhood bedroom. Colette was nearby in New Haven. She worked on a senate campaign and a mayor's race. She was good at it. When Colette had volunteered her time for the union as an undergrad at Yale, before Miami, she felt uncomfortable when black New Haven residents asked her where she'd grown up in New York. Colette had grown up in Westchester county. But sometimes she would lie and say Harlem, which her fiancé gave her hell for. After Miami, Colette didn't feel as if she had to portray herself as anybody other than who she was.

Unlike service workers in South Florida, New Haven's union members were making more than Connecticut's living wage. They were solidly middle-class. As such, the New Haven local was well staffed with labor organizers, researchers, political organizers, and executives. The perpetual desperation that had exhausted organizers at Local 355—the feeling that each campaign carried with it the future of organized labor in South Florida—wasn't present in New Haven. Organizers went on vacation because members went on vacations. Colette's mentors took the time to get to know her; they invested in her future in a way that Alex and Wendi didn't have the time to do. With that investment came higher expectations of Colette. By contrast, the pushes on her were harder in New Haven than they were in Miami. Her bosses, some of them with advanced degrees from Yale, knew how to wield onus and guilt. When Colette was accepted into law school, it took months for her to gather the nerve to tell her bosses. Law school was Off the Program. Colette's exit interviews, the pushes to get her to stay, were excruciatingly personal. After she left the local, Colette heard that one staff member, in a push on someone else, had said that by enrolling in law school Colette had put her "privilege" ahead of the "struggle."

"It's just bad organizing," Colette told me. "It's lazy to compare everything to the 'struggle' because people see right through that bullshit. All that means is that that person doesn't know me or know anything about my decision."

I had to tell Alex that I was writing about my experience as a salt. We hadn't spoken much since I'd left Miami, exchanging text messages about the Patriots and the Dodgers and congratulations when he and his wife had their second son. Mostly, I heard about Alex through Erika, who had become a full-time staff organizer for Local 355. I kept my distance from Alex on purpose, knowing that one day I had to tell him and I knew he wouldn't be happy.

I bought a plane ticket to Miami for late October 2014. A few days before my trip Alex and I exchanged text messages to set up a meeting. We agreed to watch Sunday Night Football, a much-hyped game between the 49ers and the Broncos. I rehearsed in the airport, my hotel room, and the rental car on the way to his house. I wanted to tell him clearly and quickly.

When I pulled up to his house, Alex was talking on his phone and standing at the end of his short driveway. He was pacing in his bare feet, holding a beer in one hand and his phone in the other. I could see his family in the living room. I didn't want to tell him in front of his family so I had to do it before we went inside. Leaning against my rental car for what felt like an eternity, I waited for him to finish his conversation. My heart thumped. I felt dizzy. Finally, he hung up. He threw his hand out for a shake.

"What's up, homie?" he said as he led me to his front door.

"Wait, before we go inside I need to tell you something," I said. There was a long silence as I tried to push the words out.

"Dude, what are you gonna tell me right now?" he asked, sensing my distress.

"In 2009, before I moved down here, someone told me that I should write a book on salting," I said, each word like chewing on glass. "I now have a contract to write that book." It was short and simplistic, but in two sentences I had summed up everything I had been hiding for five years. My close friends had assured me that I'd feel relieved as soon as I got the secret out. They were wrong. Alex's mouth tightened and formed a taut grin.

"So you were salting the salts," he said.

"Something like that," I said.

He nodded and took a long, dramatic pull from his beer bottle before looking at me out of the corners of his eyes, the look he gave when he was skeptical of something or someone, sizing them up. In that moment, our relationship, built on trust, respect, and mentorship, pivoted. Alex looked disappointed and dubious. No longer a comrade, I was a tourist, at best.

"You know I'm gonna tell you that you can't write that book, right?"

He was holding back. He looked tired. He said he didn't want to talk about it. We went inside to watch the game.

Before our case ever went to court, Local 355 had been developing strategies for new campaigns at Magic City and Calder. Both involved salts. Since then, workers at both casinos had voted in favor of the union. I don't know if our campaign after Mardi Gras—the newspaper stories, social media, civil disobedience, and NLRB case—influenced the campaigns at Magic City and Calder. But it was nice to think there was some silver lining to our effort. In September 2014, Magic City Casino workers ratified their first union contract. A year after winning a union vote, Local 355 was still negotiating a contract with Churchill Downs. I had heard that Alex, tasked with leading the Magic City campaign, had been practically nonexistent and the responsibility was eventually handed off to another organizer. Soon after, he took more time off to be with his family. Alex was transitioning out of his job as an organizer and into a job as a researcher.

That night Alex's fatigue stemmed from something even more personal. He and his family had just returned from a trip to California, where they were visiting Alex's mother, who was terminally ill. I had known that his mother was sick, but sitting on the couch, Alex's wife told me how bad things were, that they'd gone to California because they weren't sure how much longer she had. Not only had my revelation shocked Alex, I'd had the worst possible timing.

Inside his house, Alex and I stared blankly at the television screen as the Broncos eviscerated the 49ers. I read a children's book about bugs to his older son. We played with Thomas the Tank Engine. Alex informed me that Thomas was a puppet of the colonialists and anti-worker capitalists. I considered the handful of Thomas shows I'd watched recently with my nephew. Thomas did spend time scolding his fellow engines for being lazy. "He's anti-union, dude," Alex said smiling. The levity of his lesson did nothing to ease the tension. He and his wife exchanged text messages while I sat between them. They tried to be discreet. What was supposed to be a fun visit by a friend had turned into an uncomfortable night. I attempted to engage Alex more. He told me he was too tired to talk. We set up a meeting for the next day.

I didn't sleep that night. I had grown to admire Alex. I envied his passion. Misleading people as virtuously dedicated as Local 355's staff felt wrong. Even worse, I knew the chain of events that I had set in motion. There would be conversations about organizing me out of writing the book. *Who has the most pull with James?* There would be phone calls to higher-ups, maybe a lawyer. Word would spread to various people in the union who knew me; some people would be more shocked and upset than others. There would be brainstorming about appropriate responses to the book. There might even be conversations about how to call my credibility into question. In the end, I would be labeled Off the Program. Way Off the Program. Coming to Miami, my goal had been to convince Alex, Wendi, and the rest of Unite Here that this story might benefit the movement, but true believers are hard to persuade.

The next day I met Alex outside a French café in Buena Vista, just south of Little Haiti. As soon as he got out of his car Alex told me that he wouldn't talk until I agreed to sign a piece of paper guaranteeing our conversation would be off the record. As painful as the ultimatum was, his wariness was easy to understand. I had obliterated our trust with two sentences. There was nothing remarkable about our conversation that afternoon. He understood that I wasn't out to malign him or the union. Still, he didn't want me to write the book. But doesn't this story need to be told? I asked him. As if it were an agonizing breakup, we walked for blocks without saying anything to each other. Good at conflict, Alex was more comfortable with the silence than I was. When we got back to his car he wrote out the contract and I signed it. That was the last time Alex and I have talked.

That night Wendi and I met at a sushi restaurant on Biscayne Boulevard, not far from Jimmy's Diner. She and Alex had already talked. I didn't know what to expect. Wendi was standing outside as I approached the restaurant's patio, and she immediately recognized the torment in my face.

"Don't worry. I'm not here to yell at you," she said.

I didn't have much of a relationship with Wendi so she didn't feel betrayed, she said. Wendi, more than Alex, understood that I couldn't be organized out of writing the book. She didn't care or want to talk about personal details that might be revealed in the book. She cared about the impact the book would have on the labor movement. While Local 355's membership had almost doubled under Wendi's leadership, the union still represented only six thousand workers in all of South Florida. She described the small successes of Local 355 as being "fragile," and that was why the union was intent on keeping its messaging On the Program. She worried that anything written about salting might inspire the anti-union lobby to try to outlaw the tactic, again. I reminded her that the Supreme Court had already ruled on salting.

"We have extremely powerful enemies," she said.

She was right. Mardi Gras's parent company, Hartman & Tyner, was a minnow compared to the leviathans that were notoriously hostile toward unions. Walmart, Home Depot, Target. Every major casino in the country. All of the hotel and motel brands, fast food franchises, and restaurant chains. These companies had limitless resources. The union also battled organizations like the National Right to Work Legal Defense Foundation. Such groups enjoyed the favor of billionaires like the Koch brothers and politicians like Scott Walker, powerful people who truly believe that unions—democratic organizations full of working-class Americans—are ruining this country. More than ever, unions, the free market's check on runaway capitalism, needed to tread lightly. Something as Off the Program as an unauthorized book about the union just wasn't in Unite Here's budget.

After my beer with Wendi, I drove up to the Isle Casino. I'd heard that David, a former Mardi Gras bartender, had been working there and I wanted to ask him if he noticed any difference working in a union shop. Driving up I-95, my former places of employment were omnipresent. If billboards are any measure of South Florida's collective consciousness, casinos are in control. The billboards, advertising gambling promotions and giveaways, floated over the landscape like signal fires above strip-mall prairies. "Money Machines!" "Blinko!" "The Crappiest Promotion in Town!" "*Bienvenue á la fête!*" Ten miles north of Fort Lauderdale I heeded the billboards' call and exited.

Inside the Isle, I found a seat at the bar, ordered a beer, and played a few hands of video poker. I asked the bartender if he had a coworker named David who used to work at Mardi Gras. "David? The barback? He's around here somewhere." The bartender grabbed his radio. "David, you've got a visitor here at the main bar."

"We worked together at Mardi Gras," I said to David when he arrived.

"Oh, that's right! How are you, man?" he asked me, clearly unsure why I had gone out of my way to say hello.

David told me that he had been fired from Mardi Gras. He didn't tell me the reason for his termination and I didn't push him. He was happy to be gone. "That place was a shithole," he said.

"How do you like it here?"

"It's good, I guess. They've got seniority rules here. I've been a barback for two years but next week I start bartending."

"Yeah, seniority, with the union and all, right? I was part of that union thing at Mardi Gras. That's why I got fired."

"Oh yeah! That was fucked up, what happened to you guys," he said. "I mean, I probably would've joined, eventually."

"You like having the union here?"

"It's fine. I'm not like all union, or whatever, but the great thing is this health insurance is five dollars every week, or every two weeks or something, and I have asthma." He pulled an inhaler out of his pocket. "These things are like three hundred to three hundred fifty dollars without insurance and I need it. With our insurance it's like fifteen dollars. It really is great insurance."

Though David didn't sing the union's praises, the fact that he noticed a difference was proof of something. That difference, however incremental, multiplied by three hundred workers at four different casinos, might swell a rising tide. David and I shook hands and he went back to work. I lost a few more hands of video poker and left $20 lighter.

The next day I visited Grace, the Mardi Gras cocktail waitress who had worked in Atlantic City and whom we had tried desperately to recruit to the committee. I hadn't talked to her since she signed a card while standing on her doorstep. I wondered if Grace believed the firing of ten committee members was proof that, by not joining the committee, she had done the right thing for her and her two young children. I found her small bungalow a mile north of Mardi Gras. Her white minivan was parked outside. She answered the door in a silk slip similar to the one she had worn when Pilar and I visited a few years earlier. She didn't recognize me at first, but just as I was about to remind her, "I know you! I used to work with you," she said.

Standing on her stoop without shoes on, Grace told me that she had been fired from Mardi Gras only a few months after me.

"They told me I was fired for profanity. Do you believe that? *Profanity.* Sally had it out for me," she said through an ominous smile.

The way she explained it, Grace had gotten sick of losing lucrative shifts to younger cocktail waitresses. She had been a cocktail waitress longer than anyone else at Mardi Gras. She should have had seniority. Grace went to Sally, the food and beverage director, but nothing ever came of it. So Grace went above Sally and filed a complaint with human resources. That's when she got called into Sally's office. There was a letter written and signed by David, the guy I had visited the night before at the Isle, attesting to Grace's use of profanity on the job. Grace said her record was spotless. Sally fired her.

"For profanity?" I asked, incredulous.

"It's a right-to-work state, they can fire you for that. They can fire you for whatever they want." As she was telling her story her son slipped past her and around the corner. A few seconds later a black Dodge Challenger roared down the street with her son in the passenger seat. "There goes my lovely ex-husband," she said.

"As someone who never got a write-up, had seniority, was never late, could do every job in the place, I thought they would take care of me. Nope. Not at a place like that. It's a mess top to bottom there and they just do whatever they want."

Grace had fight in her; that's why we had tried to recruit her. She told me that she'd gotten a lawyer and brought an age discrimination suit against Mardi Gras. According to Grace, the company didn't want to go to court so they settled. She said that the company fired Sally and David shortly after the settlement. Jay, the manager who had carried out my firing, was installed as the new director of the food and beverage department.

After Mardi Gras, Grace got a job cocktailing at Dania Jai Alai, where I had gone on my first social with Dylan, the Twin Spires Tavern server from Vegas. Though Dania Jai Alai was one of the original seven pari-mutuels that won the right to operate slot machines in South Florida, it hadn't installed them until January 2014. Then, after six months of the lowest revenue of all of its competitors and a $400,000 state fine for underreporting taxes because of "software failure," Dania Jai Alai had announced it would close for a year of renovations. About three hundred people were laid off. Grace was given a sixty-day notice. David's pay and benefits hadn't drastically improved at the Isle, but his union job, with its incentives and protection, stood in stark contrast with Grace's tumbleweed livelihood.

"My last day was last week," she said. "I have no idea what I'm gonna do."

Grace's layoff came at a time when Americans were supposed to feel optimistic about the economy. In just a few months, President Obama would use the State of the Union to assure the country that "our economy is growing and creating jobs at the fastest pace since 1999. Our employment rate is now lower than it was before the financial crisis." Indeed, the national unemployment rate had dropped from 10 percent at its peak, about the time that I moved to Florida, to 5 percent. Obama went on, "At this moment—with a growing economy, shrinking deficits, bustling industry, booming energy production—we have risen from recession freer to write our own future than any other nation on earth."

The economy moves on. Churchill Downs's shareholders have reason to be cheerful; their investment has been proof of the "growing" and "bustling" and "booming." When I started at Calder, Churchill Downs's stock was selling for $38 a share. Five years later, shares were selling for $151. Meanwhile, Dan Adkins continues to operate Hartman & Tyner's properties in Florida, Michigan, and West Virginia. In August 2015, Adkins proposed a new contract to unionized workers at Mardi Gras Casino in West Virginia. The proposal included language that would prohibit the union from negotiating anything regarding health care in future contracts and required workers to pay more for insurance. Members rejected the proposal 236 to one and authorized a strike.

"I can't imagine that the bulk of the bargaining unit, the

union employees out there, would actually walk out to what amounts to about $300 a year," Adkins told *West Virginia MetroNews*. "It would boggle the mind."

Ron Brady, the head of the United Steelworkers local that represents workers at Mardi Gras (the same local once led by Randy, the official who had written a letter on Adkins's behalf in our case), told me the company's proposal would cost members an additional $1,100 annually, not $300. The fear of losing $300 or $1,100 is less mind boggling when considering how little the recovery has meant to service industry workers.

Low-wage jobs made up 22 percent of job losses during the recession but have accounted for 44 percent of job growth during the recovery. And no sector has seen more growth than the service industry. Food service jobs—the poorest of the working poor—have grown by 9 percent. But job growth has come with significant wage decreases. While the average job lost 4 percent of its annual income to the recession, service workers—janitors, housekeepers, and cooks among them— lost as much as 8.9 percent of their annual incomes. Mobility has been stymied. About 20 percent of workers making minimum wage in 2008 continued to make near-minimum wage in 2013. Union membership continues to drop and public sector jobs, bastions of high union density, are losing members at a blistering rate as states adopt right-to-work laws. Now, more than ever, Americans depend on a brittle class of service workers.

Many people are optimistic about the campaign to boost the minimum wage. Fifteen million Americans still make less than $10 an hour. Service unions have spearheaded the "Fight for Fifteen" and, as a result, some eight million workers stand to benefit from their efforts in cities like Los Angeles and New York. Yet, a minimum wage increase carries with it none of the power or protection that union membership demands. Once they're making $15 an hour, many workers may decide they don't need a union.

The fight for $15 isn't the twenty-first century's New Deal, which signaled a fundamental shift in the country's approach to the working class. In 1944, President Franklin Roosevelt, trying to avoid costly wartime work stoppages, ordered the Army National Guard to seize control of a national department store and depose its chairman because he refused to recognize the department store union. "To hell with government . . . you New Dealer!" the chairman shouted at the attorney general as two soldiers hoisted him from his chair and carried him out of the building. A decade earlier, such an intervention was unfathomable. The idea that the government would forcibly remove a company executive was revolutionary.

I liked when Alex talked about the revolution, but mostly because he was so enthusiastic about it. In fact, I never fully understood what he meant. Affordable insurance is important, but is it revolutionary? This is organized labor's challenge in the twenty-first century: When mandated minimum wage increases are possible, hours regulated, working conditions mostly humane, and conflicts litigated with some civility, what are unions fighting for? The answer was voiced over and over at the very first Mardi Gras committee meeting. Benita, Saraphina, and Harriet had all said exactly what they were fighting for: respect. I had come to Florida looking for a story about young radicals, college grads making trouble in the service industry. Instead, I found a story about the marrow of American inequality, women—most of them black, immigrants, or the children of immigrants—who have spent years sacrificing for the benefit of executives, shareholders, and consumers. At great risk to their livelihoods, the women I met demanded respect. Their efforts were inspiring; the results were shameful.

Harriet lived three miles from Grace in Liberia, a neighborhood established in the 1920s as a place for the city's black workers to live. Her apartment was in a fern-green L-shaped single-story building with two stout palm trees in the yard. Inside, Harriet welcomed me with a hug and asked how her "baby"—my dog—was doing. I took a seat at her small kitchen table. A "Bring Back the Mardi Gras 10!" poster leaned against a purple wall, half-hidden behind a faded photo of Martin Luther King Jr.

Harriet had struggled to find work. Her résumé read like an index of low-wage occupations. She had bused tables and scrubbed dishes. She had washed cars and cleared demolition sites. She had cleaned hotel rooms as a housekeeper—"harder than doing construction"—and worked as an usher at Dolphins and Marlins games. Since being fired, she had done some part-time door knocking for Local 355 during Obama's re-election campaign. She sold telephone books. She worked as a toll collector making $8 an hour. "Third shift was the worst, ten p.m. to six a.m. They got cameras on you and you're not allowed to do anything. No phone, no radio, no puzzles." She was lucky if she worked thirty hours a week. That job only lasted a few months.

Harriet had spent the better part of two years on unemployment, collecting $158 a week. Her back hurt day and night, sitting or standing. Friends and family pitched in to pay $425 for an MRI she needed. They also covered the $1,100 payment she made the day of an operation. Money from a car accident settlement was about to run out and her rent was increasing $10. Tired of asking friends for money, Harriet started using new credit cards to get cash advances to pay her rent. Aware that she was deferring the inevitable, homelessness, Harriet had reserved a space at a friend's house to store her belongings. Still, she hoped some relief might come from back pay. By the time Mardi Gras had offered Harriet her job back, she couldn't take it. Her back had gotten so bad that she couldn't work any job. She filed for disability, legally forfeiting any chance of going back to work as a slot attendant. Though

Harriet wasn't accepting the job offer, she was happy when it came in the mail. It felt good to hold in her hand material evidence of some moral order.

"I used to see Mr. Adkins at work," Harriet told me. "We used to say hello to each other and everything. I guess I hoped he'd hear our stories and give us our jobs back. I was naïve."

We went to the Moonlite Diner for lunch. The afternoon rush hadn't materialized that day, so to be fair to the waitresses, who were working in sections, the manager passed empty tables and sat us in back.

Harriet told me some Mardi Gras employees had grown wary of the union. "Some people feel let down, especially the Haitians; they feel like they were sold a dream," she said. Harriet understood their skepticism. The whole thing sort of felt like a bad dream.

"What about you?" I asked her. "What would you have done differently?"

"If I knew the way things would have played out, after all the hardship and everything, I still wouldn't have done anything differently. I can't help who I am."

Harriet ordered French toast. She talked on her cell phone while we waited for the food, coordinating the paperwork for her upcoming disability hearing. After she hung up she reminded herself to protest a traffic citation. "This is my job now," she said. "Being poor is my job."

ACKNOWLEDGMENTS

◉

This book began five years ago when Douglas Brinkley encouraged me to take a risk that most would have advised against. I'm eternally grateful for his push. Before moving to Florida I sought the advice of Ted Conover, Andrew Melldrum, and Edward Davis, who were all generous with their time and wisdom. The entire project would have been for nothing without the work of my agent, David Black, and the assistance of Sarah Smith. Thanks to David, I found Colin Harrison, an editor who patiently focused me on what was most important: writing. Many thanks to the people at Scribner, including Katrina Diaz, Sarah Goldberg, Lisa Rivlin, Aja Pollock, and everyone who helped make this story into a book.

The history in this book is largely based on the work of scholars, historians, journalists, and activists, including Philip Dray, Natasha Dow Schüll, Steve Early, Julius Getman, Richard D. Kahlenberg, Moshe Marvit, Maria Jurkovic, and Bruce Nissen. Many thanks to the kind staff at the Miami Historical Society, Alex Paslawsky, and Bob Carter, who helped with the research.

When I moved to Miami I had no friends, family, or apartment and I didn't speak a word of Spanish. Standing on Lincoln

Road like a lost child, I called Lourdes Le Batard, who found me an apartment, introduced me to friends, and became family. I still don't speak Spanish. Thanks to Alex Coello and the good people at The Corner—Chris, Manoles, and Paula—who helped me find a job after I had been fired, offered their couches when I was kicked out of my apartment, took care of Percy when I was busy, and listened to me talk about a book that probably made little sense at the time.

Perhaps the greatest debt of gratitude is due to those who read various drafts and provided feedback and encouragement along the way. Those generous folks include Don Van Natta Jr., Katharine Andres, Jay Lovinger, Larry Schwartz, Luke Elliott-Negri, Magdalene Breidenthal, and S.N. Many thanks to family and friends who shared their couches, cabins, and counsel, including the Previteras, the Fuller-Googins, and the Hollands. Most importantly, to my parents, who didn't even flinch when I told them my plan: You are on every page of this book.

INDEX

ABOUT THE AUTHOR

JAMES WALSH's work has appeared on the websites of *The New Yorker, Esquire,* and *GlobalPost.* He is on the editorial staff at *New York* magazine. This is his first book.

Printed in the United States
By Bookmasters